WISDOM LEARNED AT THE FEET OF THE LORD

33 LESSONS FOR PEACE, HOPE, LOVE, AND ETERNAL LIFE

JOHN ADAMS RIZZO, ESQ.

1

WISDOM LEARNED
AT THE FEET OF THE LORD

33 LESSONS FOR PEACE, HOPE, LOVE, AND ETERNAL LIFE

TABLE OF CONTENTS

For Maria, Christian, Gabriel, Celeste, and Irene.

And in loving memory of my brother, Frank J. Rizzo (1952-2013).

INTRODUCTION

You shall love the Lord your God with all your heart, with all your soul, and with all your mind. This is the greatest and the first commandment. The second is like it: you shall love your neighbor as yourself.

I would like to begin by thanking you for taking the time to look at this book. I hope that you will read it all the way through and enjoy the experience. I pray that reading this book will have a positive effect on your life and on the lives of anyone with whom you choose to share it. As the title of the book suggests, the thoughts I seek to share with my readers are based on what Jesus Himself says to us in the Gospels.

The thesis of my book is fairly simple: (a) Jesus of Nazareth, through His words and deeds, provided us with a blueprint for how to live our lives on this earth; and (b) our failure or refusal to follow that blueprint has serious consequences, both as to the quality of our lives on earth and, more importantly, as to our candidacy for eternal life in heaven. In the 33 chapters that follow, I will consider the effects of our adherence or non-adherence to Jesus' lessons upon our temporal and spiritual destinies. I will try, to the best of my abilities, to use my intelligence, wisdom, logic, and common sense in this endeavor while at all times remaining true to the Lord's words.[1] I hope my thoughts will resonate with most Christians. I also hope to inspire people who may have fallen away from their religion, or who never really "got" their religion.

Jesus told us that the greatest commandment is to love the Lord your God with all your heart, all your soul, and all your mind. The reality in our society today, however, is that for most people God is an afterthought, or less than an afterthought. I don't think the typical person can be said to love God with all his heart, soul, and mind; do you?

The second greatest commandment, according to Jesus, is to love your neighbor as yourself. You may ask, with a nod to Tina Turner, what's love of my neighbor got to do with this book? I am glad you asked that question. Here is my answer:

---

[1] I should point out that my training is as an attorney, a classic movie buff, and an aficionado of 1970s rock music, not as a theologian. I will endeavor to have this book not sound too much like a legal brief. Johnny Friendly is laying three to one that I fail. To the extent that students of the Bible may say that I am taking Jesus' sayings out of context, I would answer that I am conveying what I firmly believe Jesus wants the world to know, and for that reason the end justifies the means.

I recently participated in a three-part presentation and discussion series, Discovering Christ, Following Christ, and Sharing Christ, that was held at my local parish in northern New Jersey. At one of the sessions of Sharing Christ, we were challenged with the observations of entertainer Penn Jillette, an atheist, concerning evangelization. Jillette is outspoken in his belief that there is no God. Jillette states, however, that if he *did* believe in God and an afterlife, he would consider it a compelling obligation to spread that belief to as many people as possible.

So, here then is what love of neighbor has to do with this book. Jesus tells us, "Amen, amen I say to you, whoever keeps My word will never see death." And He also tells us, "Whoever drinks the water I shall give will never thirst; the water I shall give will become in him a spring of water welling up to eternal life." In other words, a person who knows Jesus' teachings and abides by His teachings, who drinks the water He gives, will share everlasting life with God. If you knew that to be the case, wouldn't you want to share that information with the people you love? Wouldn't you want the people you love to also have a share in everlasting life? If you love your neighbor as yourself, if you believe it is your Christian duty to do unto others whatever you would have them do to you, how could you **not** tell them to abide by Jesus' words, so that they too can spend eternity with God in heaven?

With that in mind, there are at least three target audiences for this book. The first target audience comprises Christians who have not yet activated their evangelization mojo. After His Resurrection, Jesus said to His disciples, "Peace be with you. As the father has sent Me, so I send you." As modern-day disciples, we are also called by God, called to be sent to those who need to hear the Word. As Jesus noted, "The harvest is abundant but the laborers are few." The harvest remains abundant. In fact, in western society the harvest is becoming ever more abundant, given the fervor of secular progressivists and unabashed atheists, and the lack of fervor and diminishing interest among many Christians. Yes, God needs laborers, both to stem the tide of the forces that deny Him, and to re-engage the masses who just don't care.

The second target audience comprises what one might call disengaged or "name-only" Christians. These folks express a belief in God and identify themselves as Christians, but don't let their religion intervene in their daily lives. Wouldn't you agree that this describes a large segment of our population?

The third target audience comprises those agnostics and atheists who may have a nagging doubt as to whether there is something else "out there". I am called to love these people, as God loves them, and as I love myself. I am compelled by the Spirit to try to reach the non-believers and the lukewarm believers, to give them an opportunity to know, and knowing, to follow, the teachings of the Lord Jesus, so that they too can merit eternal life. Some of them may resent the effort, but that does not matter.

To reiterate, at the heart of the drive to evangelize should be the desire to save souls. We have all heard that God so loved the world that He gave His only Son, so that everyone who believes in Him might not perish, but might have eternal life. But the ensuing verse from the Gospel of John, though less often quoted, is equally noteworthy, and equally reassuring: "For God did not send His Son into the world to condemn the world, but that the world might be saved through Him."

How is the world saved through Jesus? In one sense, Jesus saved the world by His death on the cross, by sacrificing Himself to atone for mankind's sins. Some people are mystified that this sacrifice 2000 years ago can atone for sins we commit today, and some people will argue that they did not ask Jesus to die for their sins. In her version of the song *Gloria*, Patti Smith sang, "Jesus died for somebody's sins, but not mine". The truth is, however, that He died for *everybody's* sins, if we but accept Him. Even if today we say, "Jesus died for somebody's sins, but not mine", tomorrow (or 40 years from tomorrow for that matter) we can still embrace Him as our Savior and receive atonement.

By His resurrection, moreover, Jesus conquered death, and, to express the theology of the cross in a colloquial manner, reopened the gates of heaven. But in another sense, Jesus saved the world, and continues to save the world, by teaching us how to live in a manner that is pleasing to God, so that at the final judgment we may be deemed worthy of eternal life. Jesus tells us to repent, for the kingdom of heaven is at hand. Jesus tells us that we do not live by bread alone, but by every word that comes forth from the mouth of God. Jesus tells us that He is the light of the world, and whoever follows Him will not walk in darkness, but will have the light of life.

Some people say that the Cross alone is all we need for salvation, that as long as we believe in Jesus we are saved. I am not convinced it's that easy. Jesus says, "No greater love is there than this, to lay down one's life for one's friends." He then continues, "You are My friends if you do what I command you." Is Jesus telling us that in order to receive the saving grace of His Crucifixion, we must abide by His teachings? I think so. It is by following the Word that we can be Jesus' friends, and it is for His friends that He laid down His life.

Jesus gives us fair warning as to the repercussions of not abiding in God's word. Do we have the sense to listen to and heed His warnings? "Everyone who listens to these words of mine and acts on them will be like a wise man who built his house on rock," Jesus says. "The rain fell, the floods came, and the winds blew and buffeted the house. But it did not collapse; it had been set solidly on rock." Then comes the warning. "Everyone who listens to these words of mine but does not act on them will be like a fool who built his house on sand," Jesus continues. "The rain fell, the floods came, and the winds blew and buffeted the house. And it collapsed and was completely ruined."

In modern, liberal theology, there is some debate as to whether or not hell exists. I have heard the theory espoused that God loves everyone, and therefore everybody goes to heaven. Those who endorse such a theory are generally willing to make a few exceptions. Adolf Hitler, for example, is generally thought to be deserving of hell, even though God loves everyone; but pretty much all the rest of us seem destined for the everlasting joys of heaven. Unfortunately, as we will explore further along in this book, Jesus' words do not support this happy view. This is why it is so important, out of love for one another, that we try to educate as many people as possible as to how God would have us live our lives.

There are a few closing thoughts I would like to share with you in this introduction. The first is to reiterate the importance of knowing, embracing, and studying the word of God. Consider the story of Martha and Mary from Luke's

Gospel. When Jesus and His disciples stopped for a visit at the home of Martha and Mary, Martha busied herself getting things ready for the guests and serving them. Mary, by contrast, sat beside the Lord at His feet, listening to Him speak. You may recall the story. Martha asked Jesus, don't you care that Mary has left me by myself to do the serving? Why don't you tell her to help me? But Jesus said, "Martha, Martha, you are anxious and worried about many things. There is need of only one thing. Mary has chosen the better part, and it will not be taken from her." As you may have inferred from the title of my book, I believe it is from listening at the feet of the Lord, as Mary did, that we can best learn how God wants us to live life. What lessons do we learn by listening to the Lord? It is a question I will try to answer throughout this book.

As an aside, I find it interesting how much discussion this little scene with Martha and Mary still generates 2000 years later. Many people seem to identify with Martha, who was so busy making arrangements for Jesus and His entourage. They indicate they would do the same. They seem to dismiss, or disagree with, what Jesus said: "Mary has chosen the better part." But listening to the Lord, learning from the Lord – this is far more important than busying oneself with domestic chores. It is important to know what Jesus – God – wants us to know. Jesus says, "Whoever obeys and teaches these commandments will be called greatest in the kingdom of heaven." He also says, "It is written in the prophets, they shall all be taught by God. Everyone who listens to My Father and learns from Him comes to Me." And what the Martha-ites often overlook is not only that Jesus Himself says Mary chose the better part, but also that Jesus says He came not to be served, but to serve.

Let me state again that the ultimate goal is eternal life with God. And Christian brotherly love mandates that we share the way to eternal life with all. So often I hear opponents of religion in general, and of the Catholic religion in particular, asserting that the goal of organized religion is to control people's lives. That's why there are all those commandments and rules, to control people's minds and bodies. Consequently, people turn away from organized religion to avoid being controlled. What is sad is that the argument is so fallacious. The Ten Commandments were given to us by God to form the fabric of our moral law.

Moreover, the Commandments, as well as the teachings of Jesus, are promulgated not simply as a moral code to control our conduct, but rather to benefit us as we journey through life.

Do you think the Pope, over in Vatican City, is concerned with controlling the lives of John Q. Catholic and Jane Q. Catholic over in New Jersey? It does not make a shred of sense to think he is. Nor is it likely that the Archbishops, Bishops, and local clergy are concerned with controlling the lives of John Q. Catholic and Jane Q. Catholic. Rather, what the clergy, and the bishops, and the Pope aim to accomplish is to encourage and persuade John and Jane Q. Catholic to live lives that will be pleasing to God. In order to exercise control over them? Of course not! In order to set them on the proper path to everlasting life with God in heaven. Because that is their vocation. Because that is what Christ-like love requires of them.

So I would ask you to keep this last point in mind as you proceed through this book. How you live *your* life is up to **you**, and your choices in that regard will likely have fairly limited consequences in *my* life. To put that another way, aside from hoping you get to heaven, I couldn't care less what you do. But I do want you to know the teachings of Jesus so that you will have a chance to apply them in your life. Because if you know them and live them, maybe you will have a share in eternal life.

To learn the wisdom Jesus would impart to us, see what He has to say. If nothing else, by the end of this book you should have a reasonable grasp of what He stands for.

QUESTIONS FOR REFLECTION OR DISCUSSION

1. What is your favorite quote from Jesus in the Introduction? Why?

2. Which of Jesus' quotes in the Introduction did you find most surprising? In what way did it surprise you?

3. How do you feel about evangelizing? About being evangelized by others?

4. Can you think of any ways in which you can spread God's word without being offensive to non-believers?

Chapter One

TELL US WHO *YOU* SAY YOU ARE, JESUS

I came into the world as light,
so that everyone who believes in Me might not
remain in darkness.

You may know that there is a scene in the Gospels in which Jesus asks the Apostles who the people say that He is. But since I am writing about the lessons we can learn from Jesus, I guess it is pertinent for us to ask Jesus who *He* says He is. Is there a reason why we should we care what He says and does?

We can describe Jesus as the Son of God, the second person in the Holy Trinity. We can say Jesus is the human incarnation of the Divine, who was sent to earth by the Father to be a sacrificial lamb to atone for man's sins, and to teach us the way to conduct our lives.   Of course the concept of Jesus as the Son of God, or as God incarnate, is a difficult concept for people who do not believe in God. But the issue of non-belief in God will be dealt with further along in this book.

Let's talk now about that conglomeration of doubters who question that Jesus of Nazareth ever existed as an historical person. In my view, the argument against an historical Jesus is a difficult one to reconcile. Consider that, within the first decade after Jesus' crucifixion, many of His followers and Apostles were martyred. For example, history suggests that the Apostle James, who was one of the sons of Zebedee and the brother of John the Evangelist, was beheaded by King Herod in or about 44 A.D. You must ask yourself, do you think James doubted whether Jesus had ever existed? Would James have said and done those things that got him martyred if he had not shared in Jesus' ministry?

Consider that, within 20 years after Jesus' death, epistles were being written by Saint Paul and by James, a brother of Jesus, and the earliest versions of the Didache, a primer for early Christian communities, were in circulation. Consider that around 49 A.D. the Emperor Claudius expelled Jews from Rome because of trouble with the followers of "Christos". Roman historians of the time spoke of Jesus and His followers, including making reference to Emperor Nero's fabricated claim that the Christians were responsible for the burning of Rome. Indeed, Nero engaged in the torture and execution of many Christians, quite probably including St. Paul and Peter the Apostle.

Peter likewise would have been quite surprised to learn that Jesus never existed, after traveling with Him for three years, spending some 30 years evangelizing, and finally sacrificing his life for his beliefs. There is also the small matter of the Gospels of Matthew, Mark, Luke, and John, written somewhere between 25 and 60 years after Jesus' earthly venture. While these are not biographies, per se, of Jesus, they do establish the time and place of Jesus' ministry. We now know there were also several other gospels that were not included in the "canonical" Bible. How and why would numerous different people write intertwined accounts about the same person if that person never existed? Finally, let me mention that the Romano-Jewish historian Flavius Josephus, writing near the end of the first century A.D., mentioned both John the Baptist and Jesus in his works concerning erstwhile recent events in Palestine.

As I see it, it is part of the incredible ego of modern man that we can decide, 2000 years later, that we are in a better position to decide if Jesus ever lived than those who lived with, traveled with, wrote about, and died for Him in the period just after His time on earth. The followers of Jesus went far and wide spreading the Gospel and converting souls, in the decades immediately following Jesus' earthly ministry. They endured hardship, persecution, and, in many cases, martyrdom. That they would have done so without knowing whether Jesus even existed seems extremely doubtful. Dare I say it is much more likely that, in accordance with ancient church tradition, they were Jesus' Apostles, they knew Him personally, and after Pentecost they undertook the mission to spread the Word.

But it is not my intention to undertake an exploration of the historical Jesus. This book presupposes Jesus' existence, ministry, and teachings. My purpose in this chapter is to consider who was Jesus, in His own estimation.

I mentioned in the Introduction that Jesus might be considered variously to have come to earth: (1) to die on the cross, thus saving the world by sacrificing Himself to atone for mankind's sins; (2) to conquer death and reopen the gates of heaven as evidenced by His resurrection; and (3) to save the world by teaching us how to live in a manner that is pleasing to God, so that at the final judgment we may be deemed worthy of eternal life. All three of these "missions" are evident in Jesus' own words. The Gospels tell us, for example, that Jesus "began to show His disciples that He must go to Jerusalem and suffer greatly from the elders, the chief priests, and the scribes, and be killed and on the third day be raised." Jesus describes Himself as "the living bread that came down from heaven", and relates further that the bread He will give is His flesh for the life of the world. He is willing to sacrifice Himself for the sake of us all. Jesus' saving mission is also expressed in the metaphor of the Good Shepherd. "I am the good shepherd," Jesus tells us. "A good shepherd lays down his life for the sheep. ... This is why the Father loves Me, because I lay down My life in order to take it up again." God sent Jesus to be an atoning sacrifice for a lost and corrupt world. "The Son of Man did not come to be served, but to serve and to give His life as a ransom for many."

Speaking of what was to be gained by His death, Jesus told His disciples, "Unless a grain of wheat falls to the ground and dies, it remains just a grain of wheat. But if it dies, it produces much fruit." Certainly we can see how this was true. Had Jesus been no more than a great rabbi who lived, taught, and died, His legacy would have most likely been self-limiting. But by His crucifixion and resurrection, He created a legacy spanning the globe and the millennia.

Jesus' mission to win souls for God and to lead them to eternal life is also manifest in His words. "I am the way and the truth and the life," Jesus says. "No one comes to the Father except through Me." [2] By these words Jesus seemed to be telling the Jewish people that the old way of following the burdensome man-made rules was no longer the way to salvation. Rather, God had sent Jesus to show the Jewish faithful the error of their ways and to encourage them to embrace Him and His teachings as the new road to salvation. "My food," says Jesus, "is to do the will of the One who sent Me and to finish His work." What was that work? "That all should believe in the one He sent." For Jesus

---

[2] It is not within the scope of this book to debate whether persons who are raised in non-Christian religions are precluded from knowing God and attaining eternal life. It is this author's view that such is not the case, and that God has revealed Himself to different peoples at different times. I envision that more than one path can lead to the Divine, so long as it is a divine path that rewards the good, not the bad. I don't think a loving and merciful God would condemn people simply because they have not been taught about Jesus.

proclaims that He is the bread of life; whoever comes to Him will never hunger, and whoever believes in Him shall not thirst.

Obviously, Jesus is not talking about physical hunger and thirst, but spiritual. And Jesus makes clear that it is God the Father who has sent Him on this missionary journey to save humanity, for Jesus also tells us that He did not speak on His own, "but the Father who sent Me commanded Me what to say and speak. And I know that His commandment is eternal life." Jesus' mighty works also testify that He was sent to us by God. There was a blind young man to whom Jesus gave sight and whom Jesus sent to wash in the Pool of Siloam. As this formerly blind young man told the Pharisees, "One thing I do know is I was blind and now I see. ... If this Man were not from God he would not be able to do anything."

Jesus speaks further about His mission to do the will of God, for which purpose He came down from heaven. "This is the will of my Father," Jesus tells us, "that everyone who sees the Son and believes in Him may have eternal life, and I shall raise him on the last day. It is written in the prophets, they shall all be taught by God. Everyone who listens to my Father and learns from Him comes to Me." I think that spells it out quite plainly; don't you? God the Father and God the Son both want us – **all of us** – to share eternal life with them. And so Jesus seeks to show us what we must do, how we are to live, to achieve this most desirable goal. "I am the light of the world. Whoever follows me will not walk in darkness, but will have the light of life." "I am the gate for the sheep. …whoever enters through Me will be saved, and will come in and go out and find pasture." "I am the resurrection and the life; whoever believes in Me, even if he dies, will live, and everyone who lives and believes in Me will never die."

Before we delve further into the specific lessons Jesus can teach us about life and death, a few more observations of who Jesus is are worth noting. Yes, God the Father and God the Son want everyone to attain eternal life. But Jesus also makes plain – perhaps to keep the righteous from getting a big head or taking the gift of salvation for granted, but undoubtedly to give hope to those who find themselves traveling down life's wrong path – that He "came to seek and save what was lost." Jesus also offers consolation to those who are a bit overwhelmed by the world, by circumstances beyond their control. "Come to Me, all you who labor and are burdened, and I will give you rest," says the Lord. "Take My yoke upon you and learn from Me, for I am meek and humble of heart; and you will find rest for yourselves. For My yoke is easy, and My burden light." What a beautiful message of comfort to all those little people beaten down by life. "In the world you will have trouble," Jesus concedes, "but take courage, I have conquered the world." We know the world can be an unfriendly and unpleasant place. Sadly, for many people it is a downright awful place from which death will be the only escape. Jesus gives us hope for something better. As Charles Dickens (and Ronald Colman) say at the end of "A Tale of Two Cities": "It is a far far better rest I go to than I have ever known." [3]

One final thought about Jesus that cannot be overstated, but is often overlooked: He isn't a sweet, lovable, cuddly Savior 24/7. He is well aware of man's evil tendencies, man's attraction to corruption, man's disobedience, man's hard heart and stiff neck. He longs for the return of the

---

[3] Many people would argue that the fact that life on earth is so awful for so many people disproves the existence of God. I understand their thinking. If God is all-powerful and all-loving, why doesn't he make the world perfect? I discuss this issue at length later in the book.

prodigal child and the recovery of the lost sheep, but He does not look kindly on sin, and by no means does He guarantee a spot in the kingdom of God for all His children. I fear that those who preach otherwise do their flocks a disservice. Jesus requires us to make a decision for good over evil, and He knows His teachings will engender conflict. Remember, Jesus says, "Do not think that I have come to bring peace upon the earth. I have come to bring not peace but the sword. For I have come to set a man against his father, a daughter against her mother, and a daughter-in-law against her mother-in-law; and one's enemies will be those of his household." How prophetic these words can be when moral and religious disagreements come about between the side of good and the side of evil.

Jesus gives little quarter to those who blithely ignore God's Commandments and refuse to change their ways. "You belong to what is below, I belong to what is above," He tells His enemies. "You belong to this world, but I do not belong to this world. If you do not believe that I am, you will die in your sins." Of those who hear His words but will not listen to His admonitions, these are His sentiments: "If I Had not come and spoken to them, they would have no sin; but as it is, they have no excuse for their sin."

If you want to earn eternal salvation, to share everlasting life with God and His angels and saints, you must listen and follow the Lord's blueprint for life. Nobody is perfect, everybody messes up. Most people mess up repeatedly. And God welcomes the repentant sinner. But God does not welcome the stiff-necked, unrepentant. Through Jesus, mankind is given a never-ceasing opportunity for salvation. But what if mankind willfully squanders that opportunity? "At the judgment, the men of Nineveh will arise with this generation and condemn it, because [the men of Nineveh] repented at the teaching of Jonah; and there is something greater than Jonah here," Jesus says. "At the judgment the queen of the south will arise with this generation and condemn it, because she came from the ends of the earth to hear the wisdom of Solomon; and there is something greater than Solomon here," He adds. It is Jesus Himself who is greater than Jonah and Solomon.

Who then is Jesus? He is our Savior, if we want Him to be. A loving word to the wise: heed His advice.

QUESTIONS FOR REFLECTION OR DISCUSSION

1. What is your favorite quote from Jesus in Chapter One? Why?

2. Which of Jesus' quotes in Chapter One did you find most surprising? In what way did it surprise you?

3. Do you doubt whether the person we know as Jesus of Nazareth ever lived on earth? Why or why not?

4. What impact does Jesus have in your own life?

Chapter Two

WHAT ARE YOUR VIEWS ON LIFE AFTER DEATH?

Now this is eternal life, that they should know You,
the only true God, and the One whom you sent,
Jesus Christ.

The question of the survival of consciousness after the end of our human existence is certainly one of the most enduring questions that humans have posed since ancient times. In Jesus' time there was disagreement among the Jews about life after death, with the Pharisees siding in favor of the dead rising again, and the Sadducees denying that this occurred. Jesus was on the side of the Pharisees, which really should settle the question once and for all, Jesus being God and all.

The Gospels tell us of Jesus being put to the test on this issue by the Sadducees, when they posed to him their ironic question: if seven brothers all married the same woman, which one would she be married to in the afterlife? Jesus deflected the absurdity of their hypothetical by observing, "The children of this age marry and remarry; but those who are deemed worthy to attain to the coming age and to the resurrection of the dead neither marry nor are given in marriage. They can no longer die, for they are like angels; and they are the children of God because they are the ones who will rise." He went on to point out to the Sadducees that they were misguided as to life after death, citing for them the Old Testament passage in which God said to the Israelites, through Moses, "I am the God of Abraham, the God of Isaac, and the God of Jacob." Jesus attested, "He is not the God of the dead but of the living."

Taking a page from those first-century Sadducees, many modern-day atheists tell us that there is no life after death, and that the notion of an afterlife is just a fantasy. Of course the people saying this are alive, so it is not clear how they come to know this. Some atheists will supplement their avowal of no afterlife with statements along the lines of "it is people who do not like their lives on earth that perpetuate the myth of life after death. It makes their miserable lives more bearable." I feel that those who make these generalizations are, like the Sadducees, sadly misguided. Because for myself, and I suspect for many people like me, the hope for life after death is not in the slightest bit a product of dissatisfaction with my human existence. Quite the contrary, it is an outgrowth of happiness on earth and the many loving relationships I have established with family and friends here. There is a genuine hope for the opportunity to continue these relationships in the afterlife. Besides that, however, there is also a sense, a perfectly logical sense I think, that a Creator who gave us the ability to form such loving relationships would not do so only to have such relationships end upon the arbitrary cessation of our mortal lives.

Getting back to Jesus' response to the Sadducees , what I find particularly enlightening about His statement concerning the children of the resurrection is that they are like angels. I am intrigued by the comparison of this statement with other events memorialized in the Gospels. For example, when Jesus took Peter, James, and John up the mountain with Him, and they witnessed Jesus being transfigured, the Apostles noted that Jesus' "face shone like the sun and His clothes became white as light". Similarly, at the time of Jesus' resurrection, when the disciples went to the tomb to look for Him, "[b]ehold, two men *in dazzling garments* appeared to them. They were terrified and bowed their faces to the ground. They said to them, 'Why do you seek the living One among the dead? He is not here, but He has been raised.'" (Emphasis mine.) I find these Biblical descriptions of unearthly (angelic?) beings dressed in dazzling garments, or having clothes white as light, to be fascinating. Fascinating because of the similarity to descriptions of visits from spirits of the deceased, in books such as Raymond Moody's "Life After Life". The visiting spirits in these modern-day accounts are generally described as being dressed in impossibly white clothing and accompanied by an unearthly bright light.

One of my few encounters with the afterlife bears a stunning resemblance to those described by Moody and others in the field. At approximately two o'clock one morning, on the day that happened to be my sister-in-law's first birthday since her death five-and-a- half months earlier, she appeared at the foot of my bed, dressed in dazzling white and surrounded by white light. As I sat up in bed, my sister-in-law told me she was very happy, asked me a question pertaining to her infant son, and then disappeared.

As real as this visit from my sister-in-law seemed – more real, vivid, and memorable than any dream – I still find myself, 30 years later, wondering if it was really a visit from the afterlife. And at the same time I also wonder why I find it so easy to be skeptical of things I really want to believe. Interestingly enough, Jesus addressed this very issue in the parable about Lazarus the beggar and the rich man. You may recall that in the parable, Lazarus dies and is carried off by the angels to Abraham's bosom. The rich man also dies, and goes to "the netherworld". The rich man, suffering the torments of hell, asks Abraham to send Lazarus to the rich man's five brothers, "so that he may warn them, lest they too come to this place of torment." Jesus has Abraham reply to the rich man, "They have Moses and the prophets. Let them listen to them." The rich man then says, "Oh no, father Abraham, but if someone from the dead goes to them, they will repent." Concluding the parable, Abraham tells the rich man, "If they will not listen to Moses and the prophets, neither will they be persuaded if someone should rise from the dead." I guess that's true for me, too. If I don't listen to Jesus when He promises eternal life, I won't be persuaded by a visit from the dead, either. Shame on me!

For the record, here are two other experiences with "the afterlife" that I can recall and pinpoint: (a) the morning after my father's death, before my father's obituary had been published, an old friend of his, a friend my parents had not seen in many years, showed up at my parents' front door. When I subsequently asked this gentleman about the timing of his visit, he said my father's spirit had visited him. (b) My daughter Celeste is named after a friend of mine who had passed away a year or so before Celeste was born. My deceased friend's birthday was August 9. When my daughter Celeste was three years old, she said to me, on August 8, "My brain told me that tomorrow is my birthday". (My daughter's birthday is September 13.)

The question of what happens to us and our loved ones when we die is such a tantalizing one that it gives rise to the "profession" of spiritual mediumship. Yes, people will pay a large amount of money to individuals who claim to be able to channel messages from the spirits of persons who have passed away. Are these mediums legitimate, blessed with a gift from God to connect with the souls of the deceased? Or are they all fakers, charlatans, and tricksters, playing on people's grief for profit? I would like to think the former. Why? Because anything that can help convince people that there is life after death is a step toward persuading people that they ought to conform their lives to God's commandments in order to attain heaven. And shepherding as many people as possible to heaven is the ultimate goal of all Christians.

At the same time, there are many Christians who maintain that an ability to channel the spirits of the dead is an ability that must come from Satan, not God. I am in no position to make that judgment. Paradoxically, however, even if this ability were satanic in origin, it would support my point, albeit in an unsavory way. For one cannot believe in Satan without also believing in God, and whether the "gift" is from God or Satan, a visit from the spirit of a deceased person would seem to show the survival of the spirit after the death of the body.

But getting back on track, for now let's disregard my reluctance to feel certain about the reality of eternal life, and move away from the mediumship industry, and focus instead on what Jesus teaches on the subject. Indeed, if we put stock in what Jesus tells us, it is difficult to deny the reality of eternal life. The Gospels, particularly the Gospel of John, are chock full of references to eternal life, which makes my personal skepticism all the more frustrating.

What is Jesus' lesson for us about eternal life? I suppose the most important lesson is quite simply this – that eternal life is a reality, regardless of what the Sadducees, atheists, and hopeful skeptics think about it. We read early on in John's Gospel, "Just as Moses lifted up the serpent in the desert, so must the Son of Man be lifted up, so that everyone who believes in Him may have eternal life. For God so loved the world that He gave His only Son, so that everyone who believes in Him might not perish but might have eternal life." Jesus goes on to tell us, "The one who is of the earth is earthly and speaks of earthly things. But the One who comes from heaven is above all. *He testifies to what He has seen and heard* … the One whom God sent speaks the words of God... Whoever believes in the Son has eternal life ..." (Emphasis added.) I don't know about you, but I find it fascinating to read that italicized verse: "He testifies to what He has seen and heard". It reminds us that Jesus has always been with God, and shares eternity and Divine nature with God. Jesus knows that eternal life exists, because He lives it.

Jesus expresses a similar sentiment near the end of John's Gospel, when He prays to God as follows:

Father, the hour has come. Give glory to Your Son, so that Your Son may glorify You, just as You gave Him authority over all people, so that He may give eternal life to all You gave Him. Now this is eternal life, that they should know You, the only true God, and the One whom You sent, Jesus Christ. I glorified You on earth by accomplishing the work that You gave me to do. Now glorify Me, Father, with You, with the glory that I had with You before the world began.

Here again Jesus tells us that He has always been with God the Father, and has shared in God's glory since before the world began. This is part of eternal life – He always was and He always will be. And He came to earth so that we can share this eternal life. What is this eternal life of which He speaks? The opportunity to know God. The opportunity to be with God, to be part of the Divine Light, forever.

Other passages in John's Gospel give further testimony that Jesus' mission is eternal life for all. Jesus says, for example, that the reaper is already receiving His payment and gathering crops for eternal life, so that the sower and reaper can rejoice together. You might paraphrase that to say God the Father and God the Son are overjoyed to have Their children join Them in eternity. Jesus readily acknowledges the quest on which He has been sent: "I came down from heaven not to do My own will but to do the will of the One who sent Me. ... this is the will of My Father, that everyone who sees the Son and believes in Him may have eternal life, and I shall raise him on the last day."

But just as clearly as Jesus tells us that God sent Him to earth for the purpose of bringing all people to eternal life, Jesus also reminds us, again and again, of the importance of obeying what He tells us. We must follow God's word in order to merit this eternal life and join in the eternal celebration. Jesus comments, "The father who sent Me commanded Me what to say and speak. And I know that His commandment is eternal life." We are directed to believe in God and believe in His Son Jesus, and further to abide in His word. Thus, Jesus told the Samaritan woman at Jacob's well, "Whoever drinks the water I shall give will never thirst; the water I shall give will become in him a spring of water welling up to eternal life."

In referring to Himself as the Good Shepherd, Jesus relates, "My sheep hear My voice. I know them, and they follow Me. I give them eternal life, and they shall never perish."

In discussing His mission with the Pharisees, Jesus made this remarkable statement: "Amen amen I say to you, whoever keeps My word will never see death. .... Abraham your father rejoiced to see My day; he saw it and was glad." Think about that. Abraham, the father of the Hebrew nation, who had lived and died many centuries before Christ, knew about Jesus' incarnation as it was happening. What an intriguing verse. It certainly speaks to the survival of consciousness after our mortal years.

Jesus repeatedly expresses to us that if we believe in Him we are on the path to eternal life. "I am the resurrection and the life," He says. "Whoever believes in Me, even if he dies, will live, and everyone who lives and believes in Me will never die." Are we willing to take Jesus at His word, and to believe His promise? For His promise is life everlasting with God the Father. He speaks further as to the destiny of those who will listen: "Whoever hears My word and believes in the One who sent Me has eternal life and will not come to condemnation, but has passed from death to life. Amen I say to you, the hour is coming and is now here when the dead will hear the voice of the Son of God, and those who hear will live..."

But again, we must heed the warning that comes with the promise of eternal life. For Jesus goes on to say, "Do not be amazed at this, for the hour is coming in which all who are in the tombs will hear His voice and will come out, *those who have done good deeds to the resurrection of life, but those who have done wicked deeds to the resurrection of condemnation*." (Emphasis added.)

The lesson Jesus teaches us about eternal life, then – if we will put aside our skepticism and listen -- is this: God the Father sent Jesus to earth to bring us the promise of eternal life. But the promise is not given freely; it comes with a corresponding obligation on our part. We must believe in Jesus, and we must live our lives in accordance with the word of God.

Having been given the promise of eternal life, what will you do with it? Will you squander it? Will you consider it a promise worth pursuing? We will discuss these questions further in Chapter 33.

QUESTIONS FOR REFLECTION OR DISCUSSION

1. What is your favorite quote from Jesus in Chapter Two? Why?

2. Which of Jesus' quotes in Chapter Two did you find most surprising? In what way did it surprise you?

3. Do you believe in the concept of eternal life?

4. Have you had any experiences with what could be called the afterlife?

5. Are you concerned with your eternal fate and the eternal fate of your loved ones? Why or why not?

Chapter Three

DOES SIN REALLY MATTER ANYMORE?

The Son of Man will send his angels, and they will collect out of His kingdom all who cause others to sin and all evildoers.

They will throw them into the fiery furnace, where there will be wailing and grinding of teeth.

When I was a child, I was taught that a sin was something wrong that a person did that hurt God, or something that a person failed to do that hurt God. There were many different sins one was prone to commit. For example, you might have strange gods before the Lord your God. You might take the name of the Lord your God in vain. You might forget to keep holy the Lord's Day. You might fail to honor your father and mother. You might kill. You might steal. You might commit adultery. You might bear false witness against your neighbor. You might covet your neighbor's goods. You might covet your neighbor's wife or husband. In other words, if you broke one (or more) of the Ten Commandments, you were guilty of sin.

Then there was a specific group of seven sins known as the capital sins, or deadly sins, of which one might also be guilty. These were anger, envy, gluttony, greed, lust, pride, and sloth. There were mortal sins, which could result in a sentence to hell if not repented and confessed, and venial sins, which were less serious but nevertheless offensive to God.

Of course all these sins still exist, at least in theory. After all, we are still guided by the Ten Commandments, to some degree anyway. And the Catechism of the Catholic Church still discusses at length capital sins, mortal sins, venial sins, and the like, and what the consequences of such sins might be. Indeed, the Catechism states at text paragraph 386:

> Sin is present in human history; any attempt to ignore it or to give this dark reality other names would be futile. To try to understand what sin is, one must first recognize *the profound relation of man to God,* for only in this relationship is the evil of sin unmasked in its true identity as humanity's rejection of God and opposition to Him, even as it continues to weigh heavy on human life and history. (Italics in original.)

Text paragraph 387 adds, "Sin is an abuse of the freedom that God gives to created persons." Wow. In other words, God gives us rules to live by, but He also gives us free will, so we can either obey the rules, or disobey the rules, which is sin.

These days, however, sin seems to have lost a lot of its swagger! Nobody seems to be that impressed by sin, nobody seems that concerned about it. Unless someone dies, that is; murder is still pretty much frowned upon (as long as the victim has made it out of the womb alive anyway). And when a bullying victim takes his or her own life, most people seem to conclude that bullying is wrong. But, by and large, these days people seem to be pretty much free to do whatever they want, short of a felony.

In the Academy Award winning movie "On the Waterfront" (1954) -- a truly great movie, and not just because it was filmed in Hoboken NJ --, Marlon Brando plays the role of Terry Malloy, who is friends with the head honchos of the corrupt local longshoremen's union. At the start of the movie, Terry is used by his "friends" to set up the murder of a longshoreman who was going to talk to the Waterfront Crime Commission. The movie follows Terry's battle with his conscience: should he tell the Crime Commission what he knows about the nefarious union leaders? In other words, should he rat out his murderous friends? In the end, he does the right thing.

Nowadays, the idea of following one's conscience, of even having a conscience, seems a tad archaic.

Nevertheless, I was a little surprised when it was suggested, in one of the sessions in the Sharing Christ series (which I mentioned back in the Introduction), that when we seek to bring souls to Christ we should not talk about sin. Apparently sinners might take offense at being called sinners!

People, this is ridiculous. I know we live in a time when it is politically incorrect to damage someone's self-esteem, but this is ridiculous. Everybody sins. From the dawn of mankind to the 21st century, everyone who has reached the age of knowing the difference between right and wrong has been a sinner.

Jesus says, "Those who are well do not need a physician, but the sick do. Go and learn the meaning of the words, 'I desire mercy, not sacrifice.' I did not come to call the righteous but sinners." If Jesus came to earth to save sinners, how can you convince someone he or she needs to come to Christ if we do not talk about sin?

We are all sinners, and those of us who are Christian sinners are called, by our duty to love our fellow man, to invite the unbelievers and the unchurched to have a relationship with Jesus. Because it is through a relationship with Jesus, in the receipt of His forgiveness and in the following of His teachings, that we attain eternal life.

Where do you think Jesus stands today about sin? Do you think Jesus feels that people are so cool these days that they needn't worry about sinning? I think there is a pretty darn good chance that Jesus does **not** feel that way. Jesus says, "Everyone who commits sin is a slave of sin." I think we can agree that being a slave to anything is not a good situation, so referring to sinners as slaves of sin was not meant as a compliment. Jesus also says, "[W]hoever breaks one of the least of these commandments and teaches others to do so will be called least in the kingdom of heaven."

I suppose if we look at the commandments logically, we can see that some of them are more serious, or important, than others. For example, "thou shall not kill" is a pretty serious commandment. It is not the place of one human to take the life of another human, to decide when that other human's time on earth should end. And as gunslinger Alan Ladd says in the classic 1953 western movie "Shane," "There's no going back from a killing." Shane didn't mean it this way exactly, but killing another person is pretty final. Life is not a video game. When you're dead, you're dead (as far as life on earth is concerned). I think we can all understand that God sees red when one of His children decides to take the life of another. It's been that way since Cain and Abel.

By contrast, coveting your neighbor's goods is a relatively innocuous sin. It just means you want something that somebody else has. This sin doesn't even require that you take any action toward possessing your neighbor's goods. Merely desiring some physical good is a sin. Yet in Jesus' words, even this little sin renders you the least in the kingdom of heaven.

Some of Jesus other comments are worth mentioning here as well. For example, there's this humdinger:

> If your right eye causes you to sin, tear it out and throw it away. It is better for you to lose one of your members than to have your whole body thrown into Gehenna. And if your right hand causes you to sin,

cut if off and throw it away. It is better for you to lose one of your members than to have your whole body go into Gehenna.

Now I do not happen to believe that Jesus really wants us to tear out our eyes or cut off our hands and throw them away. I believe He was speaking for hyperbolic effect. But that doesn't diminish the significance of His point: If you are a sinner, you are in danger of going to hell. If you do not wish to go to hell, you should do what you can to avoid sinning. Such as staying away from people or situations that are likely to lead you into sin. Or maybe summoning up the fortitude to refrain from doing something you want to do, because you know it is wrong. Imagine that!

If you bother to look at what Jesus says about the consequences of sin, you will find He doesn't pull any punches. In describing the process of separating the heaven-bound from the hell-bound, Jesus says, "Just as weeds are collected and burned up with fire, so will it be at the end of the age. The Son of Man will send His angels, and they will collect out of His kingdom all who cause others to sin and all evildoers. They will throw them into the fiery furnace, where there will be wailing and grinding of teeth." In talking about the destiny of people who lead other people into sin, Jesus is similarly forthright. "Whoever causes one of these little ones who believe in Me to sin," he warns, "it would be better for him to have a great millstone hung around his neck and to be drowned in the depths of the sea."

It is not my intention to frighten you, dear reader. God knows I am a sinner, too. But it is important, nay, critical, that we be aware of what might befall us if we persist in sinning and do not atone and seek God's forgiveness.

If we look at the Gospel of Mark, Chapter 7 verses 21-22, we find a litany of sins that Jesus was concerned about as defiling a person. The sins Jesus mentions are: evil thoughts, unchastity, theft, murder, adultery, greed, malice, licentiousness, envy, blasphemy, arrogance, and folly. A couple of those words are not commonly used these days, so let's define them. From the Merriam-Webster online dictionary, unchastity means an absence of chastity, and chastity means an abstinence from sexual intercourse, or at least from unlawful sexual intercourse (i.e., sex outside of marriage). Licentiousness means actions that lack moral or sexual restraint. In other words, premarital sex, extramarital sex, things like that, were considered sins in Jesus' time.

Hmmm. Twenty centuries later, our sins haven't changed very much, have they?

Jesus was an astute individual, and why wouldn't He be, being God and all. He was sent to earth by the Father to save sinners, to bring them to God. But He was aware that not everyone wanted to be saved. Speaking of these things, Jesus comments, "And this is the verdict, that the light came into the world, but people preferred darkness to light, because their works were evil. For everyone who does wicked things hates the light, so that his works might not be exposed." Let us not be like those who do wicked things and hate the light. Let us strive to join Father and Son in eternal life.

Sin still matters in God's eyes. Sin is still sin. We are all human and therefore prone to fall, but sinful conduct should be the exception, not the rule, and when we do sin we should be contrite and repentant. This is what God requires. So I worry about my fellow members of society when I look around and observe their behaviors, which often seem mired in sin and ungodliness.

In the film version of Robert Bolt's play, "A Man for All Seasons" (1966), Paul Schofield plays St. Thomas More. St. Thomas was a Catholic who ran afoul of his former friend, King Henry VIII, in 16th century England, when Thomas would not endorse Henry as head of the Anglican Church. Condemned to death by the king, Thomas says to the headsman who is about to execute him, "Friend, be not afraid of your office. You send me to God." When Thomas is asked whether he is sure he is going to God, he replies, "He will not refuse one who is so blithe to go to Him."

These days, I marvel that my fellow men seem so blithe to go in the other direction!

QUESTIONS FOR REFLECTION OR DISCUSSION

1. What is your favorite quote from Jesus in Chapter Three? Why?

2. Which of Jesus' quotes in Chapter Three did you find most surprising? In what way did it surprise you?

3. Do you feel that our society is less sinful or more sinful than in past generations, or about the same? Explain.

4. Where do you think Jesus stands today about sin?

5. Do you believe that Jesus died for your sins?

6. How does your answer to question 5 influence the way you live your life, if at all?

Chapter Four

THE GOOD LIFE? OR *A* GOOD LIFE?

*Abraham replied, 'My child, remember that you received
what was good during your lifetime while Lazarus likewise
received what was bad; but now he is comforted here,
whereas you are tormented.'*

Although He was the Son of God - Divinity incarnate on
earth -, Jesus did not possess earthly wealth. He was born of
humble beginnings, in a stable, because there was no room
at the inn. His first years He spent as a refugee in Egypt,
before returning to the non-descript town of Nazareth in
Galilee. His earthly father, Joseph, was a carpenter, and what
possessions they had they earned with hard, physical work.

When Jesus entered His public ministry, He was what
one might describe as an itinerant rabbi, traveling
throughout Galilee, and venturing into Judea and
surrounding provinces, proclaiming the gospel, healing the
sick, driving out demons, and performing other wondrous
works. But He did not garner wealth in the process. He lived
on what the land and sea provided, and He enjoyed the
support of patrons and patronesses who delighted in His
words and His works. Jesus' relationship to earthly wealth

might be analogized to His statement found in the Gospel of John: "You belong to what is below, I belong to what is above. You belong to this world, but I do not belong to this world." He did not know luxury in His life, and in death He was treated as a common criminal.

Despite the triumph of the Resurrection, Jesus' Apostles and other early followers were not appreciably better off themselves. From what we know, they spent much of their time moving about, evangelizing, facing persecution, avoiding capture, and, in most cases, ultimately giving their lives for their faith.

If we fast forward 2000 years, we find western civilization awash in financial corruption and unbounded greed. Many people who identify themselves as Christians slavishly pursue more, when they already have more than they could ever possibly need. And despite their supposed religious affiliation, some of these greedy people have no compunction about stretching or even breaking the law to get what they want. Nor do they display any concern whatsoever for the effects of their actions upon their fellow men and women of lesser means. We even have preachers who speak eloquently about how Jesus wants you to be rich. I surmise they have a version of the Gospels that I have never seen.

The reality is, Jesus is not a proponent of accumulating great wealth, profligate spending, and an opulent lifestyle. [4] His words seem pretty clear on this point. In a society dominated by the rich, with their luxury homes and their luxury cars and their luxury yachts, it may be radically unpopular to remind people what Jesus says about wealth. But if we are to try to get people to heaven, we can't be pulling our punches.

Let us then talk with Jesus about the type of lifestyle he envisions for His followers. I mentioned earlier that one of the capital sins is the sin of greed. According to Merriam-Webster, we can define greed as an excessive and selfish desire for more of something (such as money) than is needed. Jesus is not a big fan of greed. He says, "Take care to guard against all greed, for though one may be rich, one's life does not consist of possessions. As God said to the rich

---

[4] Certainly one of the most challenging of Jesus' teachings is this: "Every one of you who does not renounce all his possessions cannot be My disciple."

fool, 'this night your life will be demanded of you; and the things you have prepared, to whom will they belong?' Thus it will be for the one who stores up treasure for himself but is not rich in what matters to God."

In one sense, Jesus' comment about greed is a reflection of His spiritual versus temporal perspective on life. You cannot take your possessions with you when you die, so consequently the pursuit of wealth is ultimately vanity. Jesus' view is clearly that our focus should be on the spiritual, not the temporal. You will note that many of the other things Jesus says bear this out.

Jesus warns us not to "store up for []ourselves treasures on earth, where moth and decay destroy, and thieves break in and steal." Instead, Jesus urges us to "store up treasures in heaven, where neither moth nor decay destroy, nor thieves break in and steal. For where your treasure is, there also will your heart be." Jesus undoubtedly thinks that we 21st century first-worlders have our priorities all out of whack. Our focus is so strongly on what "things" can we accumulate here on earth, with relatively little regard for how our heavenly Father would have us prioritize our lives. I don't know about you, but when I see television commercials for things like luxury automobiles, and the way we, the consumers, are portrayed as covetous chumps, I cringe. Is that really the way we want to see ourselves? Would your answer be different if you knew God was watching?

One of Jesus' most famous sayings, in trying to get this point across, is "No one can serve two masters. He will either hate one and love the other, or be devoted to one and despise the other. You cannot serve God and mammon." This saying always reminds me of the 1955 movie "The Man in the Grey Flannel Suit". Frederick March plays a wealthy corporate bigwig who has sacrificed his family life and much more for worldly success, while Gregory Peck plays his younger assistant, who finds his boss's lifestyle very much at odds with what he believes his priorities should be. It is not easy for the underling to give up what he knows is a great career opportunity, but he decides he must do so in order to remain true to himself.

That is not to say that people should not work and earn money, as obviously it is important that we do both, in order to survive, support our families, do good works, et cetera. It is, rather, a question of priorities. Is the drive to make more, and to have more, consuming your life?

The main problem with money, in Jesus' view, is not the money itself, but the fact that the pursuit of money can start us on a vicious cycle of always wanting more, never being satisfied when we get it, and therefore wanting still more. There is a saying that the more money you have the more money you need, and it is true from at least these two perspectives: (1) when you attain a certain standard of living, when you can afford to travel where you want when you want, buy what you want when you want, eat dinner out seven nights a week or hire your own chef, these things become difficult to give up; (2) when you are wealthy you tend to associate with wealthy people, and in order to fit in with this circle you have to stay wealthy. Thus, facing the pressure to stay wealthy, it is difficult for the rich person to focus on the spiritual things in life. So when the word of God is sown in the heart of the rich person, it is like the seed of the sower of parable, the seed that fell among thorns. The thorns grew up and choked the seed.

As Jesus explains His parable, "The seed sown among the thorns is the one who hears the word, but then worldly anxiety and the lure of riches choke the word and it bears no fruit." If one is overly concerned with maintaining his standard of living, of getting and keeping "things", one will lose focus on what is important in the eyes of God. As a result, Jesus tells us, "Amen, I say to you, it will be hard for one who is rich to enter the kingdom of heaven. Again I say to you, it is easier for a camel to pass through the eye of a needle than for one who is rich to enter the kingdom of God."

While Jesus says it is difficult for a rich man to enter the kingdom, it is important to note that He does not say it is impossible. For as Jesus tells His disciples, with God all things are possible. It is a question of what the rich person does with his riches. Does he use his riches to live an opulent lifestyle, to lord it over the less fortunate, to make a show of his wealth? Or does he use it to contribute to the betterment of mankind? Consider again the story of the rich man and Lazarus the beggar. Do you think the rich man was consigned to hell because he was rich? Or was it not because there, right in front of him, was Lazarus, so sorely in need, and the rich man did not do a thing to help him? Remember the words of the ghost of Jacob Marley to his former partner, Ebeneezer Scrooge, in Dickens' "A Christmas Carol". When Scrooge compliments Marley as having been a good man of business, Marley's ghost wails, "Mankind was my business." Marley's lament, like the rich man in the netherworld, was that it was too late for him to use his wealth to help people.

Let us consider some of Jesus' advice that might make it possible for the rich man to enter the kingdom of heaven despite his riches. Be forewarned that this advice is not easy for those who are stuck in their ways, who are, as discussed above, stuck in a cycle of get more/spend more/get more/spend more. The Lord tells us, "To whom much is given, much is required," and this applies to our treasures as well as our talents. But the rich person will enter the kingdom of heaven if he engages in an other-directedness that is pleasing to the Lord, rather than persisting in a self-serving lifestyle.

Jesus gives this advice to the rich: "Go, sell what you have and give to the poor, and you will have treasure in heaven." And similarly, "Sell your belongings and give alms. Provide moneybags for yourselves that do not wear out, an inexhaustible treasure in heaven that no thief can reach nor moth destroy. For where your treasure is, there also will your heart be."

This statement brings us back to the question of priorities. If you are focused on your earthly riches, you are not offering the appropriate love to God and neighbor that is required as an obedient Christian. I mentioned earlier this statement by Jesus to His adversaries: "You belong to what is below, I belong to what is above. You belong to this world, but I do not belong to this world." This is the essence of the debate between living *the* good life and living *a* good life. Living *a* good life requires a focus on what is above, on using our treasures to further the kingdom of God, to love our neighbors and follow God's commands in our daily life. Living *the* good life manifests a focus on what is below, on using our treasures to satisfy our own earthly appetites. This is vanity, for as Jesus tells us in the parable of the rich fool, you will die, and what good will your treasures do you then?

Since I am not a rich guy, maybe it's easy for me to say this, but in my view this is a no-brainer. The goal is to get you all to eternal life, and therefore *a* good life trumps *the* good life, hands down.

QUESTIONS FOR REFLECTION OR DISCUSSION

1. What is your favorite quote from Jesus in Chapter Four? Why?

2. Which of Jesus' quotes in Chapter Four did you find most surprising? In what way did it surprise you?

3. Do you ever feel that you are on a treadmill of always having to acquire more "stuff"? Are there any material possessions/pursuits/hobbies/habits in your life that you feel are controlling you? If so, have you ever prayed about these things and asked God for guidance?

4. Do you find that the material world interferes with you having the spiritual life you would like to have? If so, in what way?

Chapter Five

AM I REALLY SUPPOSED TO LOVE OTHER PEOPLE? WHAT ABOUT THOSE PEOPLE WHO ARE BENEATH ME; THEM TOO?

Amen, I say to you, whatever you did for one of these least brothers of Mine,   you did for Me.

What do you think Jesus has to say to us concerning loving our fellow man and taking care of those who are less fortunate than we are? Do you think Jesus would encourage us to watch out for the other guy, and to be good to those who are in need? I am going to go out on a limb here and say that if you read the last Chapter, then you know the answer to these questions is "Yes!"

You probably know that there are millions of people in the world who are suffering from illness, poverty, loneliness, and injustice in various forms. We are called to be mindful of these people and to try helping them address their needs. You could say that's the other side of the debate between *the* good life and *a* good life. It's easy to sit back in your comfortable house with your pumpkin latte and convince yourself that these problems are too big, that there is nothing you can do that will solve the world's ills. And do you know what? You would be right. You can't stop world hunger, you can't save the world's refugees, you can't even stop the homeless from being homeless. Jesus said as much, didn't He? When the Apostles were upset that Mary had anointed the Lord with expensive ointment, arguing that the ointment could have been sold for money to help the poor, the Lord admonished them. He said, "The poor you will always have with you." And 2000 years later, with all the wealth in the world and all the advances in technology and all man's wonderful achievements over these past two millennia, the poor are still with us. Why is that? It's at least partially because people don't really care. I'm not just talking about you and me, I'm talking about people all over the world, people who might be in a position to make a difference, but choose not to.

If we take Jesus at His word, it is likely that the poor will be with us until the end of the world. But even if that is the case, even if Jesus knew that was the case, it doesn't follow that we should do nothing about it. Whatever little we can do to ease our fellow man's suffering is worth doing. Why do I say that? Well, there are at least two reasons right off the bat. The first reason is, out of compassion for those who are suffering. And you will likely find that feeding a hungry person not only helps that hungry person, it also helps you to feel a little better about yourself. The second reason is, I want you to get to heaven. That is the underlying theme that will be repeated throughout this book. And helping your fellow man is one way to get yourself on the right track for a heavenly future.

Let's take a look at some of what Jesus had to say along these lines. First, from the portion of the Sermon on the Mount that we call the Beatitudes, Jesus says, "Blessed are the merciful, for they will be shown mercy." What, you might ask, is mercy? We frequently think of mercy in a situation involving the judicial system, where a judge or someone else in authority "goes easy" on a person who is subject to some judgment or punishment. But a second definition of mercy, according to Merriam-Webster, is simply kindness or help given to people who are in a very bad or desperate situation. Thus, for example, if you donate groceries to a food bank so that a family that would otherwise have nothing to eat can put food on the table, you are being merciful. When you act in a charitable or compassionate way, you are being merciful, and God will bless you for that. Jesus also says, "If you wish to be perfect, go, sell what you have and give to the poor, and you will have treasure in heaven."

There are a couple of points worth noting here. First, as I mentioned above, even though the poor will always be with us, Jesus nevertheless advocates in favor of helping the poor. He never once says, "The poor you will always have with you, so forget about them and live it up while you can." The second point worth noting, as it has been noted before and will be noted again, doing good for the poor will improve your standing, heaven-wise. Jesus tells us that if we sell our belongings and give alms, we will have moneybags for ourselves that do not wear out, "an inexhaustible treasure in heaven that no thief can reach nor moth destroy." In His view, treasure in heaven is better than treasure on earth. If our goal is to get to heaven, we probably should put some stock in His view.

While we are talking about merciful and compassionate acts, it would be a good time to mention some other worthwhile teachings from the Lord. There is, for example, what has come to be known as the Golden Rule, which has its roots in the ancient Judeo-Christian traditions: "Do unto others what you would have them do unto you," Jesus says. "This is the law and the prophets." Then there are what Jesus terms the first and second commandments: "You shall love the Lord your God with all your heart, with all your soul, and with all your mind. This is the greatest and the first commandment. The second is like it: you shall love your neighbor as yourself."

I think you will agree there is a similarity between the Golden Rule and the second greatest commandment. Do unto others as you would have them do unto you, love your neighbor as yourself. In other words, be as good to others as you would be to yourself, or as you would hope others would be to you, in the same situation. If you were in dire need of food, drink, or clothing, you would hope someone would give you what you need. Just the same, then, you should give *them* what *they* need. There is a scene in the movie "Ben-Hur" in which Charlton Heston, as the title character, is a prisoner on a forced-march through the Palestinian desert. When other prisoners are permitted a mouthful of water, he is not. But a stranger appears – it is Jesus – and defies the Romans by giving Ben-Hur a cup of water, an act of kindness that Ben-Hur later tries to repay to Jesus on His way to Calvary. Imagine yourself as that parched person desperate for a drink of water. How wonderful the act of kindness of a stranger. We all need to be that kind stranger.

As Jesus makes clear to us, loving your neighbor is not dependent on the geographical proximity or personal familiarity between you and the needy person. One only needs think of the parable of the Good Samaritan and his encounter with the victim of a brutal robbery. The victim was a Jewish person on the road from Jericho to Jerusalem. A priest and a Levite went past the injured Jew in his time of need. But the Good Samaritan, a pariah in Jewish circles, stopped to help, and took the time, trouble, and expense to provide life-saving care. The one who was a neighbor to the robbers' victim was the one who showed him mercy. "Go and do likewise," is Jesus' command. So our acts of mercy can benefit someone who lives next door to us, or someone across the county whom we have never met, or someone halfway around the world. There are people in need, and there is a merciful God who will reward us for helping those in need. Some of the many ways we can help those in need are mentioned by Jesus in His story about the coming judgment (I'm sure you've heard this before):

> When the Son of Man comes in His glory, and all the angels with Him, He will sit upon His glorious throne, and all the nations will be assembled before Him. And He will separate them from one another, as a shepherd separates the sheep from the goats. He will place the sheep on His right and the goats on His left. Then the King will say to those on His right, "Come, you who are blessed by My Father, inherit the kingdom prepared for you from the foundation of the world. For I was hungry and you gave Me food, I was thirsty and you gave Me drink, a stranger and you welcomed Me, naked and you clothed Me, ill and you cared for Me, in prison and you visited Me." Then the righteous will answer Him and say, "Lord, when did we see You hungry and feed You, or thirsty and give You drink? When did we see You a stranger and welcome You, or naked and cloth You? When did we see You ill or in prison and visit You?" And the King will say to them in reply, "Amen, I say to you, whatever you did for one of these least brothers of Mine, you did for Me."

Food for the hungry, drink for the thirsty, a welcome for the stranger, clothes for the naked, care for the ill, a visit for the imprisoned. Once we get past the issue of our inability to solve all the world's problems, we see that there are many things we can easily do to help people in need. Donating money to churches or other charities, giving food to a pantry, coats for a clothing drive, being kind to new people in the neighborhood, visiting the sick and the homebound. Ministering to prisoners may require an exceptional level of grace that most of us do not possess, but it is another way of showing mercy. What is required mainly is a reorientation of our thinking, to care about people other than ourselves, to see and love Jesus in them, and to act accordingly. To give without expecting anything in return. [5] For the hour of judgment is coming, and Jesus tells us that when the hour comes, those who have done good deeds will proceed to the resurrection of life, while those who have done wicked deeds will experience the resurrection of condemnation. Myself, I would prefer the former.

As an example of a good-deed doer, we need look no further than Jesus Himself, for we know He not only talked the talk, He walked the walk. When the woman who suffered with a hemorrhage for a dozen years, so desperate for a cure to her affliction, merely touched Jesus' cloak, she

---

[5] "When you hold a banquet, invite the poor, the crippled, the lame, the blind," Jesus suggests to us. "Blessed indeed will you be because of their inability to repay you. For you will be repaid at the resurrection of the righteous."

was cured through Jesus' healing power. "Courage, daughter," He told her, "your faith has saved you." When Jesus went by boat across the Sea of Galilee, and the crowds heard of this and followed Him on foot from their towns, Jesus saw the vast numbers of people there. His heart was moved with pity for them, and He cured their sick. When Jesus was teaching in a synagogue one Sabbath, a woman was there who for eighteen years had been crippled by a spirit. After curing her, Jesus said, "This daughter of Abraham, whom Satan has bound for eighteen years now, ought she not to have been set free on the Sabbath day from this bondage?"

The lesson Jesus teaches us here is an easy one: "Love one another. As I have loved you, so you also should love one another. This is how all will know you are my disciples, if you have love for one another." If only all who call themselves Christians lived by that lesson! If you haven't learned it yet, please do while there is still time.

QUESTIONS FOR REFLECTION OR DISCUSSION

1. What is your favorite quote from Jesus in Chapter Five? Why?

2. Which of Jesus' quotes in Chapter Five did you find most surprising? In what way did it surprise you?

3. Have you ever given something to someone without expecting anything in return? If so, how did it leave you feeling?

4. Do you ever find yourself reluctant to share your blessings with others who are less fortunate than you are? If so, what are the reasons that standing your way?

Chapter Six

ARE YOU PLEASED WITH HOW THE ENTERTAINMENT INDUSTRY HAS PUSHED THE ENVELOPE AND BROKEN DOWN BARRIERS?

Enter through the narrow gate;
for the gate is wide and the road broad that leads to destruction,
and those who enter through it are many.

I guess you could say I'm a little old-fashioned as far as my tastes in entertainment are concerned. I was in grade school when George Carlin came out with his "seven words you can never say on television" routine. I never cared for that routine. Never much cared for old George at all, to tell you the truth, though I admit he did a commendable job as the narrator on various "Thomas the Tank Engine" videos that I used to watch with my children. His joke about anorexic girls and young women? Yeah, that's real funny, George. You're so hip.

But I digress. My point is that I grew up in an age when comedians were funny without having to use curse words, when situation comedies had to rely on cleverness rather than vulgarity. And when matters of sexual relations could be left to the imagination rather than played out in your living room for all to see.

Now I don't want to give the wrong impression that I am hopelessly outmoded. As far as television comedies are concerned, I rate "Seinfeld" right up there with "The Honeymooners" and "The Odd Couple". So I must be a little cool, don't you think? And I'm not a prude, either. In fact, although I am not proud to admit it, I was addicted to pornography for a few years back in the '80s. True, I was watching the scrambled signal from Wometco Home Theater with its squiggly lines, which increased the degree of difficulty.

Does anyone remember Wometco Home Theater? I recall it was on Channels 60 and 68 in Jersey City, whichever one came in better. Sometimes they showed music videos during the day and primetime. I saw some pretty esoteric videos on good old WHT. "Burning Flame" by Vitamin Z, "Dinero" by Joe "King" Carrasco and the Crowns, "Just Got Lucky" by Joboxers, which remains one of my favorite of all '80s songs. And I can't omit "Don't Answer Me" by the Alan Parsons Project, a truly wonderful song and video. Before it got into the esoteric music video business, WHT used to show esoteric old movies. I remember watching "The Under-pup" (1939), which was the debut of an adorable child star named Gloria Jean and also featured Bob Cummings, C. Aubrey Smith, and the always-delightful Virginia Weidler, and "The Parson of Panamint" (1941) starring Ellen Drew, Charles Ruggles, and Phillip Terry. Check them out if you have the chance.

But back to the point, at 11:00 p.m. WHT went to a scrambled signal, with all those squiggly lines on the screen, to show pornographic movies. You really couldn't see all that much through the squiggles, but, God forgive me, I did try. And the sad reality is that pornographic images stay in your brain forever. I can still visualize things I saw 30+ years ago, squiggly lines and all.

For those of us in Jersey City, the WHT days were the good old days, before Cable. Cable changed everything, and network TV has spent the last 30 years trying to catch up. We have gradually become anesthetized to vulgarity, as what once would have been shocking is now commonplace.

In the final analysis I imagine it's all about money – ratings, advertising dollars, box office revenue. To a large extent, vulgarity and corruption sell. Do you know what else seems to sell? Stupid. How else can you possibly explain the success and proliferation of "reality TV", which usually is not reality at all, but does manage to give viewers some really dumb ideas about how to behave. Vulgarity, corruption, stupidity. Tragically, the entertainment media is able to cater to the lowest common denominator quite successfully. This despite the fact that we live in a culture in which some 80% of people identify themselves as Christians. The problem here is that despite their professed religious affiliation, way too many of these Christians have allowed themselves to be co-opted by the entertainment industry. They have surrendered their ability to think, and to render their own moral judgments, in return for cheap laughs and cheap thrills.

Though we may not like to admit it, we cannot help but be influenced by what we see and hear in the media. If we watch too much gratuitous violence, we can become hardened to its effects, even though the entertainment industry protests this point. (Me think they protesteth too much.) There is a movie from 1980 called "Dressed to Kill", which is described as an "erotic thriller". The movie depicts the ultra-violent slasher killing of a woman. The first two times the movie was shown on network television, young women were stabbed or slashed to death by their sexual partners in my hometown. Whether the killers had watched the movie, I can't say. But if it was a coincidence it was an awfully brutal one. There have of course been equally horrendous crimes in which the perpetrators have *admitted* being influenced by some specific movie to carry out their acts of carnage.

Similarly, if we watch too much gratuitous sex, it becomes easier to separate the physical act from the emotional attachment that should give rise to it, pun intended. Furthermore, regardless of what the industry tells you, pornography can wreak havoc on normal sexual relationships. With the ubiquity of the Internet, I am very concerned about our young people being scarred for life by the proliferation of pornography. Moreover, there can be no question that Internet pornography has already ruined the careers, marriages, and lives of countless individuals.

One of the things that most concerns me with respect to the entertainment industry is the abdication of parental responsibility where television watching and movie attendance are concerned. I don't think most Christian parents are sufficiently on the ball as far as what their children are permitted to watch. I analogize lack of parental supervision over children's television viewing habits with this: would you invite some stranger off the street into your living room to talk to your children, without being present yourself to monitor what is being said? You probably wouldn't. But the analogy to unsupervised television watching is not that far off base. You generally have no idea about the screenwriters of prime-time TV shows, what their sensibilities are, what their agenda is, what their moral proclivities are. Let's be real, they probably don't much care if your children grow up to be depraved rather than moral. Whatever gets the ratings, baby.

So you have probably decided by now that I am quite a bit off my rocker, but enough about me. What does Jesus think of all this? We can get a pretty good idea based upon some of the things He says to us. For example, at the Sermon on the Mount, He said, "Blessed are the pure of heart, for they will see God." Purity is surely lacking in much of what passes for entertainment these days. As we have already seen, Jesus says the following in describing His mission on earth: "Amen I say to you, until heaven and earth pass away, not the smallest letter or the smallest part of a letter will pass from the law, until all things have taken place. Therefore, whoever breaks one of the least of these commandments *and teaches others to do* so will be called least in the kingdom of heaven." (Emphasis added.) Based on His comments, I would venture to say that Jesus would not approve of excessive violence, vulgarity, and depravity in the media.

Jesus also says, "You have heard that it was said, 'You shall not commit adultery.' But I say to you, everyone who looks at a woman with lust has already committed adultery with her in his heart." Certainly the prevalence of sexuality and sexual imagery in the media can lead us astray with respect to the sin of lust. To that end, remember this: "If your right eye causes you to sin, tear it out and throw it away. It is better for you to lose one of your members than to have your whole body thrown into Gehenna." Now tearing out your right eye does not strike me as being a particularly good idea; the better solution would be to stop looking at the images that will lead you down a sinful path. This takes self-discipline, as there is no question that sexual images have an addictive quality to them. But avoiding the images is a less painful solution to the problem of visual temptation than is tearing out your eye. And, in Jesus' view, both these alternatives are better than spending eternity in hell!

Even where my crazy analogy of the screenwriter as a stranger in your living room is concerned, Jesus might agree with me. Consider this pronouncement:

> Beware of false prophets, who come to you in sheep's clothing, but underneath are ravenous wolves. By their fruits you will know them. Do people pick grapes from thornbushes, or figs from thistles? Just so, every good tree bears good fruit, and a rotten tree bears bad fruit. A good tree cannot bear bad fruit, nor can a rotten tree bear good fruit. Every tree that does not bear good fruit will be cut down and thrown into the fire. So by their fruits you will know them.

Wolves in sheep's clothing. Watching that television program, going to see that movie, these activities might seem innocuous enough, but we must be careful of what is lurking there. We can so subtly be seduced by the unsavory. And if we sincerely wish to be heaven-bound, we must avoid the too-easy defense that "everybody watches that stuff, why shouldn't I?" As Jesus warns us, "The gate is wide and the road broad that leads to destruction, and those who enter through it are many. How narrow the gate and constricted the road that leads to life. And those who find it are few." In this circumstance you want to be one of the few, and I think you would want your children also to be among the few.

There are other things Jesus tells us that could easily be applied to the entertainment industry. For example, "You brood of vipers, how can you say good things when you are evil? For from the fullness of the heart the mouth speaks. A good person brings forth good out of a store of goodness, but an evil person brings forth evil out of a store of evil." Of course the entertainment industry is by no means limited to television and filmmaking. You have to include the music industry, various Internet sites, and ultra-violent video game purveyors, all of whom are all too happy to make a handsome profit from the destruction of your children's souls.

Trying to control what your loved ones allow into their brains is not an easy task, I know. God has given each of us free will, and how reluctant we are to let anyone tell us what we should do. But in pursuit of eternal life for ourselves and our families we must be strong, courageous. Jesus tells us, "Do not think that I have come to bring peace upon the earth. I have come to bring not peace but the sword. For I have come to set a man against his father, a daughter against her mother, and a daughter-in-law against her mother-in-law; and one's enemies will be those of his household." How true this statement becomes when we are embroiled in the battle to guard our loved ones' hearts and minds against the seductive attraction of depravity. But nevertheless we must battle on, for whoever is not with Jesus is against Him, and whoever does not gather with Him scatters. We want to gather our loved ones to Jesus, not scatter them among the lost sheep.

If you find yourself among the lost sheep as a result of your exposure to the unsavory influences of the entertainment industry, it is essential that you repent, change your ways, and come back to Christ. For whoever wants to come after Jesus must deny himself, take up his cross, and follow the Lord. Remember that Jesus tells us, it is he who loses his life for Jesus' sake that will find it. Consider also the shame you will experience at the judgment as a result of the bad moral decisions you have made in your life. Jesus warns us, "Whatever you have said in the darkness will be heard in the light, and what you have whispered behind closed doors will be proclaimed on the housetops." Your transgressions will be laid bare, much to your dismay.

I have previously referred to the litany of sins that Jesus cites in Mark 7, verses 21-22, as coming from the evil in men's hearts. Evil thoughts, unchastity, theft, murder, adultery, greed, malice, deceit, licentiousness, envy, blasphemy, arrogance, and folly. Pretty much the things that flood your mind after seeing the latest gory thriller out of Hollywood, viewing some Internet pornography sites, playing Grand Theft Auto, and tuning in to the latest adventures of Molly Cyrus and the music industry's bad boy or bad girl *du jour*!

While I have great concern for the effects of these things on the unsuspecting viewer, especially the impressionable children who are oblivious to the potential harm, I must also voice my concern for the producers and artists who create the garbage that poisons our minds. These are the people whose souls are in most grave danger absent a radical transformation in their lives. If you happen to be one of these people, <u>I urge you to pay attention</u>. Our modern culture is very open to the idea of artistic freedom. Society tends very strongly towards the encouragement and rewarding of outrageous performance. (There are still some limits to this; we have not yet embraced full-nudity-live-sex-acts on prime-time network television, for example. But no doubt there are many producers and artists out there who would be more than willing to give it a shot.)

When we go before God when our time on earth is done, however, I fear the "artistic freedom" defense will likely fall on deaf ears. Suppose the pornography you produced destroyed the lives of various adult entertainment performers through drug abuse, disease, and suicide? Suppose it also helped create a generation of pornography addicts, serial adulterers, and sex criminals? Suppose the music you produced helped enslave generations of young people in a cycle of street crime, violence, and early death? Suppose the video games you produced spawned a generation of young people who had no respect for law and order or right and wrong, no respect for life, including their own? Will God accept your defense of "artistic freedom", "creative license", "breaking down barriers", or however else you want to try to spin it?

If we put that question to Jesus, His answer will be "no". Why do I say that? Although Jesus died for our sins, He did not do so with the expectation that we would then lead lives of debauchery, and draw others into such lives. He did so with the expectation that we would follow His commands.

There are people who would disagree with me on this point, I know. There are people who seem convinced, as discussed earlier, that everyone gets to heaven, because God loves all His children so much that He would not want to be separated from them. If you adhere to this theory, then Hitler, Stalin, and every other murderous dictator down through the ages would have attained eternal life. And those guys who flew the planes into the World Trade Center, they would also be "up there". If this theory is accurate, the rest of us poor saps have nothing to worry about. But I cannot accept this theory. (I'm a little surprised anyone can.) I cannot accept it because Jesus does not seem to endorse it.

Specifically with regard to those who lure others into a life of sin, here is what Jesus does say: "Whoever causes one of these little ones who believe in me to sin, it would be better for him to have a great millstone hung around his neck and to be drowned in the depths of the sea. Woe to the world because of things that cause sin. Such things must come, but woe to the one through whom they come."

This statement obviously is not limited to my thesis of condemnation of modern-day purveyors of filth and violence. It clearly would apply to anyone who leads another individual into sin – drug dealers, child molesters, etc. But Jesus' words do seem to act as a warning to those individuals and conglomerates who earn their keep by perverting the morals of our society through mass entertainment.

One of the sad realities in our present age is that celebrities and executives in the entertainment world can make an obscene amount of money. They also are frequent recipients of great attention and adulation. But fame and fortune are fleeting and are of little benefit when you're dead. As Jesus says, "What profit would there be for one to gain the whole world and forfeit his life, or what can one give in exchange for his life? For the Son of Man will come with His angels in His Father's glory, and then He will repay everyone according to his conduct." Jesus also issues this warning to certain people, and I suppose today's bigger than life celebrities and mavens might well fall within its purview: "You justify yourselves in the eyes of others, but God knows your hearts; for what is of human esteem is an abomination in the sight of God."

This is what we who are sinners must recognize while there is still time. It doesn't matter how rich you are or how famous you are or how much the public adores you, it is by how you live your life that you will be judged. If you are not living it in a manner that is pleasing to God, I urge you to change your ways so that you store up treasures for yourself in heaven, and earn eternal life when your time on earth is done.

QUESTIONS FOR REFLECTION OR DISCUSSION

1. What is your favorite quote from Jesus in Chapter Six? Why?

2. Which of Jesus' quotes in Chapter Six did you find most surprising? In what way did it surprise you?

3. Do you ever give consideration to the moral implications of television shows and movies you watch or music you listen to? Do you give such consideration to television shows and movies your children watch or music they listen to?

4. Do you think God cares about what you choose to watch or listen to in your free time?

5. Are there ways in which you have found your behavior has changed for the worse as a result of something you have viewed or heard from the entertainment media?

Chapter Seven

IS THE WORSHIP OF IDOLS AN ISSUE IN THE 21ST CENTURY?

It is written, the Lord your God shall you worship,
and Him alone shall you serve.

In the Old Testament book of Exodus, chapter 20, we read about God delivering the Ten Commandments to His people, Israel. What is the very first commandment of the ten? "I, the Lord, am your God, who brought you out of the land of Egypt, that place of slavery. You shall not have other gods besides Me. You shall not carve idols for yourselves in the shape of anything in the sky above, or on the earth below, or in the waters beneath the earth; you shall not bow down before them or worship them. For I, the Lord, your God, am a jealous God, inflicting punishment for their fathers' wickedness on the children of those who hate Me, down to the third and fourth generation; but bestowing mercy down to the thousandth generation on the children of those who love Me and keep My commandments."

As this is the very first commandment God gave to the people from Mount Sinai, we can conclude that He strongly disfavors idol worship. A little bit further along in chapter 20 of the Book of Exodus, God says to Moses, "This shall you speak to the Israelites: you have seen that I have spoken to you from heaven. Do not make anything to rank with Me; neither gods of silver nor gods of gold shall you make for yourselves. ..."

Of course the ink on the tablets was not even dry before the Israelites already began worshipping an idol made of gold, in the form of a calf. I think it was some guy named Edward G. Robinson who made the idol. Can I get a witness? And elsewhere in the Old Testament there are reports of the trouble that followed when God's people took to worshipping Baal and other pagan gods. But we twenty-first century humans are far more evolved than those ancient Israelites. We wouldn't, or at least most of us wouldn't, go about worshipping images of birds, beasts, and fish made of silver or gold. So this seems to be one area, at least, in which God should be rather pleased with modern man, don't you think?

Well, you probably have figured out already that I asked that question facetiously. Because at the end of the day, the issue is not so much whether we worship gods made from silver or gold, or whether we worship idols in the form of birds, beasts, or fish. The real issue is, what in our lives receives preeminent importance? Are there things, or people, in our lives to which we give attention and adulation over and above what is deserved?

Let's consider very quickly what exactly we mean when we say the word "worship". According to Merriam-Webster, worship can mean the showing of respect or reverence for a divine being or supernatural power. But it can also mean excessive or extravagant admiration of, or devotion to, a person or object of esteem.

Taking into account the latter definition, I believe Jesus tells us, in His inimitable way, that idol worship is still a problem for us modern people despite our highly evolved condition. Jesus reminds us, for example, "It is written, the Lord your God shall you worship, and Him alone shall you serve." Jesus also instructs us that the greatest commandment of them all is, "You shall love the Lord, your God, with all your heart, and with all your being, with all your strength, and with all your mind." So the question of idolatry goes beyond worshipping carved idols; it is a question of who or what in your life is interfering with your love of God.

At this point I would like to consider this rather difficult statement that Jesus gives us: "Whoever loves father or mother more than Me is not worthy of Me, and whoever loves son or daughter more than Me is not worthy of Me; and whoever does not take up his cross and follow after Me is not worthy of Me."

What are we to make of this? Jesus tells us, throughout the Gospels, the importance of loving one another, of loving our neighbor. Therefore, I think it is safe to say that Jesus fully expects us to love our parents and our children. That being the case, we can infer that what Jesus is really saying here is that He expects us to love Him, and God the Father, a whole heck of a lot. It is when we put earthly things above God that we incur His wrath. And I much fear that we modern people put lots and lots of earthly things above God. In the final analysis, this is idol worship. God asks us not to worship anything above Him. When there are things in our lives that we admire or esteem more than God, we have broken the first commandment.

What kinds of people or things do we admire or esteem more than God? Perhaps the first and most obvious example is celebrities. We even call them idols, a fairly good hint that worshipping them could be an issue for us. There are a few different problems with this celebrity worship that afflicts our culture. Here I am directing my remarks mostly, though not exclusively, toward young people, tweens and teens, who are more likely to idolize celebrities. In the first place, the fact is that these celebrities are merely people, like all the rest of us, and therefore not entitled to worship. In the second place, as a general population celebrities are not better people than we are; furthermore, more and more these days they do not even have to be more *talented* than we are. We have reached a most absurd point in human existence where many people are celebrities for no other reason than that our idiotic media have made them celebrities. In many cases it is even worse than that: we have many people who are celebrities only because of their notorious (and I mean that in a bad way) behavior. If a culture is going to celebrate people for behaving badly, you can bet your bottom dollar that said culture has a morality problem. Every parent learns early on that it is a bad idea to reward bad behavior. In the meantime, our society acts as if it's a *good* idea.

I should take two sentences to make clear that I am not arguing against rooting for a particular sports team or player, or enjoying the work of a particular actor, actress, or musician. It is certainly natural and normal to appreciate the efforts of talented people. Rather, the problem is one of degree. If we revere people out of proportion to what their importance in our lives should be, we are engaging in idol worship. This cannot help but interfere with our relationship with God, and our relationships with our families and friends as well. Ultimately this excessive behavior comes back to hurt us, because we cannot help but be disappointed by those we idolize. Maybe they will say or do something that disappoints and hurts us. Or maybe something they fail to do will hurt us, such as not responding to our attention. Or it may be simply the disappointment of the reality of the human condition – not every performance can be great, not every season can be a success.

A more relevant and potentially more dangerous consequence of this type of idol worship is the desire to emulate those we admire. It is an unfortunate reality that many of the "stars" of the entertainment industry – actors, musicians, comedians – have a self-destructive aspect to their personality. Seeking to follow in their footsteps can lead to the adoption of harmful habits, such as excessive drinking, drug abuse, and sexual promiscuity. A high school classmate of mine wanted to be Jim Morrison, and he died of an overdose at the age of 18.

Another downside is the possibility that we will take to emulating people who, quite simply, are not good people. Many of our media celebrities are living lives filled with licentiousness, covetousness, materialism, and the glorification of violence. I can't understand why the entertainment industry promotes this type of behavior, unless the entertainment industry simply abhors a stable society. That and love of money.

It is an alarming phenomenon, though not a new one, that even celebrities who happen on the scene as clean-cut innocents frequently end up reinventing themselves as bad-ass degenerates. It has been said that even bad publicity is good publicity, so perhaps there is a method to this madness. But all too often the end result is the meteoric crash of a promising career and a premature visit to the morgue.

It is important that we and our children be aware of the pitfalls of celebrity worship and emulation. As Jesus tells us, "Beware of false prophets, who come to you in sheep's clothing, but underneath are ravenous wolves. By their fruits you will know them. Do people pick grapes from thornbushes, or figs from thistles? Just so, every good tree bears good fruit, and a rotten tree bears bad fruit. A good tree cannot bear bad fruit, nor can a rotten tree bear good fruit. Every tree that does not bear good fruit will be cut down and thrown into the fire. So by their fruits you will know them." We have to have our eyes and ears open to the influences in our children's lives. Bad influences lead to bad consequences; don't let anyone tell you differently.

Let me now circle back to the goal of this book as originally stated, to try to get all people to heaven by showing them the wisdom Jesus teaches us. When we get caught up in idol worship and the glamor of celebrity lifestyles, we lose sight of two most important lessons that

Jesus imparts upon us. First, Jesus says, "The greatest among you must be your servant. Whoever exalts himself will be humbled; but whoever humbles himself will be exalted." It is really unfair to generalize about people, so let me just say that many, though not all, celebrities are very much into being exalted; exalted by themselves, by their enablers, by the media, and by adoring fans. This is contrary to the way Jesus would have us live, and for we who call ourselves Christians, to further exalt such individuals is simply wrong. We need to pray for them; we do not need to exalt them. Second, Jesus tells us, "You justify yourselves in the eyes of others, but God knows your hearts; for what is of human esteem is an abomination in the sight of God." It hurts me to have to say it, but much of what goes on in today's entertainment media is quite accurately described as an abomination. It may sell with the public, but it does not sell with God. When the final judgment comes, God, not the public, will decide whether you will rise in the resurrection of life or fall in the resurrection of condemnation. Do not be seduced by what the world tells you is to be esteemed. Listen to Jesus, back off the adoration of human idols, and embrace God.

QUESTIONS FOR REFLECTION OR DISCUSSION

1. What is your favorite quote from Jesus in Chapter Seven? Why?

2. Which of Jesus' quotes in Chapter Seven did you find most surprising? In what way did it surprise you?

3. Are there any people or things in your life that you think you probably worship more than you should? Why is that?

4. Are there people you have worshipped as idols who have let you down in some way? How did you feel about that?

5. Do you feel there are any idols or activities in your life that detract from your relationship with God? Explain.

Chapter Eight

ISN'T IT THE GOAL TO GET MY HANDS ON WHATEVER AND WHOMEVER I CAN IN THIS LIFE?

If you remain in my word, you will truly be my disciples,
and you will know the truth, and the truth will set you
free. ...   everyone who commits sin is a slave of sin.

Lust. Covetousness. Envy. These sins have been with us since the dawn of humanity. Was it not covetousness and envy that led Cain to slay his brother Abel? Covetousness gets a place in not one, but two of the Ten Commandments. You shall not covet your neighbor's goods, nor his wife. Although not mentioned by name, lust also rings up two spots in the dishonor roll, with the commandment against coveting your neighbor's wife, and also the admonition against committing adultery, which is born of lust. Lust, you may recall, is one of the seven deadly sins of yore. So is envy. And envy is an important element in any sin that involves covetousness.

Lust can be defined as an intense or unrestrained sexual desire or an overwhelming desire or craving for something. Covetousness can be defined as a very strong desire for something that you do not have, especially for something that belongs to somebody else. Envy can be defined as discontentment and resentment caused by a desire to have something that someone else has, whether it be possessions, wealth, success, or some other advantage.

While lust, covetousness, and envy have been with us almost from day one, their ancientness has not caused them to lose any power. They are still going strong in century twenty-one. Indeed, with the invaluable assistance of our good friends, the media, these sins are as healthy and prevalent as they have ever been. With the amount of information available to us, people are more acutely aware than ever before of the gap between the rich and poor, of the lifestyles of the rich and famous. And the advertising industry will spare no expense in showing us what we could and should have, and in making us feel inadequate that we do not have it. In the entertainment media, sex and sexuality are often front and center, leading impressionable libidos down a lustful path. The advent and proliferation of Internet pornography helps further the disconnect between lust and love.

While any sin puts a wedge in our relationship with God, it is important to note how destructive these particular sins can be to ourselves and to those around us. Lust can lead to infidelity, and all the harm and mayhem that come with it. Covetousness can likewise lead to marital infidelity, if it involves coveting a person, or it can lead to instances of theft, fraud, and white collar crime if it involves trying to match the wealth or possessions of others. Envy, and the resentment it spawns, can also send us down a destructive path, as evidenced by the case of Cain and Abel mentioned above.

Since the point of this book is to help keep us all on the straight and narrow path to heaven, let's look at what Jesus teaches us about these troublesome sins.

Let's begin with this timeless, profound declaration of our Lord: "If you remain in My word, you will truly be My disciples, and you will know the truth, and the truth will set you free. ... everyone who commits sin is a slave of sin." The slavery of sin is a most appropriate metaphor for lust, envy, and covetousness. For in a very real sense we are talking here about addictions – addiction to sex, addiction to acquiring "things", addiction to feelings of self-importance.

The first step to recovery from these addictions, then, is to abide in Jesus' word in order to understand the truth of what our lives are supposed to be. First, an admonition that we have seen before: Jesus says, "Amen I say to you, until heaven and earth pass away, not the smallest letter or the smallest part of a letter will pass from the law, until all things have taken place." This bears repetition, for although Jesus came to die for our sins, that does not mean we can do whatever we want and still merit salvation. Sin is still sin, and, in order to reap the rewards of eternal life that Jesus made possible for us, we are expected to avoid, not revel in, sin.

Jesus has this to say about people who persist in their sinful ways despite hearing His word, "And this is the verdict, that the light came into the world, but people preferred darkness to light, because their works were evil. For everyone who does wicked things hates the light, so that his works might not be exposed."

Where the sin of lust is concerned, we have guidance from this Beatitude delivered by Jesus at the Sermon on the Mount: "Blessed are the pure of heart, for they will see God." Jesus also reiterates the Commandment against adultery, and takes it one step further when He says to us, "[e]veryone who looks at a woman with lust has already committed adultery with her in his heart." Jesus also advises us, in somewhat hyperbolic fashion, "If your right eye causes you to sin, tear it out and throw it away. It is better for you to lose one of your members than to have your whole body thrown into Gehenna."

Blessed are the pure of heart. Purity of heart is not an easy ideal to achieve. It becomes more and more difficult as society and our culture become increasingly sexualized, as fashions become increasingly provocative, and as the availability of sexually-charged images explodes across the media and the Internet. Successfully repelling the advances of the enemy requires the application of self-discipline, and a constant vigilance over our eyes and our minds and where we let them wander. Engaging in a continual examination of conscience is another effective weapon against the temptations we face. We are bombarded by the forces of hedonism, materialism, and consumerism at all times. The message is, if it feels good, do it; if you want it, have it. The message is never "restrain your impulses."

But the importance of listening to Jesus' message cannot be overstated, for there are both temporal and spiritual consequences to our actions. What are the temporal consequences? Divorce and the destruction of the family unit is one. Certainly the lure of the flesh has been known to cause people to seek sexual satisfaction outside of marriage, and before you know it your entire personal life has become a living hell, your marriage and family in tatters. Taking it a step further, it is not entirely unheard of for an angry spouse to exact revenge for an adulterous affair through deadly violence, bringing the temporal and spiritual consequences together in a most tragic manner.

Another possible temporal consequence from the sin of unbridled lust is jail time. If we constantly expose ourselves to messages and images of sexual libertinism, we cannot help but become immune to the underlying immorality of the messages and hardened to the impersonality of the images. So you've been watching MTV's Spring Break

Weekend with lots of bumping and grinding of scantily clad young women, and then you find yourself at a summer festival in the park with lots of scantily clad young women. What's the harm of a little touching, a little groping? Isn't that why they're dressed that way? 'Fraid not, dude, you're going to the slammer. Yes, our perverted culture has entrapped you; but no, that's not a defense, even if it probably should be.

Another consideration we must not forget is our moral obligation to our fellow human beings. If you become sexually obsessed with an individual and refuse to discipline yourself, you will go through hell and high water trying to seduce him or her. If you succeed, you have caused not just yourself but another person as well to commit sin. If you come across some prurient material that you think is worthy of sharing, and you send it to your friends, not only have you sinned, but you have now drawn others into the web of impurity. And Jesus has stern words for those of us who lead others into sin. Remember? "Whoever causes one of these little ones who believe in Me to sin, it would be better for him to have a great millstone hung around his neck and to be drowned in the depths of the sea. Woe to the world because of things that cause sin. Such things must come, but woe to the one through whom they come. "

Jesus also has plenty to teach us concerning the sins of covetousness and envy. Once again, you will note a stark contrast between what Jesus proclaims and the messages society sends us. Society pushes us to pursue worldly success, which would include the accumulation of wealth and the attainment of great attention. Fame and fortune, as Rudolph the Red-nosed Reindeer and Herbie the Elf sang about. But Jesus tells us that if these are our goals, we have our priorities misarranged. "Do not store up for yourselves treasures on earth, where moth and decay destroy, and thieves break in and steal," Jesus says. "But store up treasures in heaven, where neither moth nor decay destroy, nor thieves break in and steal. For where your treasure is, there also will your heart be." <u>Our hearts, and our eyes, should be focused on our eternal reward</u>. If we are obsessed with worldly possessions, with wanting what the other guy has, our focus will not be where it belongs. Jesus warns us, "No one can serve two masters. He will either hate one and love the other, or be devoted to one and despise the other. You cannot serve God and mammon."

It would be wrong to say that wealth itself is a bad thing, for with wealth one can do great things in service of God and man. I remember reading an article in Sports Illustrated about the most generous athletes; the article reported some staggering amount of money that race-car drive Michael Schumacher had donated to charity. As I recall, it was tens of millions of dollars. It was positively staggering, not the least because I had never heard of the man before. (OK, so I'm not a Formula One racing fan.) Think of all the people who could be helped with such donations, and think that Herr Schumacher obviously could not have donated such sums if he did not have them to donate. So the issue is not one of wealth, but of what is our relationship with wealth. Is it the be all and end all of our existence? Are we obsessed with always having more, and deathly afraid of losing what we have? Do we despise those who have more than we have? Does a lack of material possessions make us feel inadequate? If the answer to any of these questions is "yes", then we have an unhealthy relationship with wealth. And this type of envy and covetousness can cause us ruin, both temporal and spiritual, just as surely as lust can.

What great lengths people have gone to to acquire and keep wealth. Think of Enron, and Bernie Madoff. Think of the lives ruined, the confinement to prison, even the suicides in the wake of these scandals. How can the fleeting pleasures that wealth can bring possibly be worth these dire consequences? Life on earth ruined, eternal life imperiled. The lack of self-discipline, the refusal simply to acknowledge and accept that some things are right, and some things are wrong. No, it's all about getting what I want, even if I already have more than 99% of the people in the world have. Does not Jesus tell us, "What profit would there be for one to gain the whole world and forfeit his life, or what can one give in exchange for his life?" But people don't listen to the wisdom Jesus imparts.

Note the part of Jesus' parable of the sower in which He speaks of some seed falling among the thorns, and the thorns growing up and choking the seed. Jesus explains this part of the parable in this way: "The seed sown among the thorns is the one who hears the word, but then worldly anxiety and the lure of riches choke the word and it bears no fruit." No, you cannot serve God and mammon. If you are too focused on worldly success, you will surely lose your spiritual way. It is not God's desire that we spend our lives pursuing worldly riches and the adulation of the crowds. To be truly Christian, and to aspire to eternal life, it is essential that we re-order our priorities. Listen to Jesus:

> Notice how the flowers grow. They do not toil or spin, but I tell you, not even Solomon in all his splendor was dressed like one of them. If God so clothes the grass in the field that grows today and is thrown in the oven tomorrow, will He not much more provide for you, O you of little faith? As for you, do not seek what you are to eat and what you are to drink, and do not worry anymore. All the nations of the world seek for these things, and your Father knows that you need them. Instead, seek first His kingdom, and these other things will be given to you besides.

I would be remiss if I did not acknowledge that it is not only lascivious perverts and greedy scoundrels who run afoul of the sins of lust, covetousness, and envy. Jesus had to rebuke His own Apostles when their thoughts ran to worldly glory and envy of one another. Even saints are guilty of such things. Look again at the case of Martha and Mary, Jesus' friends from Bethany. Martha busied herself with much serving, while her sister Mary sat beside the Lord at His feet, listening to Him speak. Martha asked Jesus if He did not care that Mary had left Martha by herself to do the serving. "Lord, tell Mary to help me!" Wasn't it at least partly envy that drove Martha to confront Jesus? Envy that Mary was closer to Jesus? Envy that Mary was getting away with doing no work? Envy that Jesus was not attentive to Martha's self-imposed woe?

Every single one of us must be mindful of the sins of lust and envy, for they can come upon us so easily. They are never really far away, and they can damage or destroy relationships and lives in the blink of an eye.

Don't listen to what society tells you, listen to what Jesus tells you. Exercise self discipline, examine your conscience, acknowledge what is right and what is wrong, and do not let yourself become a slave to sin.

QUESTIONS FOR REFLECTION OR DISCUSSION

1. What is your favorite quote from Jesus in Chapter Eight? Why?

2. Which of Jesus' quotes in Chapter Eight did you find most surprising? In what way did it surprise you?

3. Do you worry more about catching up to the people who have more than you, or helping the people who have less than you?

4. Have you ever been in a situation where your lust for another person resulted in a problem either in your marriage or the other person's marriage, or both? If so, how did you resolve the conflict?

5. Does it bother you if someone has a nicer house or a nicer car than you have? Do you ever reflect about how God feels about your envy?

Chapter Nine

WHY WOULD I WANT TO TRAVEL ALONG THE NARROW PATH WHEN EVERYONE ELSE IS GOING DOWN BROADWAY?

Whoever wishes to come after Me must deny himself, take up his cross, and follow Me.

For whoever wishes to save his life will lose it, but whoever loses his life for My sake will find it.

One of the reasons Jesus came to earth was to provide us with a road map to eternal life. Among the more explicit directions He gives us for getting there is this: "Enter through the narrow gate; for the gate is wide and the road broad that leads to destruction, and those who enter through it are many. How narrow the gate and constricted the road that leads to life. And those who find it are few."

Two basic premises I am working from, which I hope we can agree upon, are (1) Jesus loves us, and (2) Jesus wants us to attain eternal life. In order to show us the way to eternal life, however, Jesus needs to engage in some "tough love". We human beings are gifted with free will, so we can make our own choices in life. But not all choices are good, and not all choices are pleasing to God. Often times, the more popular choice is a choice that will lead us astray. As alluded to earlier, some people theorize that God loves all His children, and therefore will welcome us all into eternal life. However, I do not believe that is what God tells us. Why should the ones who break all the rules get the same reward as those who obey the rules? Rules are made for a reason. Suppose all people lived their lives in disregard of the rules against murder, stealing, adultery, etc? What a chaotic, violent place earth would be – even more chaotic and violent than it already is. This is not the vision God has for His sons and daughters, and this is why there must be consequences for lawbreakers.

I'm sure God would prefer it if we all found the narrow path and stayed on it, so we could be with Him in heaven after our mortal journey. Unfortunately, though, that is not realistic. Because we are not a race of robots, but can exercise our free will, we often stray from the path God would have us follow. In fact, as Jesus indicates, more of us tend to follow the broad way than the narrow path. Why is this? Perhaps because the broad way is the way of least resistance, or perhaps society lures us toward the broad way. Or perhaps simply because the broad way is more fun. In "Only the Good Die Young", Billy Joel sang "I'd rather laugh with the sinners than cry with the saints, the sinners are much more fun." But Jesus' message is clear: the narrow path is the better path. What, then, is the narrow path? Let's look at some examples:

> When someone strikes me on the right cheek, shouldn't I strike him back? No! Jesus says, "Turn the left cheek to him as well."

> If I have enemies who hate me, I should hate them back, right? No! Jesus says, "Love your enemies."

> If someone is persecuting me, it's o.k. if I curse them, right? No! Jesus says, "Pray for those who persecute you."

> Do I have to love everybody? Isn't it good enough to love the people who love me? No! "Even the tax collectors do that."

> Am I supposed to be friendly to strangers? Yes! Jesus says, "If you greet your brothers only, what is unusual about that? Do not the pagans do the same?"

> Everyone I know is always trying to get ahead, to make as much money as possible, to get a bigger house, nicer clothes, a new car. Am I not supposed to do the same? No! "No one can serve two masters. He will either hate one and love the other, or be devoted to one and despise the other. You cannot serve God and mammon.... So do not say 'what are we to eat' or 'what are we to drink' or 'what are we to wear'. .. But seek first the kingdom of God and His righteousness, and all these things will be given to you besides."

> The most important thing in the world is my family. I have to take care of them. I can't be worried about the rest of the world's troubles, it's not my problem, right? Wrong! Jesus says, "Whoever loves father or mother more than Me is not worthy of Me, and whoever loves son or daughter more than Me is not worthy of Me; and whoever does not take up his cross and follow after Me is not worthy of Me. ... Whoever does the will of My heavenly Father is My brother, and sister, and mother."

Of course we do have an obligation to our families, and if you are struggling financially your family will be your primary concern. But if you are the rich guy who is storing up treasure for himself on earth, and you and your family have more than enough to get by, you must turn your gaze outward to see where you can help the rest of humanity. God requires this of us. Loving others requires this of us. Remember Jesus' words that left the rich young man crestfallen: "If you wish to be perfect, go, sell what you have and give to the poor, and you will have treasure in heaven." Like it or not, God expects much of us where our use of our treasure is concerned.

> I have to take care of my children and my spouse. I am always running somewhere, to school, to soccer practice, little league games, home-school meetings, the grocery store. I don't have time to worry about going to Church, praying, and all that religious stuff. But I'm a good person, so what's

the difference? Well! Jesus might like to remind you of His words to busy little Martha when her sister Mary was listening at His feet: "Martha Martha .... There is need of only one thing. Mary has chosen the better part, and it will not be taken from her." Busy-ness is not a valid excuse to forget about God; moreover, having God may help you through your busy-ness.

> I'm not looking to bother anybody, I just want to do my thing and have a good time, eat, drink, and be merry. I get to Church once in a while. Nothing wrong with that, is there? Yeah, there kinda is. There is more to the Christian life than doing your own thing. Jesus says, "Whoever wishes to come after Me must deny himself, take up his cross, and follow Me." Christian living ought to follow the narrow path, which includes watching out for the other guy. But there is a reward that comes with this. As Jesus says, "Whoever follows me will not walk in darkness, but will have the light of life."

Consider again the parable of the sower: some seed fell on the path, some seed fell on rocky ground, and some seed fell among the thorns. As Jesus explains, "The seed sown on the path is the one who hears the word of the kingdom without understanding it, and the evil one comes and steals away what was sown in his heart.... The seed sown on rocky ground is the one who hears the word and receives it at once with joy. But he has no root and lasts only for a time. When some tribulation or persecution comes because of the word, he immediately falls away. ... The seed sown among the

119

thorns is the one who hears the word, but then worldly anxiety and the lure of riches choke the word and it bears no fruit."

You could say that all these people are the people on the broad way. They are not bad people by any means, but they are unable, for a variety of worldly reasons, to commit themselves to Christ. The narrow path people, by contrast, are the seed that fell on rich soil. They hear the word, understand it, and bear fruit.

I have mentioned before, and will undoubtedly mention again, the corrupt and corrupting nature of the entertainment media and the Internet. As a result, these days it becomes harder and harder to find the narrow path. It takes a concerted effort to avoid the influence of the depravity in our culture. I hope I am wrong, but I fear that most people do at some point fall under its spell. It is therefore very important that we use discernment with regard to what television and the Internet bring into our homes. There seems to be almost a sense of glee among certain entertainment "artists" if they can spread indecency to unsuspecting audiences. Not surprisingly, such artists typically have nothing good to say about Christianity. For as the Gospel tells us, the light came into the world, but people preferred darkness to light, because their works were evil. For everyone who does wicked things hates the light, so that his works might not be exposed. Jesus says, "The world hates me because I testify to it that its works are evil."

In essence, those who hate Jesus are the ones who are having a grand old time on the broad way. Maybe sharing a "contract of depravity"[6], boozing it up and having commitment-free sex. By contrast, those who find the narrow path come to the light, "so that [their] works may be clearly seen as done in God."

Jesus tells us, "The hour is coming, and is now here, when true worshipers will worship the Father in spirit and truth; and indeed the Father seeks such people to worship Him. God is Spirit, and those who worship Him must worship in Spirit and truth." Those who worship God in spirit and truth are the narrow-pathers. They realize that "It is the spirit that gives life, while the flesh is of no avail."

---

[6] As Piper Laurie describes her empty relationship with Paul Newman in The Hustler (1961).

There is no denying that the narrow path is not always an easy path. It is a path of self-sacrifice and service. Those who travel it are subject to persecution, and Jesus warns them, "Because you do not belong to the world and I have chosen you out of the world, the world hates you." Yet the reward is great, for it is the path to eternal life. Therefore, it is my hope that you will search out and find the narrow path, and turn away from the seductive forces that would lead you down the broad way to hell.

QUESTIONS FOR REFLECTION OR DISCUSSION

1. What is your favorite quote from Jesus in Chapter Nine? Why?

2. Which of Jesus' quotes in Chapter Nine did you find most surprising? In what way did it surprise you?

3. When you reflect on your life, do you see yourself as more of a narrow-path person or a broad-way person? What changes do you think you need to make to be sure you are on the narrow path?

4. Most people spend some of their time on the narrow path and some of their time on the broad road. Where would you say you find more happiness?

5. Do you think more of your family members and friends are on the narrow path or the broad road? Have you made any efforts to get the ones on the broad road back over to the narrow path?

Chapter Ten

I AM ALL THAT; WHY SHOULD I GIVE THANKS TO GOD?

The greatest among you must be your servant.
Whoever exalts himself will be humbled;
but whoever humbles himself will be exalted.

We live during what has been dubbed "The Information Age", and this is truly a blessing in so many ways. For someone like me, who is nostalgic about movies and movie stars from the Golden Age of Hollywood, and who is interested in baseball, football, and basketball players from the 1960s and '70s, the amount of information that is available at the click of a mouse is staggering. Oh, the wonders of Google and Wikipedia! See an old movie, read about it on Wikipedia, click a link to read about the lead actor or actress, click some more links to read about other movies they were in.

Or go on Google and look up old baseball cards, the ones my mom threw out. Some of my favorite old cards were from the Topps 1964 collection. Jerry Walker and Sam McDowell from the Cleveland Indians. Lou Jackson of the Baltimore Orioles. Fred Valentine of the Washington

Senators. The Chicago White Sox' Tommy McCraw, with a big chaw of tobacco in his cheek. I also had a soft spot for Felix Mantilla of the Red Sox and Nelson Mathews of the Kansas City A's from the Topps 1965 collection. Why do these particular players' cards stick out in my mind? God only knows. Certainly not because of their Hall of Fame credentials. But I could go on for hours. Maybe that should be my next book, eh? "The Baseball Cards I've Loved and Lost". And then I could switch over to football and tell you about all those cards we had, too. [7] (I should admit they weren't really my cards, they were my older brothers' cards, but I loved them just the same.) I haven't held those cards since 1969, but now I can look at them again in all their glory.

That barely touches the surface of what one can learn via the Internet. For example, my uncle Dennis Adams served with the British Navy during World War II, and was killed in action when his submarine was attacked by Japanese warplanes. My brother was able to find, by Internet research, a report from my uncle's ship concerning his demise. Truly

---

[7] Interestingly, a fair number of our old football cards did survive. They must have found a better hiding place from the wrath of mom.

amazing. Likewise I have a friend who is very interested in genealogy, and he has been able to trace his ancestors back hundreds of years, largely through Internet-based resources. And then there is YouTube; oh the things you can find there. Clips of my old flame Phyllis Newman, a Jersey City girl, on "What's My Line" from the 1960s and '70s. You can watch entire old movies on YouTube, really good ones like "Orphans of the Storm" and "Great Expectations", and ones so bad they're good like "Plan 9 from Outer Space" and "Caltiki, the Immortal Monster." Ugh!

YouTube also gives me Amii Stewart in the over-the-top garish music video from her 1979 disco classic "Knock on Wood", but fast forward 30 years and you can watch Amii sing "Oh Happy Day, when Jesus washed my sins away", backed by orchestra and choir, in her adopted homeland of Italy. And I should say that most of those esoteric music videos that I watched on Wometco Home Theater back in the day (see Chapter 6, above) are now available on YouTube.

But unfortunately, all is not well on the Internet. I mentioned previously about the proliferation of pornography sites. Online gambling sites are also available. This cannot be good for people who are prone to addiction in these two areas. Makes it just a little too easy to happen upon near occasions of sin and get stuck there. I see these wonderfully upbeat ads for online gambling, and I find myself thinking, are there people who actually think this is a good idea? I guess it must be me.

What I am more concerned about in this chapter, however, are Internet social media sites, such as Facebook, Twitter, and Instagram. It seems to me that these sites have sparked an epidemic of narcissism and conceit among members of our younger generation. Now a little bit of narcissism is natural – to some degree we all tend to see ourselves as the directors and stars of the movies of our lives. But social media has taken narcissism to unprecedented levels. This epidemic of narcissism no doubt is also pushed along by the media's glorification of celebrities, especially those who have achieved celebrity status not through any particular talent or accomplishment, but through their own narcissistic exploits. The Paris Hiltons and Kardashians of the world. Make a sex tape and become a star. Impressionable young people with immature moral compasses might conclude, "hey, that's an easy way to gain some notoriety." Unfortunately, in the unforgiving world of cyberbullying, the price of such notoriety is often death. Many young people who thought, on an impulse, that it would be a good idea to "expose" themselves on social media find they are not able to deal with the consequences of such exposure. For some of these kids, death seems the only way out, so they take their own lives. How tragic for these young people, who blithely follow where the culture is leading them, but suddenly discover it is a dead end. We must pray that God has mercy on them and forgives them for their rashness and poor judgment.

But these tragic endings represent but a small minority of all the young people who are dabbling in narcissism via social media. What is the reasoning that leads one to conclude that people want to know your every thought, and to look at innumerable pictures that you have taken of yourself? (Now I have to admit that very many adults have joined in with this "selfie fascination", often to the detriment of their families, jobs, and political careers.) These kids are constantly putting themselves out there to be judged, and possibly ridiculed, by their peers. Why? Are they desperate for attention and affirmation? Perhaps some are. But I get the feeling that many of them just think they are so wonderful that of course everyone wants to see their pictures and know their every thought. In addition to the eventual pitfalls that may come from such public displays of narcissism, for our purposes it is important to note that this is anathema to the Christian life. When we are so busy being obsessed about ourselves, how can we be serving our fellow man? If you don't believe me, listen to Jesus.

We can begin by looking at a couple of the Beatitudes. For example, Jesus says, "Blessed are the poor in spirit, for theirs is the kingdom of heaven." Also, "Blessed are the meek, for they shall inherit the land." The poor in spirit and the meek are probably not going around posting a bunch of selfies and boasting about how wonderful they are. Even where doing holy things is concerned, Jesus suggests that we ought to do these things in a more quiet manner to gain God's favor. Jesus tells us:

> Take care not to perform righteous deeds in order that people may see them; otherwise, you will have no recompense from your heavenly Father. When you give alms, do not blow a trumpet before you, as the hypocrites do in the synagogues and in the streets to

win the praise of others. Amen, I say to you, they have received their reward.

Jesus also says, "When you pray, do not be like the hypocrites, who love to stand and pray in the synagogues and on street corners so that others may see them. Amen, I say to you, they have received their reward." Jesus does not want us to make public spectacles of ourselves and to go about tooting our own horns.

Consistent with His blessing of the meek and the poor of spirit, Jesus expresses discomfort with us when we think we are better, more holy, than other people. He says, for instance:

> Why do you notice the splinter in your brother's eye, but do not perceive the wooden beam in your own eye? How can you say to your brother, 'let me remove that splinter from your eye' while the wooden beam is in your eye? You hypocrite, remove the wooden beam from your eye first; then you will see clearly to remove the splinter from your brother's eye.

Along the same lines, consider the distinction Jesus made between the prayer of the Pharisee and the prayer of the tax collector. The Pharisee prayed, "O God, I thank you that I am not like the rest of humanity ..." By contrast, the tax collector stood at a distance and would not even raise his eyes to heaven, but beat his breast and prayed, "O God, be merciful to me, a sinner." Jesus tells us that it was the tax collector who went home justified, because "everyone who exalts himself will be humbled, and everyone who humbles himself will be exalted." Narcissists, you know, exalt themselves.

It is a common theme in the Gospels that people who think they are special, who think they are big shots, who think they do not need God, will have a difficult time attaining eternal life. Consider the fate of those who will not listen to God's word. "Everyone who listens to these words of mine but does not act on them will be like a fool who built his house on sand," says Jesus. "The rain fell, the floods came, and the winds blew and buffeted the house. And it collapsed and was completely ruined." Jesus says further, "Whoever wishes to come after Me must deny himself, take up his cross, and follow Me. For whoever wishes to save his life will lose it, but whoever loses his life for My sake will find it." By contrast, Jesus tells us that we are to love God with all our heart, with all our soul, and with all our mind. Further, "Everyone who acknowledges Me before others I will acknowledge before My heavenly Father." Those who think they are the greatest thing since sliced bread will likely find it difficult to make God the most important person in their lives.

Likewise, those with a single-minded determination to be the big cheese, the star of stars, the top of the world, need to change their priorities to conform to the Christian ideal. For Jesus says, "What profit would there be for one to gain the whole world and forfeit his life, or what can one give in exchange for his life? For the Son of Man will come with His angels in His Father's glory, and then He will repay everyone according to his conduct." This is not a condemnation of worldly success per se, but those who pursue worldly glory and success *without regard for the manner in which they pursue it* will come up losers in God's book. Jesus admonishes, "You justify yourselves in the eyes of others, but God knows your hearts; for what is of human esteem is an abomination in the sight of God."

What is also clear is that Jesus wants us to have an attitude of servitude towards our fellow life travelers. In His view, people who are able to put the needs and interests of others ahead of their own are the people who are worthy of praise and emulation. Take, for example, the story of the Good Samaritan, who went out of his way to be a neighbor to the victim of a brutal robbery. "Go and do likewise," Jesus urges us. Jesus also tells us, "Whoever wishes to be great among you shall be your servant; whoever wishes to be first among you shall be your slave." Those of us who carry ourselves with a sense of great self-importance may find ourselves bitterly disappointed come judgment day, for "many who are first will be last, and the last will be first. …

Everyone who exalts himself will be humbled, but the one who humbles himself will be exalted."

Think of it this way. God created the heavens and the earth, indeed the entire universe. Moreover, He ultimately provided us with whatever talents and gifts we enjoy and utilize here on earth. So it's difficult for God to be terribly impressed with our small accomplishments; it's even more difficult for Him to be impressed if we haven't accomplished anything. So when we go around acting like we're hot stuff, like we're His gift to the world, we probably rub Him the wrong way.

Jesus tells us, "Amen I say to you, unless you turn and become like children you will not enter the kingdom of heaven. Whoever humbles himself like this child is the greatest in the kingdom of heaven." Humility, not braggadocio. Don't forget what Jesus did and said at the Last Supper. He rose from supper and took off his outer garments. He took a towel and tied it around His waist. Then He poured water into a basin and began to wash the disciples' feet and dry them with the towel around His waist. Afterward, He said to the disciples, "If I, therefore, the master and teacher, have washed your feet, you ought to wash one another's feet. I have given you a model to follow, so that as I have done for you, you should also do." If the Master of the Universe is willing to wash His disciples' feet, then who are we to go about acting as though *we* are the masters of the universe?

The lesson to be learned is to live your life with humility, and to treat other people as your equals, not as inferiors. We are to love one another as Jesus loves us. This is His commandment to us, this is the basic tenet of Christian living. And how did Jesus love us? By laying down His life for us. If this is the example Jesus gave us, is it so hard for so-called Christians to be decent to each other? Must we act like we are so special and try to lord it over other folks? Jesus wants none of this. Jesus wants us to love one another and to serve one another and, in so doing, to serve Him. It is this love and service, not arrogance and conceit, that puts us on the road to eternal life. As Jesus tells us, "Whoever serves Me must follow Me, and where I am there also will My servant be. The father will honor whoever serves Me."

QUESTIONS FOR REFLECTION OR DISCUSSION

1. What is your favorite quote from Jesus in Chapter Ten? Why?

2. Which of Jesus' quotes in Chapter Ten did you find most surprising? In what way did it surprise you?

3. Have you ever visited sites on the Internet that you felt was taking you down the wrong path? If so, what if anything have you done to avoid going down that path again?

4. Are there any young people in your life who cause you concern based upon their use of social media? Are you able to discuss these concerns with them?

5. Do you think the excessive narcissism fostered by social media is an obstacle to finding God, or is it just a phase adolescents and young adults go through?

Chapter Eleven

IF EVERYBODY TICKS ME OFF,

HOW CAN I BE EXPECTED NOT TO KILL THEM?

You have heard that it was said to your ancestors, You shall not kill; and whoever kills will be liable to judgment.' But I say to you, whoever is angry with his brother will be liable to judgment.

Anger. Hatred. Violence. A senior citizen goes to the movie theater and gets upset that the young man in front of him is sending text messages. Words are exchanged, a gun is drawn, and the young man is killed.

A down-on-his-luck guy thinks his houseguest stole his iPad, so he shoots him dead and then turns the gun on himself.

A young woman finds that her boyfriend is cheating on her, so she kills him, and then herself.

A young man filled with racial hatred thinks it would be a good idea to start a race war, so he takes a gun and shoots up a black Church.

Sometimes it seems we are in the midst of an epidemic of killing. Realistically, I suppose things like this have always happened, we just didn't have the Internet to turn local tragedies into worldwide stories. Either way, let's be real, one such incident is one too many. Life is a gift from God, not to be snuffed out in a moment of anger-fueled overreaction or hate-filled passion.

While there are those who would try to change it, the United States remains a predominantly Christian nation. The title of a well-known hymn is "They Will Know We Are Christians by Our Love". It is sad, then, that our predominantly Christian nation is so full of hatred and anger. There is no shortage of people who use their religion as a *reason* for their hatred and anger. Maybe they didn't get the memo. And then we wonder why so many folks have become cynical about religion.

Anger. According to Merriam Webster, anger is a strong feeling of displeasure and usually of antagonism. Merriam Webster's online dictionary tells us that anger is a general term that includes more specific emotions such as rage or fury – which suggest loss of self-control from the violence of the emotion --, and wrath – which suggests a desire or intention to punish or get revenge. Whatever you may call it, it is an ugly emotion, and it is a sin. It manifests a lack of ability, or lack of desire, to control ourselves. And Jesus doesn't like it.

When we talk about Jesus, we often speak of His limitless love for us and His willingness to forgive our transgressions. But sometimes we forget that Jesus holds us to a high standard of personal conduct. For example, Jesus tells us:

> You have heard that it was said to your ancestors, 'You shall not kill; and whoever kills will be liable to judgment.' But I say to you, whoever is angry with his brother will be liable to judgment, and whoever says to his brother 'raqa' will be answerable to the Sanhedrin, and whoever says 'you fool' will be liable to fiery Gehenna.

So there we have a very real basis for the conclusion that anger is a sin. And as a natural progression, anger can lead to angry words and insults, and situations can escalate to the point of violence. Jesus admonishes us to stop the encounter before it starts by controlling our anger and our tongues, and lets us know that there will be consequences when we fail.

It is important to note that you do not have to be a bad person to commit the sin of anger. It could simply be a case of being in a bad mood, or a confluence of circumstances that sets you off. Think, for instance, of the Prodigal Son's brother. He was a good fellow, a hard worker, loyal to his father. But when he saw the celebration of his brother's return, he became quite angry over what he perceived to be an injustice to himself. His father instructed him, just as our Father instructs us, that anger is not a proper reaction when one loves.

Hatred is another problematic condition that plagues our society. I guess I sound like a broken record, but how can a predominantly Christian culture be so prone to hatred? We have people who hate blacks, we have people who hate whites, we have people who hate Latinos, and we have people who hate Asians. We have people who hate conservatives, we have people who hate liberals, we have people who hate libertarians, and we have people who hate socialists. We have people who hate abortionists and people who hate anti-abortionists. We have people who hate Christians, people who hate Jews, people who hate Muslims. We have people who hate anyone who disagrees with them, or is different than they are, or who lives a different lifestyle than they do. There are people who hate homosexuals, and there are people who hate people who hate homosexuals. Younger people hate older people for being older, older people hate younger people for being younger. The fact of the matter is that whether your hatred is primary hatred ("I hate you"), secondary hatred ("I hate you because you hate me"), or reactionary hatred ("I hate you because you hate green people"), it is still sin. Two wrongs don't make a right. Hating someone because they hate you doesn't solve anything. More likely, it causes hatred to escalate, eventually leading to war.

Where does all this hatred come from? It doesn't come from Jesus. Rather, Jesus says to us, "You have heard that it was said, 'An eye for an eye, and a tooth for a tooth.' But I say to you, offer no resistance to one who is evil. When someone strikes you on the right cheek, turn the other one to him as well." Jesus tells us to love our enemies, and pray for those who persecute us. He reminds us that the Father makes His sun rise on the bad and the good, and causes rain to fall on the just and the unjust. And He cautions us, "If you love those who love you, what recompense will you have? Do not the tax collectors do the same?"

The simple truth is, nobody who calls himself or herself a Christian should hate anyone, no matter what differences may exist between them. For as Jesus confirms, the second greatest commandment is to love your neighbor as you love yourself. In the parable of the Good Samaritan, Jesus greatly expands the parameters of whom we should consider to be our neighbor. But then again, Jesus also greatly expands the category of people we should love, well beyond our neighbor. For He tells us, "Love your enemies, do good to those who hate you, bless those who curse you, pray for those who mistreat you."

Love your enemies, imagine that. We have enough trouble loving our neighbors. We need to do a much better job of being Christians, that much is clear. How can we do so? I think the first thing we must do is *make a decision* to be better Christians. We are all blessed with free will. We can choose to exercise that free will by deciding to love other people, and by deciding to hate other people. The former decision is the proper decision, the one that will make God happy and society peaceful. In John's Gospel, Jesus gives us this commandment: "Love one another as I love you." He goes on to say, "You are my friends if you do what I command you."

Jesus commands us to love everyone. If we want to be His friends – and as Christians, I assume we do – we are to heed that command.

Violence. It frightens me how much our culture gets off on violence. Violent movies, violent music, violent video games. No wonder so many of our young people seem to be hardened to violence and killing. It is routinely promoted as a wonderful thing, a lifestyle to be embraced. Common sense should tell you that it is a *bad* thing if the entertainment industry promotes organized crime or a gangster lifestyle as a *good* thing! But the entertainment industry does not agree with me. Sadly, this "entertainment" is most damaging to young folks, who are immature and have not yet fully developed the ability to make wise decisions for themselves. To them, acting like the bad dudes they see, on TV shows and in music videos, may seem like a good thing to do. They need to be protected from these harmful influences. It helps if the adults in their lives have their priorities in order: Jesus is good; mainstream entertainment media are bad.

We have a lot of gun violence in America, and what always amazes me, when I hear of a shooting death, is how many people have guns. Handguns, I mean. It seems to me the purpose in having a handgun is to shoot someone. This raises the question, why are so many of us so ready to shoot someone? I understand the desire to be able to defend oneself, but it seems to me that guns are used much more often to kill someone the gunman knows than to defend the gunman from an unknown attacker. In any case, God tells us we shall not kill, and nothing Jesus says contradicts that commandment. There are certain people whose job it is to protect us or to defend our country, and naturally they must be armed. And I suppose people who hunt for food may need rifles to help them hunt more effectively. But all these private citizens and petty criminals with handguns and semi-automatic weapons, to me it's quite alarming.[8]

---

[8] Just so there is no misunderstanding, I am not talking about taking away the Constitutional right to own guns or the legal right to defend oneself and others, but I am talking about a cultural shift away from **ALL** guns, *especially the illegal ones.*

In the Gospel of John, Jesus says, somewhat prophetically, "The hour is coming when everyone who kills you will think he is offering worship to God, because they have not known either the Father or Me." As a Christian society, we need to back off the gunplay and come back to the real Jesus. If one were to embrace Christ's teaching, one would quickly be disabused of the notion that violence is a desirable response in most situations. I previously mentioned that Jesus says when somebody strikes us on one cheek, we are to turn and offer him the other as well. Jesus also offers us these suggestions: "From the person who takes your cloak, do not withhold even your tunic. ...Give to everyone who asks of you, and from the one who takes what is yours do not demand it back. ...Do unto others as you would have them do unto you. ...Be merciful, as your father is merciful." In each case Jesus advocates for peace, not violence, and proposes defusing rather than escalating a situation.

In Matthew's Gospel, Jesus warns us against behaving like the wicked servant who says to himself," My master is long delayed," and begins to beat his fellow servants and eat and drink with drunkards. For upon the master's return, he will punish the wicked servant severely and assign him a place with the hypocrites, "where there will be wailing and grinding of teeth." On the occasion of His arrest on Holy Thursday night, Jesus admonishes His own Apostles, "Put your sword back into its sheath, for all who take the sword will perish by the sword." As for those who would seek to kill, Jesus likens them to the devil, who "was a murderer from the beginning and does not stand in truth, because there is no truth in him..."

A true Christian controls his anger, loves **everybody**, and resists all urges to violence. I wish that we all, as members of a supposedly Christian society, would actually follow Christ's example and stop hating. People will annoy you, aggravate you, exasperate you, and frustrate you. But being annoyed, aggravated, exasperated, and frustrated will not make you hate someone unless you make the affirmative decision to hate. Hatred does not happen by accident. Any time you make the decision to hate, you have made the wrong decision. You need to back up and make another decision, a different decision. Love.

QUESTIONS FOR REFLECTION OR DISCUSSION

1. What is your favorite quote from Jesus in Chapter Eleven? Why?

2. Which of Jesus' quotes in Chapter Eleven did you find most surprising? In what way did it surprise you?

3. From where do you think the epidemic of hatred in this society stems? Do you think there is any solution to it?

4. Do you find there are times when you become uncontrollably angry? Are there specific triggers that cause you to become angry? Do you think Jesus feels your anger in these situations is justified?

5. It seems that many people who identify themselves as Christians in our society have a strong affinity for guns. Why do you think this is? Do you think Jesus approves?

Chapter Twelve

ISN'T IT A BIT UNREASONABLE TO EXPECT ME TO BE NICE TO PEOPLE IF I WON'T GET SOMETHING OUT OF IT?

Just so, the Son of Man did not come to be served but to serve, and to give His life as a ransom for many.

I have to admit that I worry about whether the upcoming generation is a bit callous. It may be related to the epidemic of narcissism that I wrote about earlier. Or it may be a consequence of young people spending too much time sitting in front of a computer monitor, playing with inanimate images, communicating remotely via the latest technological gizmo, rather than talking to people face-to-face and in person. Maybe it has something to do with how my generation of parents has raised our children, being overly protective, trying to prevent their fragile little bodies and psyches from being hurt by the big bad world. Whatever the case, there seems to be what I can best describe as an absence of empathy in many young folks

When my older son was in junior high school, I moderated a movie club at his school. My goal was to introduce these students to some of the great, older movies that they would otherwise likely never be exposed to (unless their parents watched Turner Classic Movies, and forced the kids to sit and watch). But when we screened the movies, I found some weird reactions from the children.

In fact, the very first movie we watched was "Sullivan's Travels", by the great writer-director Preston Sturges. The movie starts out in Hollywood, and centers on a comedy film director named John L. Sullivan, who decides he does not want to make comedies anymore. The movie is set in 1940, and with so many people suffering the after-effects of the Great Depression our hero feels compelled to make a socially conscious film about people's suffering. In order to make this *tour de force* ("Oh Brother, Where Art Thou?"), he first has to go out and do "research" about people's sufferings. He does this by living as a hobo for a while. When he feels he has done enough research, he decides to take a large amount of cash and distribute it to some of the homeless people, to thank them for what they have taught him.

However, one of his fellow hobos decides to rob John L. So the hobo follows him into a railroad yard, knocks him over the head, and takes the cash. The hobo then begins to run away across the railroad tracks, but he drops some of the money. He stops to pick up the dropped bills, and to make a long story short he gets run over by a train and killed. Well, my dear sweet junior high students thought that was just hilarious. After all, what could be funnier than a guy getting hit by a train? The sinking of the Titanic, I suppose.

What was more disturbing, however, was when we watched "West Side Story", and I was the only one in the room who was crying. Worse still, we watched "Brian's Song", and nobody cried at that one, either. Who watches "Brian's Song" and doesn't cry?

I suppose maybe I'm reading too much into their reactions, or lack thereof, to old movies. After all, I can't realistically expect everyone to be a sap like me. Just the same, empathy is a very important quality in a human person, and it would be a shame if a superficial and self-absorbed culture eliminated that quality from our souls. The ability to feel each other's pain, so to speak, is an important part of what makes us special and leads us to do things that will benefit persons other than ourselves.

According to the Merriam-Webster online dictionary, empathy is the ability to share someone else's feelings, to understand what he or she is going through, even though you are not experiencing it yourself. Empathy is an emotion that is largely born of love, for if you did not love someone it is not likely that you would bother to try to understand what he was going through. I am not necessarily referring here to romantic love or even familial love, but love in the sense of the Greek word *agape*. This is a selfless love manifested by concern for the well-being of another or others. When we are able to feel this kind of love, and to have understanding for what others are suffering, we are prompted to take action to ease that suffering. This helps explain much of the good that is done throughout the world to aid the poor, the sick, the imprisoned, the displaced, the victims of war and violence, the downtrodden.

There are millions of people who sacrifice some portion of their income or wealth to support charitable endeavors that benefit the less fortunate. This is, of course, commendable, and essential to the success of these charitable endeavors. And then there are those who are called to be directly involved in charitable service, who are right there in the midst of the pain and suffering. They sacrifice their comfort, health, and safety, and sometimes even their lives, in order to alleviate the suffering of others. They don't get much out of it, not in a material sense at least, but they are heroes.

Agape and empathy lead to sacrificial love. Would Jesus approve of this type of self-sacrifice? You know the answer to that!

Jesus came to earth to be the Lamb of God, to offer His life as a sacrifice to wash away our sins. He said to His disciples, "I am the good shepherd. A good shepherd lays down his life for the sheep." The Gospel tells us that in the time leading up to His trial and execution, Jesus had begun to show His disciples that He had go to Jerusalem and suffer greatly from the elders, the chief priests, and the scribes, and be killed, and on the third day be raised. Although He was the incarnation of God, He willingly gave up His life for humanity. As Jesus Himself tells us, "I am the living bread that came down from heaven; whoever eats this bread will live forever; and the bread that I will give is My flesh for the life of the world." So Jesus gives us the perfect example of sacrificial, unconditional love. Even as He was suffering on the cross, He prayed in regard to His executioners, "Father, forgive them, for they know not what they do."

Jesus not only talked the talk, He also walked the walk. So let's give Him the benefit of listening to His talk on this issue of sacrificial and unconditional love, as we can certainly learn from Him. We have read or heard these lessons before, but great teaching bears repeating.

Two of the most compelling lessons in unconditional love come from two of Jesus' most famous parables, the Good Samaritan and the Prodigal Son. As you know, the story of the Good Samaritan begins with a Jewish person who is robbed and beaten by bandits on the road between Jerusalem and Jericho. As the victim lies on the roadside, gravely injured, two Jewish religious figures, a priest and a Levite, successively pass him by without stopping to assist or to even check on his condition. However, a Samaritan – a natural enemy of the Jewish people – has compassion on the victim. He makes the time to tend to the victim, and he uses his money to pay for the victim's care. He had no obligation to this person, no compelling reason to help, other than love and concern for his fellow man.

No doubt the Prodigal Son is also a story that is known to you. A young punk demands his share of his inheritance even though his father is neither dead nor, by all accounts, anywhere near death. The ingrate proceeds to waste his money in rapid fashion on a lavish lifestyle and loose women. Before you know it he's down and out, and even the pigs are too good for him. So he decides to go back to his father's house and ask for forgiveness. Suppose you were the father, what would you do? Would you take him back? He essentially told you he wants nothing more to do with you except to take his share of your money; now he's coming back destitute. Of course the father in our story does welcome back his son, and is so happy to have him back that he throws him a party. The story is first a metaphor for God's forgiveness toward His repentant children, but at the same time it provides an example of the kind of unconditional love that God expects His children to exhibit toward others.

Jesus' endorsement of sacrificial love is also evident in His teaching about servitude. Jesus tells us, "Whoever wishes to be great among you shall be your servant; whoever wishes to be first among you shall be your slave. Just so, the Son of Man did not come to be served but to serve and to give His life as a ransom for many." We can paraphrase this by recasting Jesus' statement thusly: "Look, I'm God, I created the universe, but even so I came here to teach you, to minister to you, to cure your illnesses, and to die for you. So is it asking so much for you to do nice things for your fellow man?" Jesus tries to make it clear to us that our earthly understanding of sacrificial love – being good to family and friends – falls short of the standard He sets for us. Jesus asks us to take heed when He tells us to love our enemies, do good to those who hate us, bless those who curse us, pray for those who mistreat us, and do unto others as we would have them do to us. Love our enemies and do good to them. In asking us to love in this way, Jesus is essentially asking us to emulate God, "[F]or He Himself is kind to the ungrateful and the wicked." But Jesus goes on to assure us that if we do as He asks, "[our] reward will be great and [we] will be children of the Most High".

What it boils down to is something we already know: we are supposed to love everybody, care about everybody, and therefore do what we can to help whomever we can. As Jesus says, "Be merciful, as your father is merciful." Be kind to everyone you meet. Let them know you are a Christian by your love. I was taught these things very early on from the Sisters of Christian Charity at St. Nick's Grammar School in Jersey City. If everyone could learn this lesson and remember this lesson, don't you think the world would be a lovelier place to live?

QUESTIONS FOR REFLECTION OR DISCUSSION

1. What is your favorite quote from Jesus in Chapter Twelve? Why?

2. Which of Jesus' quotes in Chapter Twelve did you find most surprising? In what way did it surprise you?

3. Can you recall an experience in which someone's display of unconditional love, whether toward you or someone else, made you aware of God's presence?

4. Have you had an experience in which your kindness to another human being caused that person's mentality to become more Christ-focused?

Chapter Thirteen

IF YOU CAME TO EARTH TODAY, YOU WOULD BE A CONSERVATIVE LIBERAL SOCIALIST REPUBLICAN DEMOCRAT, RIGHT?

Render unto Caesar what belongs to Caesar,
and unto God what belongs to God.

Politics. I did not originally plan to include a chapter concerning politics. But it did occur to me that the expression of political viewpoints, particularly those that are extreme in nature, are at the root of a great deal of incivility, unchristian behavior, and worse in society today. So much of our political discourse has sunk to the level of non-fact-based emotional appeals, hate-filled rhetoric, and name calling. You're a communist, you're a fascist, you're a racist, you're a race-baiter, you're a pervert, you're a homophobe, you're an appeaser, you're an imperialist.

The thing about name-calling is that it effectively shuts down rational debate and is therefore a favored tactic for people who have a weak position. I was intrigued to learn, for example, that because I am opposed to abortion, I am a Neanderthal and a mysoginist. What about the millions and millions of women who also oppose abortion, are they mysoginists too? Is it not possible that we oppose abortion because we think the killing of an unborn child is morally wrong? Have you ever seen an ultrasound of a baby in utero? I have. That thing on the screen, it looks like it's alive. It looks kind of human. It looks kind of cute. I wonder if Neanderthal Man killed its unborn children. If not, maybe I should consider being called a Neanderthal a compliment. Because it seems to me that someone who supports the wholesale killing of our pre-birth offspring is way worse than someone who does not.

I always get a kick out of politicians and pundits who invoke Jesus' name to give support to some proposal. These are generally people who support a whole host of things that Jesus would condemn – abortion for instance – and quite possibly do not even believe in God. The purpose of their "Jesus rhetoric" is more often than not an attempt to show up certain religious groups as acting in bad faith and hypocritically on some humanitarian issue.

But just what would be Jesus' take on modern politics? We can safely say a few things about His reaction to today's political discourse. First, He would object to the name-calling and He would object to the angry rhetoric. Second, He would object to the obfuscation, misinformation, twisting of facts, and assorted other methods of distorting the truth. That is to say, lying. Third, He would surely object to the hatred displayed by political enemies, as He preaches love of enemy, not hatred and destruction of enemy.

Putting that aside, though, where would Jesus fall within the political spectrum? Left? Right? Center? I believe Jesus would be outspoken on specific issues – helping the less fortunate, fighting violence, curbing the proliferation of obscenity and unchastity. To my friends on the left I say, Jesus would be against abortion. To my friends on the right I say, Jesus would be against guns. But insofar as political philosophy is concerned, I believe He would simply stay above the fray.

Keep in mind what Jesus said when the devil tempted Him with all the kingdoms of the world in their magnificence: "The Lord, your God, shall you worship, and Him alone shall you serve." Jesus' words were in the first place a rejection of the "invitation" to worship Satan, but were also a reflection of Jesus' resistance to the lure of earthly power. Furthermore, when we get caught up in political machinations, it is easy to get sucked in to not only the temptation to seek power but also the exaltation of the political candidate of the day. Jesus does not want us to become slaves to a political affiliation or ideology.

Expressing the same point a different way, Jesus warns us, "No one can serve two masters. He will either hate one and love the other, or be devoted to one and despise the other. You cannot serve God and mammon." We use this saying as a reminder of the danger of the pursuit of material wealth, but it can just as easily apply to the pursuit of political power. Casual observation of our nation's political system at work shows this to be the case. All too often, the lust for power can cause a player to "sell his soul", so to speak, to reach the political promised land. On a lower level, we have seen many instances in which political players have broken the law and gone to jail for the sake of their party or candidate. I even recall reading about a young fellow who took his own life when President Bush won re-election. I am fairly confident (actually I'm very sure) that Jesus would not view politics as something worthy of causing someone to lose his soul or his life.

Let's take a look at some of Jesus' other experiences and remarks concerning worldly power, which I believe help prove my point. First and foremost, when Jesus is on trial before Pontius Pilate, He tells Pilate that His kingdom does not belong to this world, and that He was born and came into the world to testify to the truth. As in other contexts, Jesus shows us that His concerns are not with worldly matters, but with other-worldly matters. During the trial, Pilate states that he has the power to release Jesus, and the power to crucify Jesus. Jesus answers him, "You would have no power over Me if it had not been given to you from above." Jesus is aware that His fate is not in the hands of any governing power on earth, but is part of God's plan of salvation. Despite being on the verge of a sentence to death by crucifixion, Jesus is almost indifferent to Pilate's authority and resigned to following God's will. His resignation and indifference are also reflected in His statement following His arrest, in which He said, "Do you think that I cannot call upon my Father and He will not provide Me at this moment with more than twelve legions of angels? But then how would the scriptures be fulfilled which say that it must come to pass in this way?"

Jesus' responses to questions about taxation are reflective of a similar indifference. When questioned about paying the temple tax, for example, Jesus turned to Simon Peter and asked him, "What is your opinion, Simon? From whom do the kings of the earth take tolls or census tax? From their subjects, or from foreigners?" When Simon Peter answered, "From foreigners", Jesus then said to him, "Then the subjects are exempt." He also added, however, "But that we may not offend them, go to the sea, drop in a hook, and take the first fish that comes up. Open its mouth and you will find a coin worth twice the temple tax. Give that to them for me and you." Aside from being a rather amazing display of Jesus' supernatural powers – i.e., that He knew the fish Simon would catch was going to have a coin in its mouth – this exchange is also a fascinating look at Jesus' almost flippant attitude towards worldly power.

The more famous episode concerning Jesus and the payment of taxes relates to the question put to Him by fellow Jews concerning payment of the Roman census tax. "Is it lawful to pay the census tax to Caesar?" He was asked. And His response? "Show me the coin that pays the census tax," Jesus said. "Whose image is this and whose inscription?" It was Caesar's image and inscription, of course. So, Jesus concluded, "Repay to Caesar what belongs to Caesar and to God what belongs to God." Jesus' kingdom is not of this earth, and He tells us again and again that we must not get caught up in this life and the things of this world. We must live here, and while we live here we are subject to worldly powers and are to obey them. But our greater allegiance must be to God and to things of God; the things of the earth, like the rulers of the earth, are transitory.

Whether your political views tilt to the left or to the right, I regret to inform you that the truth is this: Jesus did not come to earth as a political activist. Rather, He came to earth to lead us home to the Father in heaven. He leads us home by showing us the manner in which we are to conduct our personal lives. Ultimately we are to be citizens of heaven, not of earth. We are to use our time on earth to know, love, and serve God, and to love others as we are loved by God. Certainly we are encouraged to take actions that will improve the lot of our fellow man, and if some of those actions are political so be it. But ideology, party affiliation, and political power are never to supplant God as the focus of our being.

We can consider two other, sadder events in the Gospel narratives that show what Jesus was all about, vis-à-vis politics and power. Number one, King Herod had John the Baptist arrested and, at the request of Herod's step-daughter, John was beheaded. John the Baptist was a cousin to Jesus. John was also a prophet, who called the Jews to repent, and paved the way for Jesus' ministry. Finally, John was, in Jesus' words, as great as any person ever born. Could not Jesus – God incarnate – have done something to save John the Baptist? Not only did Jesus not stop John's execution, but, to our knowledge, He never so much as spoke out against it, though we do know He was greatly saddened by it.

Jesus never protested against capital punishment. He never protested against any governmental action. Why? Because Jesus' concerns were and are spiritual, not temporal. The things of this world pass away, but heaven is forever. As the ultimate act of political indifference and personal self-sacrifice, Jesus was tried before Pilate, sentenced to death, and crucified, dying on the cross for the sins of humanity.

Jesus was a moral and spiritual teacher. Jesus was not a politician. When we put our politics above moral good and spiritual enlightenment, Jesus disapproves.

QUESTIONS FOR REFLECTION OR DISCUSSION

1. What is your favorite quote from Jesus in Chapter Thirteen? Why?

2. Which of Jesus' quotes in Chapter Thirteen did you find most surprising? In what way did it surprise you?

3. What is your opinion about where Jesus would fall on the political spectrum today? What makes you feel that way?

4. Are there specific political issues about which you think Jesus would be outspoken?

5. Jesus had numerous run-ins with Pharisees and scribes over what He perceived to be their hypocrisy. Do you think Jesus would clash with leaders in today's society? Give some examples.

Chapter Fourteen

DO YOU REALLY WANT ME TO LOVE EVERYONE, NO MATTER WHAT THEY MAY HAVE DONE?

I say love your enemies, do good to those who hate you, bless those who curse you, pray for those who mistreat you.

Love your enemies. That's a good one, right? When the Twelve Apostles compiled their top ten list of "the things Jesus taught that nobody will pay attention to", love your enemies was at the top. We're still choking on the bit about loving our neighbors, let alone our enemies. But I think a teaching about loving your enemies fits in very well right after a teaching about politics. Seriously, if you spend any time watching cable TV news, observing the pundits on the left and the pundits on the right, you know these jokers need a strong dose of love of enemy. Not that they should even perceive each other as enemies, but it is obvious they do.

Now I'm not going to sit here and tell you that loving your enemies is easy. When people hate you, curse you, and mistreat you, the easier response is undoubtedly to hate them, curse them, and mistreat them in return. But this is not the Christian response. We should look to Jesus as our perfect role model in this regard. He was wrongfully arrested, dragged from place to place for questioning, tried and convicted without just cause, beaten, cursed at, spit upon, mocked and verbally abused, forced to carry His cross, and crucified. The King of kings. But He did not hate His accusers, His abusers, or His executioners. He loved them. He pitied them. He prayed for them. "Forgive them, Father, for they know not what they do."

For most of us, our enemies are generally more mundane and less life-threatening. People who park in our spots or who let their dogs relieve themselves on our lawns. The boss who mistreats us or terminates us, the underling who takes our job.

More palpable enemies might be an ex-husband or ex-wife, or former in-laws who try to keep your children away from you. Yes, they mistreat you, they curse you, perhaps they even hate you, but Jesus calls us to be bigger. We are to respond in love, to turn the proverbial other cheek. In truth, responding this way can help defuse a bad situation, while responding with hatred and anger only escalates and inflames the situation. When we let anger rule the day, violence is not far behind. Then a domestic dispute turns to bloodshed, funerals, and jail. All because someone's pride or ego thought it was more important to return tit for tat than to be the bigger man and back off.

We can look to what Jesus says to us in His Sermon on the Mount for the essence of the Christian response to hatred: "But I say to you, offer no resistance to one who is evil. When someone strikes you on the right cheek, turn the other one to him as well. ... I say to you, love your enemies, and pray for those who persecute you, that you may be children of your heavenly Father, for He makes His sun rise on the bad and the good, and causes rain to fall on the just and the unjust. For if you love those who love you, what recompense will you have? Do not the tax collectors do the same?"

We are encouraged, you see, to be as much like the Father as possible, to strive for perfection in our behavior, even though we can never achieve it. God loves the bad and the unjust. He does not approve of their behavior, just as we do not like the behavior of a vexatious child. But He does love them and longs for a change in their behavior. And so we also must love them, want the best for them, and pray for them to cease their hateful, ungodly behavior. We are called, albeit on a much smaller scale, to emulate the peaceful resistance of Dr. Martin Luther King, Jr., and the Civil Rights movement.

It is key at this point to remember the Golden Rule, "Do unto others as you would have them do unto you." If we live by the Golden Rule (which we are supposed to), and if we are upset by the fact that our enemies hate, curse, and mistreat us, then it really does not make sense for us to hate, curse, and mistreat them in return. Why? Because we are not supposed to do to them what we don't want them to do to us. Two wrongs do not make a right, they usually just make a double wrong. Jesus tells us to "love one another as I have loved you". Loving one another is a choice that we are free to make or reject, but Jesus makes clear that there is no exception built into the rule. You cannot find anywhere that Jesus tells us that if somebody treats you badly, then you are no longer called to love that person. Indeed, Jesus specifically tells us that there is nothing special about loving people who love us back. That part is easy. It is choosing to love the "bad guys" that is difficult.

Jesus tells us that when somebody hurts us, if we forgive them their transgressions, our heavenly Father will forgive us. But if we do not forgive others, neither will the Father forgive *our* transgressions. So yes, if we wish to stay in God's good graces, we must forgive those who hurt us. We must love them – i.e., care about them, be concerned for them, want the best for them – despite their lack of love for us. The greatest and the first commandment is to love the Lord your God with all your heart, with all your soul, and with all your mind, and the second is like it: you shall love your neighbor as yourself. I talked earlier about the parable of the Good Samaritan, and how Jesus expects us to define the term "neighbor". It is not just the person next door or down the street, it is anybody with whom we come in contact. Again Jesus says:

> To the person who strikes you on one cheek, offer the other as well. From the person who takes your cloak, do not withhold even your tunic. Give to everyone who asks of you, and from the one who takes what is yours do not demand it back. Do unto others as you would have them do to you. Love your enemies and do good to them … then your reward will be great and you will be children of the Most High, for He Himself is kind to the ungrateful and the wicked. Be merciful, as your Father is merciful.

This is all somewhat counterintuitive. It means hoping and praying that bad people will amend their lives, and will stop hating and hurting us and others. It means praying for the salvation of everybody, including those who mock and persecute us and those who would like to see us dead, even those who are actively trying to make us dead. Our government may call for military action when it is deemed necessary to protect and defend our nation, but in our personal lives we should always hope and pray and work for peace. As Jesus knows, this requires a person-by-person commitment; one random act of hatred can inflame an entire community to seek retribution. We are each required to make the choice to love and forgive. Blessed are the peacemakers. Think of the perfect example of Christian love exhibited by the members of the Charleston church, who forgave and prayed for the person who senselessly and hatefully murdered nine church members.

I'm sure you have heard this before: "For God so loved the world that He gave His only Son, so that everyone who believes in Him might not perish but might have eternal life." But wait, there's more: "For God did not send His Son into the world to condemn the world, but that the world might be saved through Him." If we want to be saved in a spiritual sense, we are called to believe in Jesus and follow His teachings. If we want to save the world in a temporal sense, the prescription is the same. Follow the Word of the Lord. Love everyone, including your enemies. What could be more fulfilling than turning an enemy into a friend through the sheer force of love? What could be more fulfilling than turning a godless killer into a saved soul through the perfect example of Christ?

QUESTIONS FOR REFLECTION OR DISCUSSION

1. What is your favorite quote from Jesus in Chapter Fourteen? Why?

2. Which of Jesus' quotes in Chapter Fourteen did you find most surprising? In what way did it surprise you?

3. Have you had any experiences in which you were able to convert an enemy into a friend through peaceful resistance and love?

4. Do you agree with Jesus' philosophy that we should pray for people who mistreat us? Whether you agree with it or not, do you incorporate this philosophy into your regular prayer life?

5. Is the Golden Rule still viable in modern society? Why or why not?

Chapter Fifteen

AM I RIGHT WHEN I SAY THERE SEEM TO BE A LOT OF EVIL FORCES IN THE WORLD TODAY?

*He was a murderer from the beginning
and does not stand in truth,
because there is no truth in him.*

As we observe what goes on around us, we cannot help but conclude that there are evil forces at work, all over the world. The world has always been subject to evil influences, but it seems the proliferation of evil is at an unprecedented level today. I suppose people say that in every generation though. It's called getting old, right?

You cannot deny that our world is besieged by evil forces that are human in nature. Consider terrorists. It doesn't matter which persuasion of terrorist you consider. In recent years, radical Islamic terrorists have been the focus of attention, especially since the attack on the World Trade Center in 2001 that resulted in the deaths of nearly 3,000 civilians. That attack hits home for us because it took place on our soil at the hands of foreign actors. More recently we have been introduced to a singularly horrific and blood-thirsty form of evil known as ISIS. But we have also experienced domestic terrorism here in the USA, such as the attack on the Oklahoma City Federal building or, going back in time, the work of the FALN and the Weather Underground. Outside our borders, there is terrorism carried on in Central and South America by drug lords, looking to eliminate both the competition and the forces of law and order that would stop them. For very many years there were acts of terrorism carried on in Great Britain between the Catholics and Protestants in Northern Ireland, and also targeted attacks by the Irish Republican Army against the English. I suppose in each case the terrorists felt they had some justification for what they did, or some ax to grind against the perpetrators of injustice, real or perceived. But none of that justifies the intentional killing of innocent lives. Thou shall not kill, says the Lord.

We do not have to look at terrorism to see human evil, however. There is ample evidence in the acts of supposedly legitimate governments. Look at the hundreds of thousands of Syrians killed in the ongoing civil war or government-sponsored homicides. In America we still feel the sting of 9/11/2001, but see how the number of lives lost pales by comparison to the lives lost in many international situations.

Foreign governments almost routinely put down potential opposition by mass killings of their own subjects. Think of Iraq under Saddam Hussein, think of North Korea, think of the killing fields of Cambodia, think of numerous genocidal civil wars in Africa. Think of the millions killed by Hitler and Stalin.

Putting aside organized terrorists or tyrannical governments, there is also abundant evidence of human evil on the individual level. Mass murderers, serial killers, child rapists, kidnappers, persistent perpetrators of domestic violence. Also, not all human evil reveals itself in violent acts. What about people who distribute illegal drugs for profit, without regard for the lives being ruined through addiction, street violence, and premature death? What about people who create and distribute pornography, without regard for the human cost in terms of sexual promiscuity, precocious sexuality, teen pregnancy, emotionally vacuous sexual relationships, and damaged marriages that result? What about people who create and distribute for profit entertainment vehicles designed to perpetuate a culture of gangs, guns, and violence? This is evil at work, undermining the future of our children and our society.

Evil is also present in non-human manifestations in our world. I am referring to various medical maladies that plague us. The Bible tells us that God never intended for man to suffer and die, that it was man's disobedience to God that invited evil forces into our world. Suffering and death are the by-products of these evil forces and are a consequence of our fallen nature.

Is not cancer an evil force in our world? For as long as I can remember, there has been an ongoing war on cancer. There has been great research into what causes cancer, and how we can prevent cancer, and how we can cure cancer. Tremendous strides have been made. Yet, day after day, people of all ages fall prey to this dread disease and die.

When I was a kid in the 1960s, actor William Talman, who played prosecutor Hamilton Burger on the TV show "Perry Mason", appeared on TV in a public service announcement, in which he told us he was dying from lung cancer as a result of many years of heavy smoking. Mr. Talman urged us not to smoke. He died a short time afterward. Some years later, actor Yul Brynner appeared in a similar public service announcement about the dangers of smoking. I imagine these actors helped many people my age and younger in their decisions not to smoke. Nevertheless, every day people who never smoked a cigarette in their lives die from lung cancer at a young age.

No matter how young a person is, no matter how innocent a person is, no matter how nice a person is, no matter how religious a person is, cancer doesn't stop. Cancer is an ever-present killer and an ever-present threat in our midst. To some extent our lifestyle choices and environmental exposures will predispose us to developing certain forms of cancer, but at other times it appears to be completely random. And it is just as likely to strike good people as bad. But why should there even be cancer in the first place?

Cancer is just one of the almost innumerable maladies that plague humanity and are, in my view, manifestations of evil on earth. There are legions of medical disorders that strike us down. There are numerous psychiatric disorders that make sufferers' lives unbearable. Surely these are the result of evil at work in our world. There may be medical explanations for how these phenomena come about. But in a cosmic sense, why should they come about at all? Because there is evil in the world.

What does Jesus think about evil in the world? Jesus is all too familiar with it, for evil was present when Jesus walked the earth as well, and for all the thousands of years before that, since the fall in the Garden.

Before Jesus began His public ministry, while He was fasting and praying in the desert, the devil tempted Him with promises of food, power, and security. Here are Jesus' responses: "It is written, man does not live by bread alone, but by every word that comes forth from the mouth of God. … Again it is written, you shall not put the Lord your God to the test. … It is written, the Lord your God shall you worship, and him alone shall you serve."

In His ministry, Jesus came face-to-face with evil and its earthly manifestations all the time. We find these examples in the Gospels:

> They brought Him many who were *possessed by demons*, and He drove out *the spirits* by a word and cured all the sick.

He drove out a *demon* from a mute person, and the mute person spoke.

He gave the twelve authority over *unclean spirits* to drive them out and to cure every disease and illness.

He cured a *demoniac* who was blind and mute so that he could speak and see.

He freed the Canaanite woman's daughter from the clutches of *a demon*.

He cured a lunatic boy with seizures by driving out *a demon*.

He cured a man with *an unclean spirit* by driving out *the spirit*. He drove out *many demons*, not permitting them to speak because they knew Him.

He healed the Gerasene *Demon*iac. People came out to see what had happened and, when they approached Jesus, they found the man from whom *the demons* had come out sitting at His feet. He was clothed and in his right mind.

He was teaching in a synagogue on the Sabbath, and a woman was there who for eighteen years had been crippled by *a spirit*. After curing her, Jesus said, 'This daughter of Abraham, whom *Satan* has bound for eighteen years now, ought she not to have been set free on the Sabbath day from this bondage?'

I used to think that these Gospel references to demons and evil spirits were just an ignorant first century A.D. way of talking about disease. But looking again from a cosmic sense, it seems reasonable to conclude, from these Gospel anecdotes, that physical and mental illnesses may be the result of Satanic forces that have been at work in the world since the dawn of man.

As a sufferer of panic disorder, it is easy for me to see a correlation between evil spirits and human suffering. I recently read a book that I came across in my Pastor's office called "Deliver Us from Evil", which was written in 1972 by the late Don Basham. The book explored Pastor Basham's development of a deliverance ministry for casting out demons. His book included a discussion of the ways that evil spirits get inside us, which hit home for me.

When I was maybe six years old, Santa Claus came to a store on Central Avenue in Jersey City. I went to see Santa. (This was in the old days, when urban parents let their young children go out without constant surveillance. Remember?) Somehow little me got stuck in this huge crowd of people who were waiting for Santa. I couldn't move forward, I couldn't move back, I couldn't see because I only came up to everyone else's waists. I totally lost it and started screaming. I was rescued by a kid named Jimmy Cochrane, a future three-sport All-County athlete who, at the tender age of 11, was already about six-feet tall, or at least it seemed that way to me. I will never forget his act of kindness, lifting me out of the terrifying mass of humanity.

Looking back, I wonder if this traumatic experience of being lost in that crowd could have opened the door to the spirits of vulnerability, helplessness, abandonment, anxiety, and panic that occasionally plague me to this very day. Psychiatrists might describe the etymology of my disorder differently, but the end result is the same. Since I can't be expect big Jim to pull 50-something me out of the crowd, I must turn instead to the Lord in prayer and meditation to help me ward off these spirits.

Jesus did not only encounter evil in the form of demons, evil spirits, and physical maladies that plagued the people. He also saw the evil that was at work in people's hearts. He realized, for example, that some people were not capable of learning from Him, and following His way, because they had allowed evil into their lives and were not willing to exorcise that evil. Unfortunately, then as now, some people

<u>were evil because they chose to be</u>. Of such people Jesus says, "You belong to your father *the devil*, and you willingly carry out your father's desires. ... whoever belongs to God hears the words of God; for this reason you do not listen, because you do not belong to God."

Jesus also tells us that when people allow the devil to have control of their lives, it creates a barrier to their ability to see clearly in the spiritual sense. Notice this explanation regarding the Parable of the Sower, with respect to the seed that fell on the path, and was eaten by birds: "The seed sown on the path is the one who hears the word of the kingdom without understanding it, and *the evil one* comes and steals away what was sown in his heart." Similarly, in His parable about the harvesting of the wheat and the weeds, Jesus identifies the devil as the one who sows the weeds among the wheat, and the children of the devil as the weeds themselves. Thus, the devil seduces people through the glamor and allure of sin, and these, his "children", are among us in the world as a corrupting influence. We must be steadfast in our obedience to the word of the Lord in order to remain children of the kingdom.

There is indeed evil in the world, and even Jesus Himself could not eradicate the evil, nor soften the hearts of sinful man. So we humans cannot expect to be immune to evil's effects. The question is, how do we respond to it? Again, it behooves us to listen to Jesus, as His wisdom can help us through. Here are some of the things Jesus says to us. You may find that they are out of step with what many people would consider the appropriate response when evil confronts us, but listen to Jesus: "Blessed are you when they insult you and persecute you and utter every kind of evil against you because of me. Rejoice and be glad, for great will be your reward in heaven. Thus they persecuted the prophets who were before you. ... You have heard that it was said, 'An eye for an eye, and a tooth for a tooth.' But I say to you, offer no resistance to one who is evil.... I say to you, love your enemies, and pray for those who persecute you, that you may be children of your heavenly Father... "

It is also important that we know our limitations with respect to the evil we confront, and that we do not allow ourselves to be overwhelmed by things we cannot control. As Jesus says, "Do not worry about tomorrow; tomorrow will take care of itself. Sufficient for a day is its own evil."

We must be aware that ours is a fallen world, subject to evil spirits. It is an unfortunate aspect of our human condition that we suffer because of the manifestations of evil, in the form of bad people and debilitating illnesses. Jesus knows this, and He is with us in our suffering, if we want Him to be. Jesus' advice to us in dealing with the evil we face is this: answer evil with good, hatred with love, anger with kindness. Focus on what confronts you today, don't fret about what may come down the pike later. Keep your faith, worship and praise God in the face of temptation and suffering, and abide in His Word.

Evil causes all humans to suffer, but remember, this too shall pass. Life on earth is transitory. Persevere, and work for the reward that awaits you with God.

QUESTIONS FOR REFLECTION OR DISCUSSION

1. What is your favorite quote from Jesus in Chapter Fifteen? Why?

2. Which of Jesus' quotes in Chapter Fifteen did you find most surprising? In what way did it surprise you?

3. Do you agree with the author that the illnesses we suffer are the result of evil in our world? What is your opinion about why God allows us to suffer?

4. Does the promise of eternal life outweigh the suffering we endure on earth? How do you think non-believers cope with earthly suffering?

5. Have there been experiences in your life that have caused you to question whether there is a loving God? Were you able to reconcile those experiences with your spiritual beliefs?

Chapter Sixteen

SO YOU ARE NOT A PROPONENT OF 'IF YOU CAN'T BEAT 'EM, JOIN 'EM'?

The righteous will shine like the sun
in the kingdom of their Father.

What does it mean to be righteous? It is a word we hear often, and it is a word we encounter often in the Bible. But while I don't know about you, I can honestly say I have never given much thought to what it really means. I do know the Righteous Brothers had some big hits on the Top 40 charts, but that doesn't give us much insight into the meaning of the word. I know that being righteous is generally considered a good thing, and that being self-righteous is a less good thing, but just what does righteous mean?

The Merriam-Webster online dictionary defines "righteous" as "acting in accord with divine or moral law; free from guilt or sin; morally right and justifiable." "Righteous" is an adjective, while "righteousness" is a noun that means "the quality of being morally right or justifiable." "Righteous" is an antonym for "evil" used as an adjective, and "righteousness" is an antonym for "evil" used as a noun.

So at first blush, if someone called me righteous I would take it as a huge compliment. But in thinking about it some more, I suppose in modern society a person who tries to be righteous might be seen as a person to be disdained, a relic from another age, a square. Regardless of modern society's perspective, though, we are called by God to be righteous, not evil. No matter what the world around us might say, or how it might provoke us, we should strive for righteousness. Moreover, Jesus assures us that the righteous will be rewarded.

Jesus makes a couple of references to righteousness in the Beatitudes from His Sermon on the Mount. He says, "Blessed are they who hunger and thirst for righteousness, for they will be satisfied." That is to say, people who have a strong desire to see what is morally right prevail in the world will have that desire fulfilled. We know, to our consternation, that righteousness does not always prevail here on earth. But we have a promise from Jesus that our desire for what is morally right will be vindicated. We can take solace knowing that if we are not vindicated on earth, we will be in heaven.

Jesus also says, "Blessed are they who are persecuted for the sake of righteousness, for theirs is the kingdom of heaven." Although Jesus first said this some 2,000 years ago, in one way or another many righteous people are still being persecuted today. The persecution may be in the form of violence against, or imprisonment of, people working for the human rights of others. Think, for example, of people who try to further the rights of women living under repressive regimes – e.g., the rights to be educated and kept safe from abuse. Or the persecution may be less extreme, but nevertheless wrong, such as insulting and ridiculing people for choosing not to have sexual relations prior to marriage, or for otherwise refusing to give in to the lure of a corrupt society. When I think about people who are being persecuted for doing God's work, it gives me pangs of inadequacy. Sure, finding a job and keeping a job, supporting a family and raising children, and instilling moral values in them, this is all hard work. But it pales in comparison to those who are putting their lives on the line every day for the Lord's sake.

Nevertheless, we are all, in our own way, called to righteousness and challenged to live our lives in a manner pleasing to God. Jesus tells us, "You are the light of the world. A city set on a mountain cannot be hidden. Nor do they light a lamp and then place it under a bushel basket. It is set on a lampstand, where it gives light to all in the house. Just so, your light must shine before others, that they may see your good deeds and glorify your heavenly Father."

What is special about this passage is how it shows us the three blessings that emanate from our righteous living. First, it curries favor for us in heaven. God loves the righteous. Second, it blesses those people who are the beneficiaries of our righteous behavior, whether they be the poor or the sick, or widows or orphans, or whomever else we minister to. Finally, it blesses those who see our righteous acts and are brought closer to God as a result. As expressed in a quote attributed to St. Francis of Assisi, "Preach the Gospel at all times; when necessary, use words." We can teach and inspire others by our selfless actions.

Now I will admit, I have at times been confused by the apparent inconsistency between: (1) Jesus' instruction to us to let others see our good deeds so that our light shines before others, and (2) Jesus' admonition "not to perform righteous deeds in order that people may see them; otherwise, you will have no recompense from your heavenly Father." Jesus also says,

> When you give alms, do not blow a trumpet before you, as the hypocrites do in the synagogues and in the streets to win the praise of others. Amen, I say to you, they have received their reward. But when you give alms, do not let your left hand know what your right is doing, so that your almsgiving may be secret. And your Father who sees in secret will repay you.

Is it not somewhat confusing to try to decipher just what it is Jesus expects of us when we serve others? I think the best way to reconcile these statements is to consider not the circumstances under which we perform righteous deeds, but rather our motivation. If we come upon someone in public who is in need of assistance, Jesus does not want us to say, "I won't help that person because I shouldn't be seen doing good." Of course Jesus wants us to help people in need, even in public. As I said above, this is good for us, good for the person we are helping, and good for those who observe us, as they may be inspired to do likewise, and so do the Father's will. On the other hand, if we look to help people in public **in order** that people will see us, rather than **despite the fact** that people will see us, our motivation for helping becomes suspect. It appears in this case that we are doing good so that we will be praised, rather than doing good for the glory of God.

Jesus wants us to help others because it is the right thing to do, not because we want to get a pat on the back or for some other ulterior motive.

Jesus indicates to us that doing what is right should be a primary goal of our existence. Jesus tells us, "So do not say 'what are we to eat' or 'what are we to drink' or 'what are we to wear'. All these things the pagans seek. Your heavenly Father knows that you need them all. **But seek first the kingdom of God and His righteousness, and all these things will be given to you besides**." This raises the question, what are our priorities? Are we focused on doing God's will, following His commands, and serving our fellow man? Or are we focused on our material comforts, satisfying our worldly desires, with all that religious stuff just an afterthought? God does not want to be our afterthought. Material comforts are transient, and when our lives on earth are over they will not mean anything. Jesus says to us,

"What profit would there be for one to gain the whole world and forfeit his life, or what can one give in exchange for his life? For the Son of Man will come with his angels in his Father's glory, and then He will repay everyone according to his conduct."

In other words, you cannot buy your way into heaven. Your possessions have no value in the afterlife. It is how you behave in your earthly life that matters. "Just as weeds are collected and burned up with fire," Jesus says, "so will it be at the end of the age. The Son of Man will send His angels, and they will collect out of His kingdom all who cause others to sin and all evildoers. They will throw them into the fiery furnace, where there will be wailing and grinding of teeth. Then the righteous will shine like the sun in the kingdom of their Father. Whoever has ears ought to hear."

I think it is pretty clear then, all other things being equal, that Jesus would be just delighted if we all conducted ourselves in a righteous manner. It should make no difference to us that society appears to be promoting and honoring the unrighteous. Our call to righteousness remains. If we live righteously, we will be rewarded.

There is just one caveat I must issue to you with respect to righteous living: you must develop thick skin. First, you will need thick skin because the unrighteous will mock you for your goody-goodiness. Secondly, like the prodigal son's older brother, Jesus will not have you in His sights. Metaphorically speaking, the righteous are the "well" Jesus speaks of when He says, "Those who are well do not need a physician, but the sick do." Jesus continues, "I did not come to call the righteous but sinners." This is why Jesus associated with the tax collectors and sinners, to lead them back to God. Jesus tells us, "There will be more joy in heaven over one sinner who repents than over ninety-nine righteous people who have no need of repentance. ...I tell you, there will be rejoicing among the angels of God over one sinner who repents."

As the forgiving father tells the unprodigal older brother, "My son, you are here with me always; everything I have is yours. But now we must celebrate and rejoice, because your brother was dead, and has come to life again; he was lost, and has been found." This can be a little difficult to swallow for those who are in the habit of doing God's will and living righteously. It is as if the sinners somehow get preferential treatment. But remember, righteous dudes and dudettes, the goal is that **ALL** God's children be welcomed into heaven and share eternal life. If we love our brothers and sisters as God wants us to, then we should **want** them all to repent, to come back to God and merit everlasting happiness in God's holy presence. If this seems unfair to us, then we need to look in the mirror and ask ourselves, do we really love our fellow man as God calls us to? Or is it really all about us?

The lesson to be learned is this: live a righteous life, and pray to God that the evil will repent and also come to live righteously, so that they will be welcomed along with us in God's kingdom. Remember, if you are righteous you will shine like the sun in the kingdom of your Father. What more could you want? If some less righteous people make it there too, who cares? The more the merrier.

QUESTIONS FOR REFLECTION OR DISCUSSION

1. What is your favorite quote from Jesus in Chapter Sixteen? Why?

2. Which of Jesus' quotes in Chapter Sixteen did you find most surprising? In what way did it surprise you?

3. Do you consider yourself a righteous person? Why, or why not?

4. Do you think in today's society it is easier to get along if you are righteous, or unrighteous?

5. Would the world be a better place if more people lived righteous lives?

6. Does it bother you that unrighteous people who repent can share eternal life with people who have always striven for righteousness?

Chapter Seventeen

ARE YOU TROUBLED BY THE PROLIFERATION OF GOSSIPING AND BULLYING IN SOCIETY?

By your words you will be acquitted,
and by your words you will be condemned.

The Eighth Commandment says, "Thou shall not bear false witness against your neighbor." Jesus tells us, "[U]ntil heaven and earth pass away, not the smallest letter or the smallest part of a letter will pass from the law, until all things have taken place. Therefore, whoever breaks one of the least of these commandments and teaches others to do so will be called least in the kingdom of heaven." We can easily conclude, therefore, that Jesus opposes – nay, condemns – us bearing false witness against our neighbors. Yet there has probably never been a time in the history of mankind more rife with bearing false witness than our time. Digital media and social media were practically tailor-made for it.

What do I mean by this? Digital media can be manipulated in such a way as to enable one to take a "sound bite" completely out of context, and thereby totally distort the meaning of what was said. News organizations take a one-sentence clip from a lengthy presentation and then sensationalize the clip by ignoring the context. This can harm the speaker's reputation by making it seem to the public that he or she is saying something awful, when the "editor" of the clip knows this was not the case. Liberal media organizations do this to conservatives, and conservative media organizations do it to liberals. Making it seem that a person was saying something that he wasn't really saying is bearing false witness. It is slanderous and malicious.

The Internet is another breeding ground for false witness. E-mail, chat, texts, and social media sites like Facebook and Twitter make it very easy to initiate and spread false rumors, malicious gossip, and innuendoes. This can become like an avalanche against the poor victim of this false witness before he has any chance to respond and defend himself. Reputations are ruined; tragically, those who lack the emotional framework to contend with this may take their own lives. This is part of the cyber-bullying epidemic, in which most of the perpetrators and victims are mere high school students, or younger.

I have to wonder how many of the young perpetrators who engage in this cyber-bullying would self-identify as Christians. Based upon the demographics of our nation, quite a lot, I would think. Even if their parents choose to overlook or excuse their behavior, their Savior may be less kind in His evaluation. "Do unto others as you would have them do unto you," Jesus instructs us. "This is the law and the prophets." Would the bullies like to be on the other side, driven to the point of suicide by relentless rumor, gossip, and torment? I doubt it.

Unfortunately, the opportunities for bearing false witness via the Internet are not limited to social media sites. Most news organization websites allow readers to comment on news articles. All you really need in order to comment is a computer with a keyboard and an Internet connection. You don't need a sense of decency, a sense of shame, a sense of compassion, or any sense at all, for that matter. And not having to face the people you are talking about makes it so much easier to speak your mind, so-called, doesn't it?

There was an incident not too long ago that made the national news, in which a young teacher was brutally murdered by one of her high school students. Among the "comments" posted by readers on a news site about the story was an assertion (in reality wild speculation, but stated in a bold, assertive way) that there must have been a sexual relationship between the teacher and the student, and when she broke off the relationship he killed her. Was the purpose of this comment to somehow suggest that she deserved what she got? Have we become so callous to the value of human life that a comment such as this should be our reaction to this tragic story? The bigger problem, however, is that there was not a shred of truth behind this comment, and the only "evidence" that would even support such an assertion was the fact that the student had murdered his teacher. Isn't it bad enough that this young woman, who was devoting her life to teaching our children, was heartlessly killed by one of her lieges? Do we have to kill her reputation as well by starting unfounded rumors about her personal life? One hopes the deceased is with God and beyond caring about such cruelty, but I'm pretty certain her family would be devastated to read such garbage.

Another recent tragic news story concerned a young married couple out Christmas shopping at a suburban mall.

Upon returning to their vehicle in an unsecured parking garage, they were accosted by vicious criminals, who shot the husband to death and then made off with the couple's automobile. Again the brilliant minds, safe behind their computers, take to the Internet to comment on this horrendous story. Well, since the bad guys shot the husband and not the wife, the wife must have arranged the whole thing. After all, what young bride hasn't fantasized about taking her husband on a shopping trip at Chrismastime and hiring some thugs to meet them in the garage, kill her husband, and take her car with all the presents in it? The perfect crime, no? The police would never suspect. Thank goodness we have heartless Internet innuendo-throwers to crack the case.

Just like those who transmit vile emails, texts, and tweets designed to destroy reputations, those who sit at their computers sharing their thoughts with us about current events would do well to read the Gospels. Not only is there a little matter known as the "Golden Rule" --- how would you like someone making such comments about **you** on the day of your greatest personal tragedy? – there is also a none-too-subtle warning from Jesus, which goes like this: "[F]rom the fullness of the heart the mouth speaks. A good person brings forth good out of a store of goodness, but an evil person brings forth evil out of a store of evil. I tell you, on the day of judgment people will render an account for every careless word they speak. By your words you will be acquitted, and by your words you will be condemned."

Thus, gossiping and cyber-bullying can be considered analogous to bearing false witness against one's neighbor, which is verboten. Furthermore, gossiping and cyber-bullying are also contrary to another aspect of God's word, to wit: when you come right down to it, gossiping and cyber-bullying are a form of judging others. When we talk behind peoples' backs, aren't we in essence making judgments about them, about the things they do or say, or rather about the things we have been told they did or said? Of course we are, and we have decided that whatever they are supposed to have done or said is somehow blameworthy, otherwise we wouldn't be talking about it behind their backs!

But even though the people we are gossiping about may be unaware of what we are saying, God knows. And Jesus tells us, "Whatever you have said in the darkness will be heard in the light, and what you have whispered behind closed doors will be proclaimed on the housetops." If you are saying bad things about people, it will be made known, and you will be judged accordingly. "Stop judging and you will not be judged," says our Lord. "Stop condemning and you will not be condemned."

Who are you to talk about others, anyway? Are you so special? Remember what Jesus said concerning the woman who was caught committing adultery: "Let the one among you who is without sin cast the first stone."

There is an old adage that says if you can't say something good about a person, don't say anything. Some people still live by that adage, but fewer and fewer, it seems. Saying bad things about others seems to be some people's favorite pastime. And I cannot claim to be innocent in this arena, for I have often been drawn into negative conversations about absent friends. [9]

---

[9] Now that I think of it, I may have been guilty of bearing false witness in this very book Remember when I talked about my mother throwing out our old baseball and football cards? Well, I did not actually see her do that. For all I know, one day while I was at school a flying saucer might have landed in our backyard, and little green men may have

But the fact that it is commonplace does not excuse the wrongdoing. "Enter through the narrow gate," Jesus advises us, "for the gate is wide and the road broad that leads to destruction, and those who enter through it are many. How narrow the gate and constricted the road that leads to life. And those who find it are few." Better to be the few than the many in this instance, methinks. In other words, when people are gossiping, be the one who decides to put a stop to it.

This calls to mind the heart-to-heart talk between John Garfield and Dorothy McGuire in "Gentlemen's Agreement" (1947). Sure, Dorothy found it very upsetting and disturbing when her WASP-y friends were making anti-Semitic comments. "But what did you do about it?" John wants to know. Because being upset and disturbed and sitting quietly by doesn't change anything. The same is true for bullying and gossiping. Not liking these behaviors, being disturbed by them, will not change anything unless you speak up. When the mob was going to stone the adulteress, Jesus did not stand by in silent disapproval of their plan. He spoke up.

---

chloroformed poor mom and made off with the loot!

Cyber-bullying is similarly a form of judgment, a judgment that some person is worthy of ridicule or condemnation, or simply that a person should not be associated with. This behavior too will not be overlooked when we go before God. "Stop judging, that you may not be judged," Jesus admonishes us. "For as you judge, so will you be judged, and the measure with which you judge will be measured out to you." How much more terrible will that judgment be if you bully someone to the point of suicide?

Are you a cyber-bully? Are you using the Internet and social media to make someone you know miserable, to ruin his or her life? Jesus says stop! Jesus instructs us, "I give you a new commandment: love one another. As I have loved you, so you also should love one another. This is how all will know you are my disciples, if you have love for one another." You cannot call yourself a Christian and be engaged in bullying, or you are a liar. Jesus calls us to love, and bullying is not love!

Are you aware of someone who is being bullied by friends of yours, even though you yourself are not a bully? Then intervene and put a stop to it before it is too late. For as

Jesus also tells us, "Blessed are the peacemakers, for they will be called children of God."

Yes, Jesus is dismayed by the gossiping and cyber-bullying that goes on all around us. It is a distinctly uncharitable and distinctly unChristian way of behaving. If you want to stay on the path to eternal life, you would be well served to stay away from these troubling, destructive behaviors, and to speak out against them when you encounter them.

QUESTIONS FOR REFLECTION OR DISCUSSION

1. What is your favorite quote from Jesus in Chapter Seventeen? Why?

2. Which of Jesus' quotes in Chapter Seventeen did you find most surprising? In what way did it surprise you?

3. Have you been either a perpetrator or victim of cyber-bullying? What if anything did you learn from the experience?

4. Have you ever lied about someone in a situation that caused him or her to be harmed by your lie? Has anyone ever lied about you in a similar situation? Can you understand why God issued a Commandment against this behavior?

5. Have you ever attempted to stop a group of friends from gossiping about someone who was absent? If so, were you persecuted for it?

Chapter Eighteen

I TEND TO BE JUDGMENTAL AT TIMES, BUT THAT'S OK AS LONG AS MY HEART IS IN THE RIGHT PLACE. ISN'T IT?

Why do you notice the splinter in your brother's eye,
but do not perceive the wooden beam in your own eye?

I think that gossiping and cyber-bullying are both, to some degree, born of judgmentalism. Of course there are other factors that must be in play as well. To gossip about someone requires some amount of dislike and/or resentment of that person, and probably some amount of insecurity in oneself. To take it a step further and begin harassing and bullying somebody requires more again: meanness and an utter lack of sensitivity or compassion. But it begins with a judgment – a judgment that something the other person did or said is worthy of scorn and condemnation, or deserving of ridicule. So let's continue briefly with the theme of judgmentalism. Of all my sins, it is surely the one that I have committed most consistently.

When I was an innocent young lad, I didn't used to judge people. Even if someone did something that was not nice, I would always give him or her the benefit of the doubt. As I got a little older, however, I found that I developed a habit of pre-judging people, of thinking badly of them even though I didn't really know them. Often times I would be proven wrong. Somebody I didn't like from afar turned out to be a genuinely nice person when I got to know him or her. Yet even being proven wrong again and again, I would repeatedly fall into the same trap of assuming certain people were not nice or were not good, without taking the time to know them.

What I believe, although I do not like to admit it, is that my judgmentalism is often the result of other sins. If someone is smarter than I am, stronger than I am, wealthier than I am, better looking than I am, or more spiritual than I am, I might judge that person by looking for and focusing on his flaws. Why? Because in reality I am envious that he is better than I am. If I think someone is less intelligent or less spiritual than I am or has multiple tattoos and piercings, I might rush to judgment because of the sin of pride. "Oh, I'm so much better than he is." If I think someone is better then I am, I judge him. If I think someone is not as good as I am, I judge him. Only people on an equal plane with me are safe.

Of course I am exaggerating a bit. Nevertheless, it is a serious flaw, and one that Jesus is not happy with.

In what ways does Jesus indicate to us that He does not want us to be judgmental? Let me count the ways! In the first place, if we are judgmental towards people because of bad things they have said or done to us and others, remember that Jesus tells us, "Blessed are the merciful, for they will be shown mercy." Jesus also tells us, "Stop judging and you will not be judged. Stop condemning and you will not be condemned." Clearly, Jesus does not want us to be judgmental, and essentially instructs us that, for our own good, we ought to stop. [10]

---

[10] I think I should insert a quick explanation of what I mean when I speak of being judgmental, and what I believe Jesus means as well. Basically I am talking about making a value judgment and a moral judgment about another person. When I decide that I am better, holier, more special than the other person, and that when all is said and done I am going to heaven but he or she probably is not, I am being judgmental. It is not my place to make those decisions, and Jesus warns that if I am going to put myself in the position of deciding who should get to heaven, I am going to have to live up to the standards I set for others. What I *don't* mean, when I speak of being judgmental, is giving people advice about things they are doing or not doing. If I tell someone he should stop smoking, I am doing so for the benefit of his health, not because I think I am better than he is. If I tell a recovering alcoholic he shouldn't have an alcoholic beverage, it's not because I think I am better than he is. If I tell someone he should read the Bible, it's not because I think I am better than he is. Making suggestions to people about things they can do to improve themselves is not being judgmental. By contrast,

If we judge people because we think we are better than they are, Jesus has some choice words for us as well. Remember, the Pharisees thought they were better than everyone, too. Jesus reprimanded the Pharisees for their arrogance and their pride. And just so, Jesus says, "I tell you, unless your righteousness surpasses that of the scribes and Pharisees, you will not enter into the kingdom of heaven." Jesus tells a story of a Pharisee and a tax collector praying in the temple: "The Pharisee prayed, 'O God, I thank you that I am not like the rest of humanity ...' But the tax collector stood at a distance and would not even raise his eyes to heaven, but beat his breast and prayed, 'O God, be merciful to me, a sinner.' " It is important that we remember that it was the tax collector's prayer that Jesus found worthy. The tax collector went home justified, not the Pharisee. Jesus does not want us to be proud, arrogant, and superior, like the stereotypical Pharisee. He tells us, "Everyone who exalts himself will be humbled, but the one who humbles himself will be exalted."

---

saying, "You're going to hell because you drink too much" **IS** being judgmental.

Consider again the case of Jesus' friends, Martha and Mary. Surely, when Martha sought the Lord's intercession, she thought she was coming from a place of moral superiority vis-à-vis her sister Mary. After all, Martha was busying herself serving others, while Mary was just sitting at Jesus' feet, doing nothing. I'm sure Martha was taken by surprise when Jesus took her sister's side and said, "Martha Martha, you are anxious and worried about many things. There is need of only one thing. Mary has chosen the better part, and it will not be taken from her." Just so, we may be in for a rude awakening ourselves when we look to condemn others. Jesus just might give us a gentle chastisement, as He did to Martha.

Another fault of the stereotypical Pharisee of Jesus' day was that he was hypocritical, and this is another issue that faces those of us who are judgmental. In other words, where do we get off being judgmental of others? Are we so perfect? We most certainly are not. Therefore, Jesus questions us: "Why do you notice the splinter in your brother's eye, but do not perceive the wooden beam in your own eye? How can you say to your brother, 'let me remove that splinter from your eye' while the wooden beam is in your eye? You hypocrite, remove the wooden beam from your eye first; then you will see clearly to remove the splinter from your brother's eye."

One problem with casting aspersions upon others is that you make yourself a target anytime your own conduct does not measure up to proper Christian standards. Jesus warns us, "Stop judging, that you may not be judged. For as you judge, so will you be judged, and the measure with which you judge will be measured out to you." If we judge others harshly, we run the risk of facing harsh judgment from God when it is time for us to go before Him and give an account of our lives. If we look to the example of Jesus, we will see how inappropriate it is for us to pass judgment on our "inferiors". Many tax collectors and sinners sat with Jesus and His disciples, as there were many who followed Him. Jesus, the King of kings, God incarnate, did not condemn the tax collectors and sinners, but welcomed them. He said, "Those who are well do not need a physician, but the sick do. I did not come to call the righteous but sinners." And as to the woman caught in adultery, Jesus says to those who would condemn her, "Let the one among you who is without sin cast the first stone." Who then are we to condemn, when we don't even know if God Himself would condemn?

Back in 1969, the wonderful singer and songwriter Joe South sang, "Before you abuse, criticize and accuse, walk a mile in my shoes." Similarly, in the book and movie "To Kill a Mockingbird", Atticus Finch teaches his children that you can't make judgments about someone unless you've walked around in his shoes. Yet how often we judge a person while knowing little or nothing of what that person is going through, or has gone through, and how that impacts his or her behavior. It is easy for us to judge from afar; how easy would it be for us to live the judgee's life?

As if it isn't enough that our judgmental behavior will run afoul of God when we face our own judgment, we also run the risk here on earth of being chastised by the enemies of Christianity, who are just itching to point out how flawed we Christians are. Accusing Christians of being judgmental and blind to their own faults is a favorite tactic of God-deniers everywhere. That "take the beam out of your own eye" stuff hurts.

More importantly, however, judging and condemning people is bad because it violates the spirit of Jesus' most meaningful lessons. "I give you a new commandment: love one another," Jesus says. "As I have loved you, so you also should love one another. This is how all will know you are My disciples, if you have love for one another." When we put ourselves on a higher moral plane and deign to judge others, are we acting out of love? Asking the question another way, would we appreciate being judged by people who do not know our full situation, but have nevertheless concluded that we are worthy of condemnation?

I wish I could be more like Jesus as I go through my daily walk, instead of judging everyone I meet. I really really need to remind myself to love them as Jesus does, and to keep my trap shut unless I've walked a mile in their shoes.

QUESTIONS FOR REFLECTION OR DISCUSSION

1. What is your favorite quote from Jesus in Chapter Eighteen? Why?

2. Which of Jesus' quotes in Chapter Eighteen did you find most surprising? In what way did it surprise you?

3. Is there a particular subset of the population that brings out the judge in you? Why do you think that is?

4. The author indicates he falls into the habit of being judgmental towards people by whom he feels threatened. Have you had a similar experience?

5. Have you ever experienced being unfairly judged by someone? What were the circumstances, and how did you react to it?

Chapter Nineteen

LORD, HOW WOULD YOU HAVE US LIVE?

Just so, your light must shone before others, that they may see your good deeds and glorify your heavenly Father.

It seems to me that it is easier to write about the things God wants us **not** to do than to write about the things God affirmatively wants us to do. Perhaps that is because of my judgmental nature (see Chapter 18), or perhaps it is because I have more experience in doing bad than in doing good. In any case, it is important to talk about how God wants us to live our lives.

As I see it, Jesus gives us a primer for living a holy life. Many of the lessons have parallels in Judaism and other religious traditions, but if we are to live a Christian life we should know Jesus' take on a holy life. So here are 14 of Jesus' sayings that we ought to apply in our daily lives. We have seen or will see some of these sayings in other contexts throughout this book, but for now let's just focus on them as our Christ-like instruction manual.

> ➤ "You are the light of the world. A city set on a mountain cannot be hidden. Nor do they light a lamp and then place it under a bushel basket. It is

set on a lampstand, where it gives light to all in the house. Just so, your light must shine before others, that they may see your good deeds and glorify your heavenly Father."

Earlier I mentioned a saying often attributed to St. Francis of Assisi, which I first heard when I made a Cursillo weekend. It goes like this: "Preach the Gospel at all times; when necessary use words." The concept behind this saying is quite simple. If we are living a truly Christian life, it will be obvious to those we encounter, by the way we treat others and the good works we perform. Ideally, people who do not already "know" Jesus will come to know Him and follow Him because of our example. This is what Jesus is saying to us here. To reiterate a point made earlier, it is not about showing other people how wonderful we are. We must be careful to be humble and sincere in our good works, rather than boastful about them. It is by walking the walk, not talking the talk, that we will demonstrate what Jesus is doing in our lives.

> ➤ "Amen I say to you, until heaven and earth pass away, not the smallest letter or the smallest part of a letter will pass from the law, until all things have taken place. ... whoever obeys and teaches these

commandments will be called greatest in the kingdom of heaven."

This is an important saying that I fear often gets overlooked by the "la-di-da everything is groovy" brand of Christianity. Yes, Jesus is a God of love, and yes, Jesus is a God of peace, and yes, Jesus is a God of forgiveness. But, gosh darn it, Jesus is also a God of rules, regulations, and commandments. He did not come to earth to tell us the Ten Commandments no longer apply. Rather, He made clear that they still *do* apply, despite His coming. Therefore, living a Christian life means: Loving God with your whole being; putting no strange gods or idols before God; keeping the Lord's Day holy; honoring your father and mother; not killing anyone; not stealing anything; not committing adultery; not telling lies against your neighbor; not wanting what your neighbor has; and not desiring your neighbor's spouse. If we are violating any of these commandments, in action, in thought, or in spirit, we are not living a truly Christian life.

> ➢ "You have heard that it was said to your ancestors, 'You shall not kill; and whoever kills will be liable to judgment.' But I say to you, whoever is angry with his brother will be liable to

218

judgment, and whoever says to his brother 'raqa' will be answerable to the Sanhedrin, and whoever says 'you fool' will be liable to fiery Gehenna."

With this saying, Jesus calls us to practice the virtues of temperance and restraint. He is teaching us the importance of avoiding not only violence, but also the near occasion of violence. As true Christians we should neither incite arguments, nor act or speak in a manner that will escalate arguments. This should not come as a surprise, inasmuch as we are called to love one another, which naturally includes being kind to one another. We do of course encounter situations on a daily basis that bring us annoyance, frustration, and exasperation. In these situations we must call on God to help us control ourselves and hold our tongues, so as not to inflame these situations. It is not our Christian duty to prove we are right in any disagreement that arises; it *is* our Christian duty to act charitably towards others when disagreements arise.

> ➤ "Therefore, if you bring your gift to the altar and there recall that your brother has anything against you, leave your gift there at the altar, go first and be reconciled with your brother, and then come and offer your gift."

We are called to love God with our entire being; we are also called to love our neighbors as ourselves. When I was in elementary school, the Sisters of Christian Charity and their lay colleagues emphasized the point that the Spirit of God is in all people. If we are to love God, therefore, we must also love *all* His children. So what Jesus is telling us is this: if you are not in a good place vis a vis your relationship with your earthly brethren, it is pointless to worship and honor God. Your words and your offering will have little meaning if your worship of God does not carry over to your dealings with man. Similarly, coming to Church on Sunday is a somewhat a empty act if what God teaches us is falling on deaf ears.

> ➤ "You have heard that it was said, 'You shall not commit adultery.' But I say to you, everyone who looks at a woman with lust has already committed adultery with her in his heart."

When I read this statement by Jesus, I say to myself, "Wow, did He really say that?" It seems to me that I have been looking at girls and women with lust since I was 12 years old. If God didn't want me to look at them, then why did He make them so attractive? I think the definition of lust helps with this conundrum. The Merriam-Webster online dictionary defines lust as "intense or unbridled sexual desire".

It is natural to have some amount of sexual desire for members of the opposite sex. The question we must answer for ourselves is, when does that sexual desire cross the line and become "unbridled"? There are times when our desire for someone can start to control our lives, to make us do stupid things we *know* we shouldn't be doing. What we are called to do in such situations is harness ourselves, and refrain from doing those stupid things. Even if we do not engage in sexual relations with the object of our lust, we have committed adultery in our heart if the non-sexual things we do for the "desired one" make it clear that our sexual desire has skewed our priorities in an unacceptable way. It is our duty as Christians to exercise self-control and bridle our sexual desire when its object is an inappropriate one. In the same vein, it is important that we keep away from the near-occasions of lust, such as pornography. There is no question that pornography can definitely skew your views of what is morally right and wrong in a sexual context. Refrain. Be respectful of others, and of yourself.

> "Not everyone who says, 'Lord, Lord' will enter the kingdom of heaven, but only the one who does the will of My Father in heaven. Many will say to Me on that day, 'Lord, Lord, did we not prophesy in Your name? Did we not drive out demons in Your name? Did we not do mighty deeds in Your name?' Then I will declare to them solemnly, 'I never knew you. Depart from Me, you evildoers.'
"

There is more to loving and worshiping God than giving Him lip service. Those who talk a great game are not assured of a place in the Kingdom if their hearts are not right with God. Jesus wants us to realize that our prayer and worship may be in vain if the rest of our lives are out of synch with God's will. Do we obey God, do we follow His commandments? Do we act charitably towards our fellow man? Or do we have an in-Church life in which we praise God, but an out-of-Church life in which we do what we please, no matter how off course from the Father's will it may lead us? I think of the movie "The Godfather", of the video montage that juxtaposes scenes of the mobsters at Mass with scenes of their murderous crimes. Do they think God is going to overlook their heinous crimes because they attend Sunday Mass?

> ➤ "You shall love the Lord your God with all your heart, with all your soul, and with all your mind. This is the greatest and the first commandment. The second is like it: you shall love your neighbor as yourself."

In Fr. Robert Barron's excellent series, "Untold Blessings: Three Paths to Holiness", he talks about the importance of having Christ at the center of our lives. It keeps us centered, it keeps our lives in balance. And considering what Jesus calls the first and greatest commandment, it is an essential component of a true Christian life. But how many of us can say we love God with all our heart and all our soul and all our mind? I think it must be a very small percentage. It is a sure thing that our society does not foster in us a loving, committed relationship with God, which is a significant change for the worse over the past half century. It seems as if we have gone from a society in which Sunday morning worship was an expected thing, to one in which "who can be bothered with going to Church," and "who really cares?" Church attendance is just one component of a Christian life, but if that basic component fails, it is hard for the other components – love of neighbor, charity towards all – to thrive. We the people, we who comprise "society", must turn this around by restoring God to the center of our lives.

> ➤ "Be sure of this: if the master of the house had known the hour of night when the thief was coming, he would have stayed awake and not let his house be broken into. So too, you also must be prepared, for at an hour you do not expect the son of man will come."

People have been waiting for the second coming of the Lord since the first century A.D. The early followers of Jesus expected Him to return during their lifetime. But our time is not God's time. He is eternal, and a second for us could be like a thousand years for Him. So despite speculation and predictions, nobody knows when Jesus will return. Jesus Himself tells us that only the Father knows. As it has been nearly 2,000 years since Jesus' death and resurrection, it is easy to become complacent in our spiritual life and doubt whether He will ever return. But the point is, we do not know when Jesus will return, and perhaps more importantly, we do not know when *our* last day will be. It is important for us to live our lives in a manner that is pleasing to God, so that when our time on earth is up we can be found to merit eternal life. What could be more important?

> "The King will say to those on His right, 'come, you who are blessed by My Father. Inherit the Kingdom prepared for you from the foundation of the world. For I was hungry and you gave Me food, I was thirsty and you gave Me drink, a stranger and you welcomed Me, naked and you clothed Me, ill and you cared for Me, in prison and you visited Me. Then the righteous will answer Him and say, 'Lord, when did we see You hungry and feed You, or thirsty and give You drink? When did we see You a stranger and welcome You, or naked and clothe You? When did we see You ill or in prison and visit You?' And the King will say to them in reply, 'amen, I say to you, whatever you did for one of these least brothers of Mine, you did for Me.' "

There is really not much I can add to this passage. It makes clear that Jesus expects us to be charitable and merciful to the people we encounter in our lives, whether they be family, friends, neighbors, or strangers. We thereby share God's love for us with others, and we shall be rewarded.

> "The Sabbath was made for man, not man for the Sabbath."

The Sabbath was established to commemorate that on the seventh day, after creating the universe and the earth, and the flora and fauna, and man, God rested. Likewise, in the

Jewish faith men were expected to work six days and observe a day of rest on the seventh. However, Jesus was dismayed by the numerous rules the Jewish religious leaders had imposed on the people regarding the Sabbath, in essence taking what was to be a day of rest and turning it into an administrative burden. Jesus' words have just as much meaning today, but for a far different reason. As society has become more and more secularized, the very notion of a day of rest has been rendered obsolete. The Sabbath is supposed to be a day of rest, and a day to keep Holy. But aside from attendance at Church services by those who still bother, Sunday has become much like any other day. People work on Sunday, people shop on Sunday, people do chores on Sunday, people hurry around to their children's sporting events on Sunday. It is no longer a day of rest at all, nor is it Holy. I think we need to heed Jesus' words on this subject now more than ever, because our world is so crazy, and everyone makes themselves so busy, that we dearly **need** a day of rest. And more than that, we need a day on which to focus our attention on the things of God, instead of on the things we focus on the rest of the week. We Christians need to take back our Sundays.

> "Forgive and you will be forgiven."

We hear the words all the time. Our God is a forgiving God. Our God is a God of second chances. The parable of the lost sheep, the parable of the prodigal son. If we are truly sorry for our sins, God will forgive us and welcome us back into the fold. Oh but wait, there's one more thing. Yes, God will forgive you if you are sorry, but you likewise must forgive those who have trespassed against you. That is imperative.

Don't we acknowledge as much every time we pray the "Our Father"? "Forgive us our trespasses, *as we forgive those who trespass against us,*" we beseech God. But how often have I heard someone say, at a religious gathering or retreat, "No, I can't forgive whatshisname, that's one thing I can never do"? Forgiveness is a basic tenet of Christianity, right up there with love. God loves us, God forgives us, God calls us to be like Him. Yet we cannot forgive? Why not? "Because he hurt me too much." More than we hurt God every day? As much as you hurt God when He asks you to forgive and you say, "No, I won't"? If someone who has hurt you is truly sorry for what he did and has apologized, it is your

Christian duty to forgive him. Could it be your Pride that stands in the way? Don't forget, pride is one of the seven "deadly sins". Swallow your pride and forgive, for God's sake, and for the sake of your immortal soul.

> ➢ "Blessed are those who hear the word of God and observe it."

Some Catholics go to Mass every Sunday for their whole lives, hear the Gospel being preached, receive the sacraments religiously, yet never quite seem to "get it". They live their lives filled with anger, hatred, pride, arrogance, envy, resentment, lust, greed, gluttony, self-centeredness, dishonesty, vindictiveness, and any other attribute you can think of that is contrary to the Commandments, the Beatitudes, and all the other lessons from our Lord. But enough about me, let's talk about them. I wish there were some way to break through their hard heads and hard hearts and say to them, "Listen to what Jesus says and obey what He asks of you, that's what your religion is all about." So now I'm asking you: listen, absorb, reflect, and then live your life in accordance with what you heard. (See, there I go being judgmental again.)

➢ "Do not work for food that perishes but for the food that endures for eternal life, which the Son of Man will give you. ..."

Not surprisingly, we here on earth tend to get caught up in life on earth. We have responsibilities to our families, to our communities, and to our nation. We have to make a living in order to put food on our tables and a roof over our heads. But Jesus wants us to remember that our earthly home is a temporary arrangement. We should be more concerned with where we will spend eternity than we are with what happens in this world. When we set our priorities, Jesus wants to make sure we prioritize appropriately, for whatever we garner here on earth will ultimately come to nothing. So, He tells us, we should store up our treasure in heaven.

➢ "If you love Me, you will keep My commandments. ... Whoever has My commandments and observes them is the one who loves Me. And whoever loves Me will be loved by My Father. ... This is My commandment: love one another as I love you. No one has greater love than this, to lay down one's life for one's friends. You are My friends if you do what I command you."

I have to admit, I think it would be grand if Jesus considered me to be His friend. I'm not sure I've earned His friendship yet. I fear I still need a good deal more sanctification. But I do hope one day to merit being called His friend.

In any case, what is noteworthy in these passages is that this is really Jesus' ultimate command to us, His disciples: love one another. In other words, be concerned about one another's feelings and well-being, learn to put one another's needs ahead of our own. Radio personality Harry Harrison, a WMCA good guy back in the '60s and a cornerstone of WCBS-FM for decades, used to say, "If you see someone without a smile, give him one of yours." My fifth grade teacher, Miss Lois Moran, taught her students the same thing. She encouraged us to walk up Central Avenue and smile at people who seemed downcast, to brighten their days. Simple enough, isn't it? These days most people you pass on the street won't even look at you. They are too busy looking at their Smartphones or whatever, and listening to something through their earbuds. As part of Christian living, we should endeavor to reestablish contact with our fellow humans, to acknowledge and encourage each other whenever we meet.

Jesus laid down His life for us, and in this He gives us the ultimate example of love. Most of us will never be called to give our lives for others, but we can take the first step in that direction by putting others' needs ahead of our own. That is really the essence of Christianity.

QUESTIONS FOR REFLECTION OR DISCUSSION

1. What is your favorite quote from Jesus in Chapter Nineteen? Why?

2. Which of Jesus' quotes in Chapter Nineteen did you find most surprising? In what way did it surprise you?

3. In what areas of your life do you struggle most in modeling Christ-like behavior? What efforts have you made to improve in these areas?

4. Are there specific sins you find yourself committing repeatedly despite resolving to stop? Can you figure out why that is?

5. Would you say that you usually keep the Lord's Day holy? If your answer is no, do you wish you could change that, or does your life work better if Sunday is just another day?

6. Do you think you are Jesus' friend, and if not, what about you do you think you should change to attain His friendship?

Chapter Twenty
AND WOULD YOU HAVE US LIVE THIS WAY
EVEN IF IT HURTS?

Whoever does not carry his own cross
and come after Me cannot be My disciple.

There are occasions – more frequent than I like to admit –
when my Christian faith wanes a bit, and I find myself
asking myself, "Was Jesus really the Incarnation of God? Did
He really rise from the dead?" It is at times like these that I
like to think back to the first century Christian martyrs, who
gave their lives for their belief in Jesus.

Start with Jesus Himself. Think about when He was
arrested and brought to trial, before the high priests, then
Pilate, then Herod, and finally Pilate again. Jesus knew He
was facing a humiliating and torturous death by crucifixion.
If He were just a misguided rabbi, and not God in the flesh,
would He have been so defiant in front of the Jewish leaders,
and so passively defenseless in front of Herod and Pilate?
Wouldn't He have broken down, and said it was all a
mistake? Wouldn't He have said He was just a Jewish
teacher trying to get the Jews to turn back to God? Wouldn't
He have begged for mercy and said He never claimed to be a
Messiah or God, it was just the people who said that? But He

didn't do that. He went all the way to Calvary, according to God's will.

Most of Jesus' Apostles and many other disciples also wound up dying for the faith. If they had not actually encountered the risen Jesus, if they did not really believe He was the Son of God, why would they pretend to cling to such a belief in the face of execution? Would you? I know I wouldn't! Even if I had seen the risen Lord I probably would have denied it to save my hide. It's counterintuitive to think people would spread such a story, **and die for such a story**, if they knew it to be untrue. Therefore, I must conclude that Peter and James and the other martyred Apostles truly did see Jesus after the Resurrection, and knew that He was God.

All of which brings us to the issue of being persecuted for your faith. Jesus tells us, "Blessed are they who are persecuted for the sake of righteousness, for theirs is the kingdom of heaven." Jesus also says, "Blessed are you when they insult you and persecute you and utter every kind of evil against you because of Me. Rejoice and be glad, for great will be your reward in heaven. Thus they persecuted the prophets who were before you." Jesus promises us a heavenly reward if we suffer persecution on His account. But how persuasive is that promise when your life on earth hangs in the balance? As I already said, if someone were threatening my life for my Christian beliefs, I think I would cave. It's not just that I'm a coward, but there's also the practical problem of leaving my three children fatherless. My religion is important to me, but there are limits.

Fortunately, there are many people, better Christians than I, who are willing to make great sacrifices, and even give their lives, for their faith. Surely their reward will be great, for Jesus says, "[W]hoever loses his life for my sake will find it." For the less courageous among us, we must take solace in the knowledge that there are other forms of persecution, short of martyrdom, that we can endure for our God. These include being scorned, reviled, mocked, insulted, or simply ignored when we try to share or stand up for our beliefs. Or, in the case of Tim Tebow, it means knowing NFL teams may not sign you as a quarterback despite your history of winning whenever and wherever you've been given the chance to play. Granted, in the whole scheme of things these types of persecutions are trifling. Nevertheless, the fact that we are willing to endure them is commendable, compared to the alternative of hiding our faith.

For example, in His parable of the sower, Jesus speaks of the seed sown on rocky ground. This seed represents the one who hears the word and receives it at once with joy, but has no root and lasts only for a time. "When some tribulation or persecution comes because of the word, he immediately falls away." Not only are there those who fall away as soon as tribulation or persecution comes, there are those who will never make their faith known outside the safe confines of their home and church, so as to avoid having to face such tribulation or persecution.

Unfortunately, based upon the way our society is evolving (some might say DEvolving), it is probably reasonable to expect that Christian believers will face increasing persecution in the coming years. As the intolerant forces of progressivism continue to disavow that quaint notion formerly known as differences of opinion, and instead cast such differing opinions as hatred, people with "traditional" points of view are likely to come increasingly under attack. Jesus Himself painted a disturbing portrait as

235

follows: "Brother will hand over brother to death, and the father his child; children will rise up against parents and have them put to death. You will be hated by all because of My name." Let us hope that in our somewhat enlightened society nothing quite so dire will come to pass. At the same time, we must realize that we live in an environment in which a good-faith, religion-based opposition to "social progress" in its various forms may someday result in criminal prosecution for hate speech. Can we be sure that our traditional opinions, rooted not in hatred but in religious belief, will not eventually come under such scrutiny? Can we be sure our "wrong is right/right is wrong" culture will not someday reach the pinnacle of its deluded state by exterminating those who stand for moral values and righteousness? And think it is justified in doing so? "The hour is coming," says Jesus, "when everyone who kills you will think he is offering worship to God, because they have not known either the Father or Me." Ai Caramba! What a statement! Did you know Jesus said that?

<u>All of which is to say that sharing our religious beliefs always carries with it the specter of persecution</u>. But as Jesus tells us, "Whoever does not carry his own cross and come

after Me cannot be My disciple." There are of course many types of crosses we must bear when we choose to live as true Christians. For example, we must lovingly encounter people who are not particularly loveable. We must respond to hatred and mistreatment with passive resistance and civil disobedience. We must reach out to help our neighbors who are in need. But one of the largest crosses to be borne is the intolerance and persecution that comes with living and spreading the Christian faith.

I suppose it is easier to get along in the world if you are quiet and secretive about your faith. You can go to Church on Sunday, and then just go about your business the rest of the week, never letting on that you believe Jesus has the words of everlasting life. Certainly you would not have to worry about people feeling intimidated by you, or uncomfortable around you, when their words and actions are decidedly unchristian. You wouldn't have to worry about people despising you out of their own insecurity that you may be judging them, or that you may believe yourself superior to them. But if you believe that Jesus has the words of everlasting life, isn't that something worth sharing with your fellow travelers? Even if some of them may despise you for it? For the sake of their immortal souls, people need to know that it is better to have a friend in Jesus than a companion in Satan.

"If the world hates you, realize that it hated me first," Jesus tells us. "If you belonged to the world, the world would love its own; but because you do not belong to the world and I have chosen you out of the world, the world hates you." In the end, it is worth risking the world's hatred in order to save souls. I hope you agree with that assessment. Tribulations and persecutions are disturbing, but like life itself they are transient. If we are on Jesus' side, we will overcome the tribulations and persecutions in the end. Jesus tells us as much: "In the world you will have trouble, but take courage, I have conquered the world."

QUESTIONS FOR REFLECTION OR DISCUSSION

1. What is your favorite quote from Jesus in Chapter Twenty? Why?

2. Which of Jesus' quotes in Chapter Twenty did you find most surprising? In what way did it surprise you?

3. Have you ever been persecuted for something you believe in? Have you ever persecuted another for his or her beliefs? If so, what impact did these experiences have on you?

4. How do you think you would react if you were given the choice to renounce your faith or be killed?

Chapter Twenty-One

WHAT ARE YOUR SUGGESTIONS FOR ATTAINING PERSONAL PEACE IN A MAD MAD MAD MAD WORLD?

Are not two sparrows sold for a small coin? Yet not one of them falls to the ground without your Father's knowledge.

Get the kids to school, go to work, pick up the kids from school, make dinner, run to soccer practice, make sure the homework's done, get the kids to bed, think about exercising – nah, too tired, think about taking a shower – maybe tomorrow, collapse into bed. Repeat.

What a life! I think one of the best lessons we can learn from Jesus, and also probably the most overlooked, because who has the time to think about it, is how to remain placid amid the madness. There are at least three components to this particular lesson: (1) our attitude towards others; (2) our attitude towards the world; and (3) our relationship with God. Let's have a listen.

1. Others

Jesus says, "Therefore, if you bring your gift to the altar and there recall that your brother has anything against you, leave your gift there at the altar, go first and be reconciled with your brother, and then come and offer your gift." Oh brother. We all seem to have some kind of issue with our families, whether it be our parents, our siblings, our children, our aunts and uncles, or our cousins. Many times the issue is related to money. I've seen siblings whom I never thought would have problems with each other suddenly be at war over dad's survivor social security benefits. At other times the issue is a personality clash. "Brother, I can't stand your wife." "Sister, I can't understand why you ever married that man." "Oh yeah? Well I ain't talking to you no more."

Basically Jesus tells us to stop the nonsense. Don't come worshiping and praying to Me when you're not even getting along with your own family. I told you to love one another. So go patch up your differences, make amends; if the situation cannot be resolved, forgive the other one and move on, and then come back to Me. You, and your life, will be that much more peaceful if you do.

Jesus also tells us (I know you've heard this one before):

You have heard that it was said, 'An eye for an eye, and a tooth for a tooth.' But I say to you, offer no resistance to one who is evil. When someone strikes you on the right cheek, turn the other one to him as well. If anyone wants to go to law with you over your tunic, hand him your cloak as well. Should anyone press you into service for one mile, go with him for two miles.

Oh brother again. Here He goes with the 'love your enemies' bit!

Well yes, precisely. As Marvin Gaye sang, only love can conquer hate. When someone confronts you with anger, respond with calm. When someone confronts you with hatred, respond with love. When someone seeks to incite violence, respond in peace. Do what Jesus would do. The result will likely be to defuse rather than escalate the situation. Believe me, I know this is not as easy as it sounds. When someone comes at you full of negative emotions, it is difficult not to flare up with your own emotions. What it requires is personal restraint, which is greatly aided if we get in the habit of seeing God in everyone we meet, as the Sisters of Christian Charity taught me. Again, not easy when tempers are flaring, but it is what Jesus asks of us. Take a step back and breathe deeply. It will help cure you of that knot in your stomach, and in extreme cases it might protect you from a murder charge.

Another way of attaining and maintaining peace in your life is by staying out of trouble. Live a moral life, avoid sin as much as possible, and avoid leading others into sin as well. Don't be caught up in what the world thinks is cool. Instead stay grounded in what Jesus thinks is cool.

Our society is so mixed up right now, if you drop out of school and become a small-time hustler and drug dealer people will act like you're the man, you're a warrior, you're all that. But they don't know what they are talking about. You'll be constantly looking around to see who's after you, and chances are you'll wind up prematurely dead or in prison. But that's only half the problem. Beyond the temporal punishment there is also the issue of spiritual loss. Not only your own, but also those who naively seek to emulate you. Jesus says, "Whoever causes one of these little ones who believe in me to sin, it would be better for him to have a great millstone hung around his neck and to be drowned in the depths of the sea. Woe to the world because of things that cause sin. Such things must come, but woe to the one through whom they come." Jesus realizes that we are all prone to sin, that we are subject to evil influences and evil urgings, and that we are weak humans. The bigger problem faces the one who knowingly leads others into a sinful life, who *is* the evil influence. Don't be that guy. Your life on earth will be full of misery and pain, and your eternal life will be in peril.

2. The World

Did I say before that the world is a crazy place? I think I did say that.

Our own little world can be a beautiful place when we are filled with the love of God and surrounded by loving family and friends. But the bigger world "out there" is still crazy, and scary. Don't get me wrong, there are good people, wonderful people, all over the world. But there is also a lot of evil and hatred in the world, and on a smaller scale we all have to deal with evil and hatred, sickness and injury, and financial burdens from time to time in our daily lives. So how do we deal with it and retain our composure?

First, Jesus wants us to keep our sense of proportion as to what is truly important. Worldly things and material possessions should not be preeminent in our minds. Second, Jesus wants us to avoid letting ourselves become anxious and worried about things   that are *not* truly important.

Listen to Jesus:

> If even the smallest things are beyond your control,
> why are you anxious about the rest? Notice how the
> flowers grow. They do not toil or spin, but I tell you,
> not even Solomon in all his splendor was dressed like
> one of them. If God so clothes the grass in the field
> that grows today and is thrown in the oven
> tomorrow, will He not much more provide for you, O
> you of little faith? As for you, do not seek what you
> are to eat and what you are to drink, and do not
> worry anymore. All the nations of the world seek for
> these things, and your Father knows that you need
> them. Instead, seek first His kingdom, and these other
> things will be given to you besides. Do not be afraid
> any longer, little flock, for your Father is pleased to
> give you the kingdom.

In the same vein, Jesus also says, "Is not life more than food
and the body more than clothing? Look at the birds in the
sky; they do not sow or reap, they gather nothing into barns,
yet your heavenly Father feeds them. Are not you more
important than they?"

Jesus urges us to trust in the providential nature of the
Father, and not to be overly concerned with worldly things.
"Can any of you by worrying add a single moment to your
life span?" Jesus asks. "Why are you anxious about clothes?"

245

Jesus also tells us to focus on the matters we are facing in the present time and not trouble ourselves about things that may (or may not) happen sometime in the future. "Do not worry about tomorrow; tomorrow will take care of itself. Sufficient for a day is its own evil." There is great wisdom in these words. Tomorrow is not promised to any of us; the entire world as we know it could be changed in a heartbeat by one lunatic with a nuclear warhead. Does it make sense to be excessively concerned about things that may never come to pass? We can use our God-given intelligence to make the most of our present and to plan for our futures, but if we trouble ourselves with fears and anxieties about what might be, we uselessly expend energy and deprive ourselves of tranquility. Learn from what Jesus tells us about the sparrows: "Are not two sparrows sold for a small coin? Yet not one of them falls to the ground without your Father's knowledge. Even all the hairs of your head are counted. So do not be afraid; you are worth more than many sparrows."

We are all God's children. He knows us, and He wants what is best for us. If we surrender ourselves in trust to Him, we can have peace in the midst of our crazy world.

I should clarify that what Jesus is talking about here is an attitude of trust and a prioritizing of our relationship with God, not an abdication of personal responsibility. I think it would be imprudent of you to stop doing whatever it is you do to support yourself and your family, and instead sit at home waiting for God to deliver food and clothing to you.

One other thing Jesus wants us to know with respect to attaining peace on earth is to stop focusing on material wealth. It is clear throughout the Gospels that Jesus wants us to focus on those aspects of our lives that will help us gain eternal life, rather than those aspects that will help make us rich in the world's eyes. "Do not store up for yourselves treasures on earth, where moth and decay destroy, and thieves break in and steal," Jesus advises us. "But store up treasures in heaven, where neither moth nor decay destroy, nor thieves break in and steal." God would prefer that we enjoy the peace that comes with living a modest life, rather than chasing after wealth, a chase that becomes a vicious cycle as one strives always to maintain the standard of living that is his god. "Take care to guard against all greed," warns the Lord, "for though one may be rich, one's life does not consist of possessions."

We have all heard the saying, "You can't take it with you," and Jesus echoes this sentiment when He tells us of the rich fool, to whom God said, "This night your life will be demanded of you; and the things you have prepared, to whom will they belong?" When wealth becomes your god, you may very well sacrifice your peace of mind, your health, and your very soul pursuing it. When you die, and come before God to be judged, will He be impressed by your wealth? Not likely. In amassing (or trying to amass) a fortune, you may wind up condemning yourself to Gehenna. This is not the end God desires for us, but Jesus cautions us, "Thus it will be for the one who stores up treasure for himself but is not rich in what matters to God."

For many people, the pursuit and maintenance of their gaudy lifestyle is a death sentence, as they work and worry themselves into an early grave just to be wealthy. What a sad waste of life that is!

3 God

It seems to me that another key to finding peace on earth is to have a right relationship with God. This is, to be sure, an over-generalization. Undoubtedly there are many people who are not God-fearing individuals, but who have nevertheless found peace in their lives. And there may be just as many people who think they have a good relationship with God, but who nevertheless worry about everything. However, I do believe that, in general, if you listen to God and follow His "suggestions", you will be at peace. Here are a few things Jesus tells us that lead me to that conclusion.

First, let's consider this parable:

> Everyone who listens to these words of Mine and acts on them will be like a wise man who built his house on rock. The rain fell, the floods came, and the winds blew and buffeted the house. But it did not collapse; it had been set solidly on rock. And everyone who listens to these words of Mine but does not act on them will be like a fool who built his house on sand. The rain fell, the floods came, and the winds blew and buffeted the house. And it collapsed and was completely ruined.

This parable is open to different interpretation, but here is one that I think rings true. If we listen to Jesus' words, we will come away with certain directions about conducting our lives. For example, don't mistreat people. Don't cheat people. Don't take what is not yours. Don't kill anyone. Don't tell false stories against people. Don't be consumed over things you don't have. Don't be unfaithful to your spouse. Don't be chasing after your neighbor's spouse. That's a relatively small sampling, but it covers a lot of the important points. Now if you are the guy who hears Jesus' words but decides not to act on them, what will happen? If you mistreat people, people will dislike you. If you cheat people, people will distrust you. If you take what is not yours, you will be dragged into Court and subject to civil liability and criminal prosecution. If you kill someone, the police will hunt you down, and you will spend your days in prison. If you lie about people, you will be despised, and possibly subject to liability for slander and perjury. If you are consumed over things you do not have, you will fritter away your time and energy trying to "keep up with the Joneses", and if you are lucky enough to surpass the Joneses you will find someone else to try to keep up with. If you are unfaithful to your spouse, he or she will divorce you, and your children will become estranged from you. If you chase after your neighbor's spouse, you will destroy your reputation and become a local pariah, and there is some small possibility that your neighbor or your spouse will kill you. This is not exactly a recipe for attaining peace.

On the other hand, if you listen to Jesus, you will treat people well, you will be honest with people, you will not take what is not yours, you will not hurt or kill anyone, you will not lie about people, you will not care about what you do not have, you will be true to your spouse, and you will leave your neighbor's spouse alone. Then people will like, trust, and respect you, you will be content, your family will love and keep you, and your neighbor will not kill you.

Jesus says to us, "Come to Me, all you who labor and are burdened, and I will give you rest. Take My yoke upon you and learn from Me, for I am meek and humble of heart; and you will find rest for yourselves. For My yoke is easy, and My burden light." In the context of first century Judaism, Jesus was setting the people free from the burdens placed upon them by the innumerable rules imposed by Jewish law. By comparison, what Jesus asked of them was fairly simple, and aimed more at living a substantively moral life than at complying with onerous nonsense. In 21st century society, the burden Jesus places on us is still light, in the sense that if we listen to Him we will be happy, we will be content, and we will be at peace with ourselves. Why? Because what He asks of us is what we already know, in our heart of hearts, we should be doing, or not doing, as the case may be.

And there's one more thing: if we live as Jesus asks us, we will be ready when the day of judgment comes. As Jesus tells us, nobody knows when this will be, only the Father. We would be well advised, therefore, to be ready at all times for that day. Jesus tells us, "Be sure of this: if the master of the house had known the hour of night when the thief was coming, he would have stayed awake and not let his house be broken into. So too, you also must be prepared, for at an hour you do not expect the Son of Man will come." Listen to the Lord, and be ready. This advice applies whether we are talking about **the** final day, or just about **our** final day.

Consider also the following statements made by Jesus, and how they relate to the importance of our relationship with Him vis a vis our personal peace.

(1) "For God so loved the world that He gave His only Son, so that everyone who believes in Him might not perish but might have eternal life."

(2) "Whoever hears my word and believes in the One who sent Me has eternal life..."

(3) "Do not work for food that perishes but for the food that endures for eternal life..."

(4) "I am the resurrection and the life; whoever believes in Me, even if he dies, will live, and everyone who lives and believes in Me will never die."

(5) "In My Father's house there are many dwelling places. If there were not, would I have told you that I am going to prepare a place for you?"

The significance of these verses goes back to the concept of eternal life that we explored early on in this book, and the related concept that if we love one another we must want each other to attain eternal life – i.e., heaven. If we believe in Jesus, and in the things He tells us, then we must believe that He was sent to earth by God/as God Incarnate. Thus if we believe in Him and in God, we know that by taking Him into our hearts and following His words we will be with Him in Paradise when our time on earth is over. This belief, this promise, should bring peace to all who believe, regardless of our earthly plight.

Before I close this chapter I would like to return once again to our friends Martha and Mary. (I guarantee you will be sick of Martha and Mary by the time you get to Chapter 33!) As you already know, Martha had a sister named Mary who sat beside the Lord at His feet, listening to Him speak. Martha meanwhile was rushing about setting the table, getting dinner ready, putting things in order. Martha, somewhat annoyed with her sister, asked Jesus if He did not care that Mary had left Martha by herself to do the serving. Martha wanted Jesus to tell Mary to help her. But Jesus said, "Martha Martha, you are anxious and worried about many things. There is need of only one thing. Mary has chosen the better part, and it will not be taken from her."

You have probably figured out by now that I am more a fan of Mary than of Martha. And realistically, if you are looking for the peace Jesus wants us to have, Mary is the way to go. Why do I say that? Because Jesus wants to have a personal relationship with us, and in order to have a relationship with Him we have to know Him. How best to know Jesus? By listening to what He wants us to hear, not by telling Him what *we* want *Him* to hear. Mary listened to what Jesus had to say. Martha was too busy to listen. Of course there is nothing wrong with being busy. We are all called to serve God and each other, and this requires effort.

But it is a question of proportion. If you are too busy with your busy-ness to hear what Jesus wants to tell you, then your busy-ness will not bring peace, only frustration and aggravation. If you don't believe me, ask Jesus.

QUESTIONS FOR REFLECTION OR DISCUSSION

1. What is your favorite quote from Jesus in Chapter Twenty-one? Why?

2. Which of Jesus' quotes in Chapter Twenty-one did you find most surprising? In what way did it surprise you?

3. What is your recipe for keeping peace with people? For finding peace in the world? Does your relationship with God play any part in your recipe?

4. Have you ever found yourself so caught up in some worldly pursuit that you made yourself miserable? In retrospect, was the goal of your pursuit worth the misery?

5. Does your relationship with God (assuming you have such a relationship) bring you peace? If so, in what way?

6. As you go about your daily routine, do you spend any time thinking about the afterlife, and what you must do to attain heaven? Do you think focusing your attention on the salvation of your soul would cause you to change your routine and habits in some way?

Chapter Twenty-Two

DO YOU HAVE ANY OTHER ADVICE
THAT MIGHT HELP LIGHTEN OUR LOAD?

Forgive and you will be forgiven.

As you read this, are you holding a grudge against anybody? If so, why? Grudges, resentments, and lingering anger against people who have hurt you fester inside you and make you ill, emotionally and spiritually, if not physically. They do not accomplish anything, really. And no matter what the offending party may have done to you, grudges and resentments do not enable you to claim the moral high ground. On the contrary, they are a distinctly unchristian way of approaching the world.

Don't get me wrong, I understand the importance of learning from our past experiences so as not to repeat our mistakes. Once bitten, twice shy. I am not suggesting that you give someone who has burned you the opportunity to burn you again. I am suggesting, however, that you forgive people who have hurt you and move on with your life. There are at least two good reasons for doing this. One is that you will feel relieved of the burden of anger and negativity that you direct to those who have hurt you whenever you think about them. The second is that it is your Christian obligation.

Jesus makes it clear that He expects His followers to have a mentality of forgiveness. When Peter approached Jesus and asked Him, "Lord, if my brother sins against me, how often must I forgive him? As many as seven times?" Jesus answered, "I say to you, not seven times, but seventy-seven times." (When I was a schoolboy the favored translation was seventy times seven times, or 490. Either way, Jesus' point is well taken.) You may recall the parable of the unforgiving servant. That is the story Jesus tells of the servant who owed his master a great debt and begged for additional time to make good on it. Having compassion, the master forgave the servant his entire debt. However, that same servant, when confronting a fellow servant who owed him a relatively small amount, refused to forgive his fellow servant, but instead had him sent to prison. When the master heard of it, he punished the unforgiving servant. Commenting on the story, Jesus warns us, "Unless each of you forgives your brother from your heart, My heavenly Father will hand you over to the torturers until you have paid back your whole debt."

Jesus makes it plain throughout the Gospels that our forgiveness will be rewarded, but our lack of forgiveness will come back against us. "Blessed are the merciful," Jesus said at the Sermon on the Mount, "for they will be shown mercy." Similarly, Jesus tells us, "If you forgive others their transgressions, your heavenly Father will forgive you. But if you do not forgive others, neither will your Father forgive your transgressions." As I previously mentioned, we are reminded of this Christian obligation each time we pray the Our Father, as we say "forgive us our trespasses, as we forgive those who trespass against us."

In Jesus' philosophy, there is no place for holding grudges. Each Sunday at Mass we gather together to pray to God. And Jesus tells us, "When you stand to pray, forgive anyone against whom you have a grievance, so that your heavenly Father may in turn forgive you your transgressions." So any grudges we might be holding against those who hurt us should not last beyond the next time we stand up in Church to pray!

By His words and actions, Jesus was always trying to give us an example of forgiveness, and a demonstration of the Father's forgiveness, that we might have something to emulate. "Those who are well do not need a physician," Jesus says, "but the sick do. Go and learn the meaning of the words, 'I desire mercy, not sacrifice.' I did not come to call the righteous but sinners." Just as Jesus seeks to reach out in forgiveness to those who have sinned, He expects us to forgive anyone who has sinned against us. Jesus seeks out the lost sheep who have gone astray, to forgive them and bring them back to the fold. If we can forgive our own lost sheep, it will be a blessing both to them and to us.

Consider again the parable of the prodigal son. When the younger son demands his share of the inheritance and leaves home, he is in essence saying that his father may as well be dead. "I don't want you, I don't need you, just give me the money and I'm out of here." What a slap in the face. Imagine, if you are a father, particularly a father who loves his children, how hurtful that would be. The prodigal son runs off and squanders his inheritance, lives what you would have to consider a very sinful life, and then comes back to the father he had insulted, because he has nowhere else to turn. The older son is angry that his father has welcomed back this ne'er-do-well. Who among us who have loved, respected, and obeyed our parents can blame him? But Jesus says the power of love and forgiveness must be stronger in our hearts. "My son," dad tells number one son, "you are here with me always; everything I have is yours. But now we must celebrate and rejoice, because your brother was dead, and has come to life again; he was lost, and has been found."

This is a very hard lesson, especially for those of us who have a degree in righteous indignation. But now pause for a moment and think of someone you have loved – a sibling, a childhood friend, a parent, even a favorite entertainer or movie star – whose life came to ruin because of drugs, alcohol, pornography, or any other vice we could name. If you truly loved that person and were saddened by her fall, wouldn't you want God to welcome her home with loving arms? Of course you would! In the same way, if someone who has hurt you badly comes back to you asking forgiveness with genuine contrition, you must forgive. Forgiveness heals, it lifts a weight off your life, and it brings peace.

I should close this chapter with one last thing: "Father, forgive them, they know not what they do." You are hanging on a wooden cross, with spikes through your wrists and ankles, you are publicly humiliated, you are in excruciating pain, and each time you pull yourself up to fight for breath your bare back scrapes raw against the rough wood of your cross. It doesn't get much worse than this.

But He forgave those who did this to Him

QUESTIONS FOR REFLECTION OR DISCUSSION

1. What is your favorite quote from Jesus in Chapter Twenty-two? Why?

2. Which of Jesus' quotes in Chapter Twenty-two did you find most surprising? In what way did it surprise you?

3. Think about a grudge you held against someone, and think about when you let go of that grudge. When did you feel more peace and joy, while holding the grudge, or when releasing it? When do you think you made God happier, when you held the grudge, or when you released it?

Chapter Twenty-Three

WHAT DO YOU WANT TO SAY TO THOSE WE MIGHT CALL "NAME-ONLY CHRISTIANS"?

Whoever is not with me is against me,
and whoever does not gather with me scatters

This is one of those chapters that is going to make people angry at me (again), because they are all going to think I am trying to tell them how to live; and that I am judging them, which Jesus says I'm not supposed to do; and that I'm being all morally superior, which Jesus says I am not supposed to be. To this I respond: (1) I am not trying to tell you how to live, I am just letting you know how *Jesus* wants you to live; (2) I am not judging you. I am in no position to judge you. I am a sinful person who hopes God will have mercy on me and let me into His kingdom. However, I do want you to be prepared for when *God* judges you; (3) It is not my intention to come across as morally superior, it is only my intention to make suggestions that will help you attain eternal life. Only God knows if I myself am moral enough to deserve the same.

So now that you know where I'm coming from, the bigger question is: why, in a nation where three-quarters of the people purport to be Christians, are we plagued by so much un-Christ-like behavior? The easy answer is that way too many people who identify themselves as Christians do not seem to know what being a Christian means. Which only leads to another question: if you are not going to act as a Christian should, why do you bother to identify yourself as a Christian? Is it because you think it sounds better than saying you are a Jew, or a Muslim, or an atheist? Or is it by force of habit? Or is it because you think it is what is expected of you by your parents or your spouse?

I can tell you that my father was a registered Democrat. What else would you expect from a son of Italian immigrants who was living in Jersey City? But I'm pretty sure that in every Presidential election I can remember, he voted for the Republican candidate. His beliefs seemed much more in line with the Republican platform as well. Dad always said he was a Democrat, but at some point didn't he become a Republican, regardless of what he or his voter registration said?

In the same way, if you do not know what Jesus says, or do not care what Jesus says, and do not listen to what Jesus says, are you still a Christian just because you call yourself one?

This question is important, because there is a lot more to Christianity than calling yourself a Christian. Christianity is a call to holiness, a call to follow Christ. It is a call to walk the walk. Let's take a quick look at some parts of that walk that many of us who call ourselves Christians would just as soon walk away from.

Evangelization. Ugh! The dreaded E word. Jesus says to His disciples, "Come after me, and I will make you fishers of men." We are supposed to share our faith and our belief in Jesus with others. Not in an obnoxious, judgmental way, but in a loving and encouraging way, the goal being not to offend people, but to save souls. It is a difficult task, one that will open us up to abuse, derision, and at least some level of persecution. But people do need to be told about God and the gift of eternal life, and to be instructed about how God would have them live their lives. Come to think of it, that's why I am writing this book. So buy copies for all your friends.

The Commandments. Remember that Jesus tells us:

> Until heaven and earth pass away, not the smallest letter or the smallest part of a letter will pass from the law, until all things have taken place. Therefore, whoever breaks one of the least of these commandments and teaches others to do so will be called least in the kingdom of heaven. But whoever obeys and teaches these commandments will be called greatest in the kingdom of heaven.

Jesus also says, "If you love Me, you will keep My commandments. ... Whoever has My commandments and observes them is the one who loves Me. And whoever loves Me will be loved by My Father." So obeying the Commandments is a basic requirement of being a Christian. I also think it is a basic requirement for meriting eternal life. We are all fallible humans and all sinners to one degree or another, because we are human. God understands that, and is always ready to offer His forgiveness. He does, however, expect us to *try* to live a holy life. But how many of us (present company included) take a rather cavalier attitude toward some of the Commandments? We take the Lord's name in vain, we do not keep the Lord's day holy, we want what is not ours, we talk bad about people like it's going out of style. Perhaps we even cheat on our spouses or, worse yet, are responsible for the deaths of other people, born or unborn. If so, we are not living a Christian life.

Listen again to what Jesus tells us:

> ➤ "Not everyone who says, 'Lord, Lord' will enter the kingdom of heaven, but only the one who does the will of my Father in heaven."
> ➤ "Why do you call me, 'Lord, Lord,' but do not do what I command?"
> ➤ "Blessed are those who hear the word of God and observe it."

Ask yourself this, what does it accomplish for us to say we believe Jesus is the Christ, but not to listen to what He tells us? It doesn't do us any good, nor does it do any good for the world around us. The world would be a better place, and our souls would be *in* a better place, if everyone obeyed the Commandments. There would be peace, love, justice, and harmony.

Unloving Others.   Harmony does seem to be in short supply in society these days. Everybody has an ax to grind with somebody. People are divisive and pugnacious, and what's worse is they seem to be proud of it. Until somebody gets a gun and starts shooting, that is. Then everyone gets somber and subdued for a few days. Our thoughts and prayers go out to the victims, blah blah blah. Then we're back to being at each other's throats. Such a Christian society.

"You have heard that it was said to your ancestors, 'You shall not kill; and whoever kills will be liable to judgment,'" Jesus instructs us. "But I say to you, whoever is angry with his brother will be liable to judgment, and whoever says to his brother 'raqa' will be answerable to the Sanhedrin, and whoever says 'you fool' will be liable to fiery Gehenna." Do we listen? Nah!

What else does Jesus say? "I give you a new commandment: love one another. As I have loved you, so you also should love one another. This is how all will know you are My disciples, if you have love for one another." As Christians we really do need to take those words to heart. Some people like to say, "God wants us to love everybody, but that doesn't mean we have to *like* everybody!" And that is a funny comment, I admit. But even if we don't like a person, love still requires that we treat him or her well. We're like, "just because I berate you and put you down doesn't mean I don't love you. It's true that I wish horrible things would happen to you, but I still love you." Uh-uh, 'fraid not. If you love a person, you treat that person with kindness and charity, even if you don't really like him, even if you're a liberal and he's a conservative, or vice versa.

Jesus goes on to tell us what God requires of us in relation to others:

> Love your enemies, and pray for those who persecute you, that you may be children of your heavenly Father, for He makes His sun rise on the bad and the good, and causes rain to fall on the just and the unjust. For if you love those who love you, what recompense will you have? Do not the tax collectors do the same? And if you greet your brothers only, what is unusual about that? Do not the pagans do the same? So be perfect, just as your heavenly Father is perfect.

Jesus knows talk is cheap, so it's not enough to *say* we're Christian. Instead, Jesus calls us to strive for perfection in our lives. How do we treat our fellow man? How do we treat the people we disagree with? How do we treat the people who screw up our day? How do we treat the people who cut us off on the road? Do we curse and scream at them and wish they were dead? If so, we have failed the test.

Materialism and Greed. Jesus admonishes us, "Do not store up for yourselves treasures on earth, where moth and decay destroy, and thieves break in and steal. But store up treasures in heaven, where neither moth nor decay destroy, nor thieves break in and steal. For where your treasure is, there also will your heart be."

Jesus also observes, "No one can serve two masters. He will either hate one and love the other, or be devoted to one and despise the other. You cannot serve God and mammon." He warns us to guard against all greed, "for though one may be rich, one's life does not consist of possessions." As God said to the rich fool, "this night your life will be demanded of you; and the things you have prepared, to whom will they belong?" Jesus tells us **not** to store up treasure for ourselves, but to be rich in what matters to God.

In the parable of the sower, Jesus reinforces the problem of being too caught up in worldly things. "The seed sown on rocky ground is the one who hears the word and receives it at once with joy," Jesus cautions. "But he has no root and lasts only for a time. When some tribulation or persecution comes because of the word, he immediately falls away." Explaining further, Jesus speaks of those who lose their Way: "The seed sown among the thorns is the one who hears the word, but then worldly anxiety and the lure of riches choke the word and it bears no fruit."

Now I admit we are up against it in terms of resisting the lures of materialism and greed. We live in a society that is saturated with advertising that is designed to make us think we are missing out on something if we are not "filthy rich". The appallingly opulent lifestyles of the rich and famous are thrust in our faces as something fabulous, and the lives of simple folk are portrayed as something to be scorned and shunned. There is a sociological concept known as relative deprivation that posits that even people who are pretty darn well off will feel that they don't measure up if they don't have the "best things in life", so-called.

However, living in the advertising age does not excuse us from using our common sense and our morals. Greed, gluttony, and pride are sins, and are especially egregious when those having an excess of wealth allow their neighbors to suffer want. There is no shortage of want in our world.

"You justify yourselves in the eyes of others," says Jesus, "but God knows your hearts; for what is of human esteem is an abomination in the sight of God." The rich jet-setters are portrayed in our world as super-cool, and the humble poor are portrayed in our world as suckers and losers. But God doesn't see it that way, and when we die it is God, not the world, Who will be our judge. Hedge fund billions and private jets will count for nothing when you give your account to the Lord.

"Whoever wishes to come after Me must deny himself, take up his cross, and follow Me. For whoever wishes to save his life will lose it, but whoever loses his life for My sake will find it." Heed the Ghost of Jacob Marley while there is still time. If you are a Christian, mankind is your business.

Judgment and Hypocrisy. "Stop judging," Jesus tells us, "that you may not be judged. For as you judge, so will you be judged, and the measure with which you judge will be measured out to you.

"Why do you notice the splinter in your brother's eye, but do not perceive the wooden beam in your own eye?" He continues. "How can you say to your brother, 'let me remove that splinter from your eye' while the wooden beam is in your eye? You hypocrite, remove the wooden beam from your eye first; then you will see clearly to remove the splinter from your brother's eye."

As Christians, we should want our lives to say something to the world. Our behavior should proclaim our belief that Jesus is Lord and should demonstrate our resolve to walk in His footsteps. We want people to know we are Christians by our love. If we are judgmental towards others, we are not acting in a Christ-like manner. Rather, we are acting as hypocrites. And hypocrisy is the bane of the Christian, because there are scores of unbelievers out there just waiting for you to be a hypocrite so they can say, "Aha! See, there is no God, because you did not behave as Jesus wanted you to."

Of course such a conclusion is ludicrous. Being Christians, we should strive for holiness; being human, we will always fall short of the mark. We are sinners, just as humans have always been sinners. Otherwise, we would not need a Savior. But the point remains the same: we should live our lives in a manner that proclaims our faith, and being judgmental betrays our calling.

As Jesus told those who were ready to stone the adulteress, "Let the one among you who is without sin cast the first stone." If He can forgive such transgressions, who are we to judge our fellow humans?

Serving Others.   We have all heard Jesus' words concerning the importance of serving others as part of our Christian duty. "Do unto others as you would have them do unto you," Jesus says. "This is the law and the prophets." He further teaches us, "The greatest among you must be your servant. Whoever exalts himself will be humbled; but whoever humbles himself will be exalted."

You will recall (I hope) the account from the Gospel of John concerning Jesus washing the feet of His Apostles on the night of the Last Supper:

> Jesus rose from supper and took off his outer
> garments. He took a towel and tied it around his
> waist. Then he poured water into a basin and began
> to wash the disciples' feet and dry them with the

273

towel around his waist. … "If I therefore, the master and teacher, have washed your feet, you ought to wash one another's feet. I have given you a model to follow, so that as I have done for you, you should also do."

To reiterate what we heard earlier in this Chapter, Jesus is not merely looking for people who will go about saying they are Christians and calling after Him, "Lord, Lord." Christianity is a call to action for the betterment of our neighbors and all of mankind. Granted there is only so much each one of us can do. We are not expected to save the world. But each of us doing our part for those less fortunate or troubled people that life puts in our path will surely make the world a better place.

It would be nice to think that all Christians will be persuaded to serve those around them simply because it is what our Lord asks of us. But unfortunately we know that is not the reality. Too many of us are so wrapped up in our own lives (raises his hand) that we don't give a second thought to others around us who are suffering. It is good, therefore, that Jesus gives us a little extra incentive to be nice by describing the fate that might await those who don't care. Here is a scene Jesus describes from the final judgment:

"Then He will say to those on His left, 'depart from Me you accursed, into the eternal fire prepared for the devil and his angels. For I was hungry and you gave Me no food, I was thirsty and you gave Me no drink, a stranger and you gave Me no welcome, naked and you gave Me no clothing, ill and in prison, and you did not care for Me.' Then they will answer and say, 'Lord, when did we see You hungry or thirsty or a stranger or naked or ill or in prison, and not minister to Your needs?' He will answer them, 'amen, I say to you, what you did not do for one of these least ones, you did not do for Me.' And these will go off to eternal punishment."

Eternal punishment. That's what we are trying to avoid here. That's why I am writing this book, so that we can all share eternal joy, not eternal punishment. Be charitable to those who are less fortunate than you are. Don't thumb your nose at them, lest it come back to haunt you.

Admitting to Your Faith. Do people know that Jesus is your Lord and Savior? Is it evident to them by the things you do and say and from the way you live your life? Or are you one of those who go to Church on Sunday, and then forget what they heard the minute they're out the door, having satisfied their obligation for the week? I guess a preliminary question I should ask first is, *do you want people to know* that Jesus is your Lord and Savior? Because being a religious person is not particularly cool. I guess it never was, but certainly it used to be more acceptable than it is now. We need to change that.

We Christians are the soldiers in Christ's army. But it is not an army of war, it is an army of peace and love. We aim to conquer people's hearts and souls, to encourage them to lead holier lives and strive to attain heaven. Christians have the strength of numbers on their side, but most of the time that is not evident in how society operates. Oh, it's true that lots and lots of Christians – maybe even more than 50% -- will take umbrage if someone says "Happy Holidays" instead of "Merry Christmas", but in the whole scheme of Jesus' message that's a pretty inconsequential issue. As a matter of fact, I don't think Jesus ever mentioned it. Let's get real people, we don't gain followers by being righteously indignant over inconsequential issues. If Christians really acted like Christians, nobody would even care about "Happy Holidays". You don't want to get me started on the commercialism of the Christmas season, it's the ultimate casting of pearls before swine. For Christ's sake, let the heathens have the holiday season. Spending a month's salary at the mall isn't saving *any*body's soul.

Jesus tells us that the greatest commandment of all is this: "You shall love the Lord, your God, with all your heart, and with all your being, with all your strength, and with all your mind." But how many of us can say we follow that commandment? I fear a lot of us barely give God a passing thought now and then. That is unfortunate, and certainly is not the way Christians should conduct their lives. Our love for God should manifest itself in how we behave, and it should be apparent to others that our faith shapes us. But too many of us either choose not to know, or choose not to care, what Jesus asks of us. And again we are warned that there may be eternal repercussions. For Jesus warns us, "At the judgment the queen of [Sheba] will rise with the men of this generation and she will condemn them, because she came from the ends of the earth to hear the wisdom of Solomon, and there is something greater than Solomon here. At the judgment the men of Nineveh will arise with this generation and condemn it, because at the preaching of

Jonah they repented, and there is something greater than Jonah here."

What exactly is Jesus saying here? He is saying that the Creator of the Universe came to earth to teach His people how He wants them to live their lives, and way too many of them didn't want to hear it and didn't want to conform their lives to His vision. That is to say, if you're not going to listen to God Himself, you have only yourself to blame for the consequences.

We read in the Gospels that Jesus says, "Everyone who acknowledges me before others I will acknowledge before my heavenly Father. But whoever denies me before others, I will deny before my heavenly Father." And elsewhere it is written, "I tell you, everyone who acknowledges Me before others the Son of Man will acknowledge before the angels of God. But whoever denies Me before others will be denied before the angels of God." Jesus wants followers who are real, sincere, and steadfast, not followers who will blow with the winds. Even if your commitment to Him causes some friction and tension in your life, His cause is worth the fight.

Not everyone likes a Christian vision of life, not everyone wants to think they are supposed to live a moral life. Righteousness be damned, they want to have fun, or worse! So a commitment to Christ and an admission that He means something to you will not be welcomed in all precincts. But if we believe, it is our calling to follow where He leads. Jesus says, "Whoever is not with me is against me, and whoever does not gather with me scatters." So gather with Jesus, or go change your voter registration card to say secularist.

QUESTIONS FOR REFLECTION OR DISCUSSION

1. What is your favorite quote from Jesus in Chapter Twenty-three? Why?

2. Which of Jesus' quotes in Chapter Twenty-three did you find most surprising? In what way did it surprise you?

3. What aspect of a Christian's duty do you find most intimidating? Why?

4. Do you think most of the Christians you know are living up to the ideal Jesus sets for them? In what ways do they fall short?

5. Assuming you are a Christian, do you think people know you are Christian based on either the way you behave or the things you say?

Chapter Twenty-Four

WHAT ABOUT THE APPARENTLY GROWING NUMBER OF ATHEISTS IN OUR SOCIETY?

Although You have hidden these things from the wise and learned, You have revealed them to the childlike.

What is it that makes someone decide to identify him or herself as an atheist? What makes someone come to the conclusion that God does not exist? From my limited experience with the subject, there is no one, easy answer, but by observation I suspect there can be several reasons.

For one thing, some people are undoubtedly taught from a young age that there is no God, just as most of us who are believers have been taught from a young age that there IS a God. Other people are taught to question God's existence at a later age, in high school or college, for example. Paradoxically, often times these anti-God lessons come from our Catholic high schools [11] and universities. I have heard many stories from parents who shelled out big bucks to send

---

[11] If you think about it, this really puts God up against it. In public high schools, His existence is curricularly ignored, and in Catholic high schools, where He can at least be mentioned, His existence is questioned. It must make God rather sad.

their children to religious learning institutions, only to have their children come out irreligious. I suppose you could argue that it is a good thing that these Catholic institutions of learning teach their students to think about and question the essential underpinnings of the Catholic religion. However, I don't think that argument holds up to the mission of the Catholic Church to get its members into heaven. It's also worth noting that high school and college students are at a very impressionable and somewhat rebellious age, at which they may blindly accept whatever indoctrination a teacher puts forth, especially if it is something that would confirm the stupidity of their parents!

I can only hope and pray that children who are taught that there is no God will undergo an epiphany as their minds mature and they begin to apply common sense to what they observe.

Part of the indoctrination into an atheist worldview is undoubtedly a refusal to believe in a Being Who cannot be seen. As if that proves something. I can't see the air I breathe, but it's there. People have never seen a dinosaur, but they have no problem believing in their (former) existence. Ahh, you say, but there are fossils. Even though I have never seen a dinosaur, the fossils prove to me that they exist(ed). Well, even if I can't see God, I can see you and I can see me, and I can see the world and the universe. This indicates to me that there must be a Creator. I can read the Bible and the Bhagavad Gita, and this indicates to me that God has sought through the ages to reveal Himself to man. And God continues to be revealed to us through, among other things, Marian apparitions, such as in Lourdes, Fatima, Medjugorje, etc. Who am I – indeed, who are you -- to conclude that Saint Bernadette and the other youngsters who claim to have seen and conversed with the Blessed Mother were lying, or were delusional? These seers were examined thoroughly, and their stories were investigated fully. Bernadette et al. were found to be neither untruthful nor insane.

Yes, God reveals Himself to us in countless tangible ways, even if He Himself is Spirit.

Another noteworthy aspect of the apparent increase in atheism is that it is very much a "first world" phenomenon. Where people are financially and socially comfortable, religious fervor dwindles. We see this in western European nations like The Netherlands and Sweden, and to a lesser extent here in the United States. It is as if folks find that when they have creature comforts, and society provides them all that they need to be "happy", God is shown the door. This phenomenon is not new, though; in the Old Testament Book of Proverbs, we read, "provide me only with the food I need, lest, being full, I deny you, saying, 'Who is the Lord?' " Creature comforts beget religious indifference. Conversely, just as there are less likely to be atheists in the proverbial foxhole, belief in God remains strong where people are less insulated from financial hardship and social strife; that is, where people have not come to the conclusion that they no longer *need* God.

Considering further the spread of atheism, I sense that there are some super-intelligent individuals whose view of the universe simply does not allow for the existence of a Supreme Being or Creator. I honestly don't know why that should be; maybe these really intelligent people can't accept the existence of God because that would require them to acknowledge that there is someone smarter than man. But at the same time, let's face the fact that there has been a whole host of really intelligent people throughout the ages who have concluded that there *is* a God.

As I see it, the fact that things exist, and that we humans have the ability to think and feel, would seem much more to prove that there *is* a Creator than that there is not. For if nobody or nothing created *stuff*, how did *stuff* come to exist? I recently read an online comment that suggested there is not a shred of evidence of the existence of a supernatural creator. I thought that was funny. How about CREATion and CREATures? Don't they count as some evidence that there might be a CREATor? It is not just coincidence that those words share the same root. The more logical conclusion would be that if things exist, someone (i.e., a Creator) must have brought them into existence.

Most of my personal interactions with self-identified atheists have been with folks I would characterize not as super-intelligent, but rather as of above-average intelligence. Perhaps they are under the influence of the super-intelligent atheist thinkers in choosing to believe there is no God. Many atheists may come across as snarky and arrogant, and perhaps even insulting to those who are stupid enough to think there could be a God. They come across as somewhat perturbed that God-fearing people still exist. Often they will support their argument against God's existence by talking about evil things that humans do – the events of September 11, 2001, or the sexual abuse of children by members of the clergy, for example. I must confess, it is a mystery to me how the fact that humans do bad things can be thought to disprove God's existence, but more on that later.

I also sincerely think there are many so-called atheists whose "decision" about God's existence is based on their desire to live a sinful life. They have chosen to conform their religious beliefs (or lack thereof) to their behavior, rather than to conform their lifestyle to a religious belief that stresses morality. "God doesn't want me to lead a licentious and unchaste life; but I want to lead a licentious and unchaste life; therefore, there is no God." See the logic? Hopefully these atheists of convenience find their way back to God and ask forgiveness once they have had their fill of "sowing their wild oats".

Lastly, I imagine there are some young members of the population who haven't given the whole God thing a lot of thought, but think it is cool to buck the establishment. Disavowing the traditional religious beliefs that their dimwitted, unevolved parents followed is one of the ways they can do so.

On a more serious and somber note, undoubtedly a subset of all these atheist groupings are people who are bitter about some aspect of their upbringing or life experiences. Perhaps they have suffered a personal tragedy or endured some form of abuse, or perhaps they have observed the evil and tragedy that plagues the world, and have decided as a consequence that there cannot be a God. Why would God let bad things happen? (I treat this issue at length in Chapter 30, which is devoted to the topic.) Some of these people may actually believe in God, but are so angry at Him that they prefer to say He does not exist. I would like to be able to change their minds and soften their hearts. Despite our differing views of the world and the universe and everything in them, I love all my atheistic brothers and sisters, and sincerely hope they will one day come to accept God. For their own sake, not mine.

I think one of the problems with modern man is we have become so advanced that we no longer see a need for God. Look at all the wonderful things we have accomplished, scientifically and technologically. Obviously, man is the brilliant progenitor of all these advances. The fact that God gave man the brainpower and resources to accomplish these things does not occur to our bloated, prideful egos. Religion, you see, is for the common sucker, not the wise and learned.

But wait, doesn't Jesus tell us as much? Listen: "I give praise to You Father, Lord of heaven and earth, for although You have hidden these things from the wise and learned you have revealed them to the childlike." In fact, this is a sentiment that Jesus repeats a few times in the Gospels. If we think too much, we might think ourselves right out of religious belief. It is easy, I fear, when you are of a certain level of intelligence and education, to become skeptical about *every*thing. Stories that resonated with you as a child now seem somewhat far-fetched, too supernatural to be true, or maybe too good to be true. Jesus knows this, too. Does He not also tell us, "Let the children come to me, and do not prevent them; for the kingdom of heaven belongs to such as these." And this: "Amen, I say to you, whoever does not

accept the kingdom of God like a child will not enter it."
Jesus knows that if we try too hard to reason it out, we may
trip ourselves up. Some things we must accept with
simplicity, not through over-analysis.

That is not to say one must be a simpleton to believe in
God. As I alluded to above, extremely intelligent and
learned men and women throughout the ages have believed
in God and in Jesus the Christ, His Son. It is more a question
of *how* you choose to use your reasoning power. Two people
could look at the same data and come to opposite
conclusions, but many times they come to the conclusion
they *want* to reach.

I think for many people the biggest stumbling block to
belief in God is the distance God keeps from us. As Anthony
Quinn says as the hopelessly confused title figure in the
movie "Barrabas", "Why can't God make Himself plain?"
God does not often push Himself on us in our daily lives,
and when He speaks to us He does so in such a way that we
can easily miss it if we are too busy or distracted, or if we do
not want to hear it. But God does want to communicate with
us. It is helpful if (1) we believe in Him! (2) we make

ourselves available in quietude to hear Him, and (3) we listen without our own preconceived agenda of what we want to hear.

From my perspective, there are so many indications of God's existence, of a Divine creator, or an intelligent Designer if you will, that the application of reason to the facts presented can't help but lead to the conclusion that He *does* exist. I am not even taking into account those things that are probably the strongest evidence of God's existence to people of faith -- personal revelations, messages that seem to have come directly or indirectly from God, people that seem to have been put into your life's path for a special reason, insights from a death or near-death experience -- because these experiences either cannot be externally corroborated or are subject to interpretation. But let's look at tangible, indisputable "evidence". Start with the fact that we are here on earth, placed in an environment that is perfectly suited to our existence and survival. Add the fact that we are able to think and feel, laugh and love, mourn and cry. Ponder a moment the phenomena of laughter and tears. If we humans came into existence as a result of some random cosmic explosion millions of years ago, what's the explanation for why we should laugh or cry about things? Why should random creatures spawned out of chaos think anything was funny, or sad? Why would we even care about anyone or anything? Does it make sense to think that all our emotions just randomly happened?

Consider some other, more tangible phenomena of our earthly existence. How refreshing is a drink of water on a hot day? That just happened, by chance? How about a glass of cold milk after a fudge brownie? Okay, that's probably cheating. What about a juicy, sweet/tart grapefruit on a winter day? Or a semi-sweet, juicy bing cherry on a summer afternoon? Maybe I'm prejudiced in favor of grapefruits and bing cherries, but you can substitute your own favorite fruits or vegetables or whatever. Watermelon, honeydew, mangoes. And you needn't stop at things we consume. Think about all the varieties of trees and flowers and plants that decorate our world. It's hard to fathom that all these wonderful things would come about from a random explosion of cosmic chaos.

I also find it rather impossible to think that a slender, shapely girl with long brown hair is a cosmic accident. Oh, you prefer blondes? Too bad, this is my book. Go write your own. But seriously, can you honestly think all the beautiful things we enjoy in our lives came about by random chance?

Another phenomenon through which God seems to proclaim His existence to us is procreation. We have all experienced the "miracle of birth" in one way or another, but how often do we stop and think about the whole process? How many times my wife has remarked, in looking upon our handsome six-foot tall son, upon the amazing reality that the uniting of a sperm cell and an egg could develop into a fully-grown human person. I understand that there are scientific explanations for this wonder of nature, but let's keep some perspective here – the phenomenon preceded the scientific explanations by a whole bunch of millennia. So while science can reverse engineer the process and give crazy names to the intricate details, science did not invent the miracle of birth. So how did this incredible process come about? A random explosion of cosmic gases? Or the design of some really brilliant Creative Force who knew exactly what He was doing?

In discussing procreation, it would be appropriate to also mention human sexual relations. The sexual relationship between a loving couple is certainly the most physically pleasurable and emotionally unitive experience a couple can enjoy. Did the magic of the sexual experience just randomly come along? Isn't it yet another marvelous proof of the actions of a loving Creator?

In a random, chaotic worldview, why should the act that leads to human reproduction be pleasurable? I suppose one could theorize that the Cosmos (meaning the universe, not the soccer team) wants us to procreate, to keep our species going. But that begs the question, how can the Cosmos "want" anything? [12] Can something that is not alive and does not have thoughts or emotions want something? Isn't saying the universe wants us to propagate the species sort of like saying my pet rock wants me to propagate the species? And if in fact an unthinking, unfeeling Cosmos *did* want us to propagate the species, we still wouldn't need sex to do it. After all, there are cell-dividing amoebae and segmenting worms, and things like that. Frankly, I doubt that an

---

[12] Unless you are saying the Cosmos is a living, thinking being, kind of like a creator God.

unthinking, unfeeling Cosmos would care if there were any pleasure involved in the process.

By my reckoning, human sexual relations are a Divine gift from God to mankind. Albeit a gift to be used prudently, responsibly, and lovingly. [13]

It is puzzling to me that people can actually think an explosion of gases, with no Divine direction, led to rivers, streams, and oceans; trees, shrubs, grass, and flowers; sparrows, chipmunks, puppy dogs, puffins, and Thomson's gazelles; beautiful women and lemon meringue pie (oops – I'm cheating again); laughter, romance, and Steve Howe's pedal steel guitar solo on the Yessongs version of "And You and I". And sex. Without God it's incomprehensible.

Now I have to admit the last page-and-a-half did not really derive from anything I learned at the feet of the Lord. I figured these things out all on my own. Ain't I smart?

---

[13] It is sad that so many in our society view sex as a recreational sport. They get the transient fun but miss the transcendent beauty. It doesn't help that the entertainment media portray sex as something to be engaged in indiscriminately.

Before I move on, I would like to offer one more piece of evidence for God's existence: this book. Why am I writing this book? There are estimated to be 317,000,000 people living in the United States of America at the present time. This is just a wild guess, but that probably means there are more than 316,950,000 people here whom I have never properly met. Add a bunch of billions to that, and that's how many people in the *world* I haven't met. And probably never will, I might add. So let me ask you this rhetorical question: Do I care if some of those billions of people take things that are not theirs? Or have sex with people they are not supposed to have sex with? Or lie about people behind their backs? Or don't believe in God? Or jet-set around the world without giving a nickel to the poor? Or even go around killing people, provided they don't kill anyone I care about? In a godless vacuum, the rhetorical answer would be "No". Generally speaking, how people whom I don't know choose to live their lives doesn't make the slightest bit of difference to me. As long as it does not adversely affect my life, I have no stake in what people do, and no interest in *telling them* what to do.

So let's return to my prior question: why am I writing this book? The answer is, because I want people to live lives that will help them merit heaven. But why, you may ask, should I care about that? The only reason I can give you is that God **wants me** to care. And the only reason I can give you as to why I have spent years writing this book is because I believe God has spoken to my heart that He wants me to write it. So in my mind, this confirms that God exists. To recap: (1) absent God and His promise of heaven, I couldn't care less how you lived your life; and (2) absent God urging me to encourage people to strive for heaven, I would have no reason to advise you how to live your life. (I think what I'm really saying is, if you don't like this book, don't blame me, blame God.)

I spoke earlier about why someone might decide he or she is an atheist. Let me now posit the theory that it is not entirely an individual's decision to be a non-believer. And for this theory I will actually revert back to the plan of this book and use lessons I learned from Jesus!

The theory I am talking about vis a vis a person becoming an atheist is this: Fairly recently, I came to the realization that the devil plays a large part in the proliferation of atheism. Two totally diverse occurrences synergistically came together to awaken me to this point. One of these occurrences was the despoliation of Miley Cyrus. Raised by Christian parents (though I can't comment on how well they raised her), she seemed to decide one day that there was no God. At around the same time she also decided that her musical career would now feature live sex acts. Looking at her "in action", I came away with the strong opinion that not only did she look repulsive rather than alluring, but also that she looked downright demonic. What exactly am I saying here? I'm saying I believe it is possible that the changes in Ms Cyrus' religious outlook and style of performance are the result of evil spirits taking hold of her. And I pray for her to be set free from these demons in case I am right.

The other unrelated but synergistic occurrence that convinced me of the devil's hand in atheism was a closer reading of Jesus' parable of the sower, which I had read and/or heard probably a hundred times before. On my closer reading of the parable, I noticed – I mean *really* noticed -- for the first time -- what Jesus says by way of explanation of the seed that fell on the path and was eaten by the birds. Jesus says, "The seed sown on the path is the one who hears the word of the kingdom without understanding it, and *the evil one* comes and steals away what was sown in his heart." The evil one! I swear I never noticed that before. It's the devil. The devil can actually make someone disbelieve in God! I had always before thought of the devil leading people astray in terms of their thoughts and actions; I had never before thought of the devil in terms of influencing one's religious convictions. But as always, Jesus nails it. If the devil wants our company in hell, what easier way than to steal away our belief in God?

The other portions of the parable of the sower are also pertinent to modern society's struggle with theism vs. atheism. For example, take the seed that fell on rocky ground. The seed that fell there sprang up at once because the soil was not deep, and when the sun rose it was scorched, and it withered for lack of roots. Jesus tells us, "The seed sown on rocky ground is the one who hears the word and receives it at once with joy. But he has no root and lasts only for a time. When some tribulation or persecution comes because of the word, he immediately falls away."

People who view their religious belief as a kind of spiritual panacea or lucky amulet will have trouble sustaining their faith, because trouble comes to us all in life. If we think believing in God makes us immune from such trouble, we are sadly mistaken. Indeed, the early history of the Church proves that the converse is true. In those days. Christian faith often resulted in persecution and martyrdom. One who deludes himself into thinking that God will protect him from all harm is greatly mistaken, yet this is the gospel that is preached by some Christians today. You can easily imagine a believer, thus deluded, quickly morphing into a non-believer.

Then consider the seed that fell among thorns, which grew up and choked the young plant. Jesus explains, "The seed sown among the thorns is the one who hears the word, but then worldly anxiety and the lure of riches choke the word and it bears no fruit." It is fair to say, with the pervasiveness of advertising and the ubiquity of all media through the Internet, that there has never been a time in human history in which the push for material goods and the phenomenon of relative deprivation have been so powerful. So many people want want want; we want what the other guy has, what the advertisers are selling, whatever there is. Sadly, these covetous Christians are just as delusional as those Christians who think no harm will ever come to them. All the possessions in the world do not bring happiness, and God doesn't give a good goddam how much "stuff" you have. But again, there are preachers out there who tell you the opposite, that God just wants you to be filthy rich. I mean, if a fleet of Ferraris, a home on every continent, and a private jet isn't abundant life, I don't know what is. All you have to do is ask Him. (I guess I'm asking wrong.) If that is your belief system – faith in God will make me rich –, then the inevitable reality that most people who believe in God are *not* rich can make you feel duped and dubious about this God who promised you abundant life.

The more significant lesson to take from the story of the seed that fell among the thorns, however, is that our striving for material wealth and worrying about attaining and maintaining such wealth will quickly knock us off course from where God wants us to be. When wealth becomes our god, pursuit of spiritual treasures is no longer in the picture. Since we cannot serve God and mammon, one has to go. If God will not take a backseat to our pursuit of wealth, many of us would just as soon drop Him off at the next corner. If God won't abide my lifestyle, then I won't abide God.

My concern, as stated many times before, is this: what will happen to our atheist friends when they die? Will they have a chance to share eternal life with us? I like to think that "sincere atheists", those who would like to believe in God but are for whatever reason incapable of doing so, but who nevertheless lead good and moral lives, will be forgiven and welcomed into the kingdom. So too those whose miserable, loveless life journeys have rendered them incapable of conceiving that there could be a loving God. But of this I am, candidly, unsure. When Jesus commissioned His Apostles to go into the world and preach the Gospel, He said, "Whoever believes and is baptized will be saved; whoever does not believe will be condemned." We are also told in the Gospel of John that God sent His Son into the world to save it, but that whoever does not believe has already been condemned, because he has not believed in the name of the only Son of God.

We must also be mindful that we have the Gospels, the New Testament Epistles, and 2,000 years of great Christian thinkers and writers available to us, to lead us to Christ and, through Him, to God. As Jesus said of His own contemporaries:

> An evil and unfaithful generation seeks a sign, but no sign will be given it except the sign of Jonah the prophet. Just as Jonah was in the belly of the whale three days and three nights, so will the son of Man be in the heart of the earth three days and three nights. At the judgment, the men of Nineveh will arise with this generation and condemn it, because they repented at the teaching of Jonah; and there is something greater than Jonah here.

Will God have mercy on *our* contemporaries who do not believe? True, we did not have the benefit of having Jesus walk among us, teaching and healing and doing miraculous things. But even if we did, would we have believed? Or would we, like the Jewish leaders, be obstinate and skeptical, and look for reasons to disbelieve? For despite evidence of all God's great works, and knowledge of all Jesus' great wisdom, more and more of our brethren nevertheless fail to embrace God in their lives.

Note that Jesus also says, "There are some of you who do not believe. For this reason I have told you that no one can come to Me unless it is granted him by My father." **I submit**

to you – if you are a believer – that it is our unending Christian duty to pray that God will open the eyes of all non-believers, and enable them to accept Him. For this in fact is God's will. As Jesus tells us, "I came down from heaven not to do My own will but to do the will of the one who sent Me. … this is the will of My Father, that everyone who sees the Son and believes in Him may have eternal life, and I shall raise him on the last day."

Notice that when Jesus prayed to the Father for the benefit of His disciples on Holy Thursday night, He also prayed that *all* might come to believe; listen: "I pray not only for them, but also for those who will believe in Me through their word, so that they may all be one, as You, Father, are in Me and I in You, that they also may be in Us, that the world may believe that You sent Me." Jesus would like for all the world to believe in God, and to be saved. This is why I say we, too, must pray for this conclusion.

But what about those who choose not to believe simply because they want to be evil? We all know there are many people like this in the world. How do we deal with the people who simply do not want to be saved? Jesus has said this: "And this is the verdict, that the light came into the world, but people preferred darkness to light, because their works were evil. For everyone who does wicked things hates the light, so that his works might not be exposed."

Similarly, Jesus also tells us this:

> I came into the world as light, so that everyone who believes in Me might not remain in darkness. And if anyone hears My words and does not observe them, I do not condemn him, for I did not come to condemn the world but to save the world. Whoever rejects Me and does not accept My words has something to judge him: the word that I spoke, it will condemn him on the last day, because I did not speak on My own, but the Father who sent Me commanded Me what to say and speak. And I know that His commandment is eternal life.

For these, too, we must pray, try to share God's Word, and hope that something in their lives will open their eyes to the truth.

Can I say one last thing before we leave our treatment of atheism versus theism? Since I'm the author I guess I can.

There has recently developed a more virulent strain of atheism, an aggressive form that feels it has an obligation not just to poo-poo and laugh at the God-fearing, but to actively seek to eradicate religion (read Christianity) from society. But consider this. If a religious person manages to persuade an atheist that there is a God, the result is that the former atheist gets to heaven. In other words, the evangelizer has done the ex-atheist a tremendous favor. But if an atheist manages to persuade a theist that there is **not** a God, the result is that the formerly religious person will *lose* heaven. In other words, the atheist has utterly ruined the other person's life/afterlife.

I find difficult to understand that atheists don't grasp the significance of this distinction, given how much smarter than believers they claim to be. It should be pretty easy to comprehend why Christians (a) want to spread the Word, but (b) shy away from atheists who try to spread their non-word. It all has to do with getting to the Promised Land. If the reason atheists can't grasp this distinction is that they refuse to entertain any argument that assumes the existence of God, then they are sadly the victims of their own arrogance.

Regardless of all that, the closing point is that Jesus is very sad about the growing number of non-believers in society and the peril in which they place their immortal souls. Jesus needs us to continue preaching His truth and praying for a change in the hearts, minds, and souls of all atheists.

QUESTIONS FOR REFLECTION OR DISCUSSION

1. What is your favorite quote from Jesus in Chapter Twenty-four? Why?

2. Which of Jesus' quotes in Chapter Twenty-four did you find most surprising? In what way did it surprise you?

3. a. If you are an atheist, what is the biggest obstacle to you believing in God?
   b. If you are a believer, what is the biggest obstacle to you trying to persuade atheists that God exists?

4. Are you persuaded of God's existence by the argument concerning sex and reproduction?

5. Do you think the devil and/or his minions are present in our world? If so, do you think they are capable of preventing people from believing in God?

6. Are there features in creation that convince you that God exists or doesn't exist?

7. Assuming you are a believer who used to be, or are personally acquainted with, atheists, what do you think are the primary reasons atheists are unable or unwilling to believe in God?

Chapter Twenty-Five

DO YOU WANT YOUR PEOPLE TO EVANGELIZE?

The harvest is abundant but the laborers are few;
so ask the master of the harvest to send out laborers for his
harvest.

Coincidentally, the closing paragraphs of the last chapter segue nicely into the new chapter, as it examines Jesus' call to us to spread the Word.

Evangelizing is a daunting task that most of us would rather not think about too much. It's hard enough to talk about religion to our friends and family without being mocked, insulted, or ignored, let alone talking about religion to people we barely know, or don't know at all. What sort of reaction will we get? Will they, too, mock us, insult us, or ignore us? Will they yell at us? Will they get violent with us? It is easy to be intimidated by the possible fallout from efforts to spread God's word. There is also a certain amount of internal conflict that comes with the thought of attempting to evangelize. Jesus wants us to be humble and polite. Is it humble and polite of us to impose ourselves and our beliefs on someone who may not want to hear it? We are supposed to do unto others as we would have them do unto us. If we would like Jehovah's Witnesses to stay away from our door, wouldn't the corresponding obligation upon us be to leave other people alone as well?

The call to evangelize is both unnerving and a bit perplexing. Nevertheless, as Jesus Himself makes clear, evangelization is indeed something to which we are called. I guess the best way to reconcile ourselves to this call is to fall back on the importance of saving souls. Maybe it is annoying and a little obnoxious for us to try sharing our faith with others, but our ultimate goal is to help them attain eternal life. Can we put aside our reservations and self-consciousness for the sake of this most important of all goals? Let's listen to what Jesus has to say.

<u>The Call to Evangelize</u>

There is no denying that part of the Christian's duty is to share the word of God with other people. One of the very first things Jesus said to his first Apostles was, "Come after me, and I will make you fishers of men." From the first, the Apostolic duty was to go out and save souls. The word of God was out there, had been out there for many centuries, but it seems that most of the Jewish people weren't "getting it". So first John the Baptist, and then Jesus, were sent by God to stir things up, to rekindle the word. Jesus enlisted his twelve Apostles to help, and implored them to find more help. "The harvest is abundant but the laborers are few," Jesus told them, "so ask the master of the harvest to send out laborers for his harvest."

We should also take another look at the Parable of the Sower for further confirmation of the call to evangelize. For Jesus tells us there that some seed falls on rich soil, and produces fruit, a hundred or sixty or thirty fold. Jesus explains, "The seed sown on rich soil is the one who hears the word and understands it, who indeed bears fruit." When we understand what God is saying to us, it becomes incumbent on us to spread the word so that others will also have the opportunity to hear and understand. Jesus also says to us, "Whoever is not with Me is against Me, and whoever does not gather with Me scatters."

Just as some of Jesus' earliest words to His Apostles were a call to evangelization, so too were some of his last words to them. After His Resurrection, before ascending to the Father, He said to them, "Peace be with you. As the Father has sent

Me, so I send you." He further instructed them, "Go, therefore, and make disciples of all nations, baptizing them in the name of the Father, and of the Son, and of the Holy Spirit, teaching them to observe all that I have commanded you." The importance of this Great Commission is reflected in this additional instruction to His disciples: "Go into the whole world and proclaim the Gospel to every creature. Whoever believes and is baptized will be saved; whoever does not believe will be condemned." Where the quest for eternal life is concerned, therefore, this becomes a matter of life and death. This is why the call to evangelize remains so important. It is about securing eternity with God for the people we encounter, including our friends and loved ones.

We should keep in mind that when we answer the call to evangelize, we do not go it alone. As Jesus told His disciples, "You will receive power when the Holy Spirit comes upon you, and you will be My witnesses in Jerusalem, throughout Judea and Samaria, and to the ends of the earth." We need, therefore, to pray for the help and guidance of the Spirit in our efforts to save souls.

Methods of Evangelizing

We can recognize three distinct but complementary ways of sharing God with others. The most basic and most obvious is by sharing the Gospel itself, the words of God as brought to us by Jesus, His Son. Jesus said to His disciples, "What I say to you in the darkness speak in the light. What you hear whispered, proclaim on the housetops." Jesus does not want us to keep the word to ourselves; it is to be shared with others so that all may benefit from the Lord's Wisdom and receive the words of eternal life. Make no mistake about it, Jesus realizes this is not an easy task. As He told his Apostles, "Behold, I am sending you like sheep in the midst of wolves; so be shrewd as serpents and simple as doves." At the same time, Jesus had some harsh words for those to whom the Gospel was presented, but who chose to reject it: "Whoever will not receive you or listen to your words – go outside that house or town and shake the dust from your feet. Amen I say to you, it will be more tolerable for the land of Sodom and Gomorrah on the day of judgment than for that town." When we speak God's word to people, therefore, it is helpful to keep in mind that God is with us in our mission, and it is also important to keep in mind the importance of what we are trying to accomplish: harvesting souls for eternal life.

A second method of evangelization derives from the story of the healing of the Gerasene Demoniac. This is the story of the man who was possessed by many demons, and who would cut himself on the rocks in the wilderness in the region of the Gerasenes. When Jesus encountered this possessed man, Jesus commanded the demons to come out of him, and sent the demons into a nearby herd of swine. The swine proceeded to kill themselves by running down a cliff into the sea. The entire population of the region, on learning what had happened, asked Jesus to leave, because they were seized with great fear. But what of the man from whom the demons had been expelled? When Jesus got into a boat to leave, the man from whom the demons had departed begged to remain with Him. But Jesus would not permit it. Rather, Jesus sent the man away, saying, "Return home and recount what God has done for you."

You might say this event gave birth to the "witness talk" method of evangelization. Certainly, one of the most powerful ways of bringing God to others is through an individual who recounts what God has done for him or her. There have been countless stories of people whose lives were totally out of control until they accepted God, changed their ways, and turned things around. Such talks can be profoundly powerful and inspirational. If you are one of these people, please do not hesitate to share your story with those who would benefit from it!

The final method of evangelization I will mention here is living a Christian life in order to set a good example. There is a movement in the Catholic Church known as Cursillo. Cursillo is a Spanish word that means "a short course" – i.e., a short course in Christianity. One joins Cursillo by attending a weekend retreat in which fellow Catholics provide instruction on living a Christian life and sharing one's faith with others. It was when I went on a Cursillo weekend that I first heard the saying, "Preach the Gospel at all times; when necessary, use words." I have since seen and heard the saying in other contexts (and you, you lucky duck, you've seen it at least three times just in this here book). I have been told that this saying is attributed to Saint Francis of Assisi. But really, it stems from Jesus Himself. For Jesus tells us, "You are the light of the world. A city set on a mountain cannot be hidden. Nor do they light a lamp and then place it under a bushel basket. It is set on a lampstand, where it gives light to all in the house. Just so, your light must shine before others, that they may see your good deeds and glorify your heavenly Father." Similarly, Jesus says, "Whoever lives by the truth comes to the light, so that his works may be clearly seen as done in God." And of course we have this legacy that Jesus left us: "I give you a new commandment: love one another. As I have loved you, so you also should love one another. This is how all will know you are My disciples, if you have love for one another."

This evangelization method is reflected in the title of the song "They Will Know We Are Christians by Our Love". Indeed, one of the points of this book is to remind Christians that their lives should stand for something, should be a beacon of light in a dark world. If people cannot tell that you are a Christian by the way you act, then what is the point of your religion? We should be living according to Jesus' teachings in order to inspire others to do likewise and thus, hopefully, lead them to salvation.

In conclusion, then, Jesus does want us to continue the work of evangelization that His Apostles started 2000 years ago, so that as many souls as possible will be saved and raised up to heaven for eternity. Whichever method of evangelization you employ, keep in mind that it must follow the words and actions of Jesus in order to bear fruit. For as Jesus says, "Just as a branch cannot bear fruit on its own unless it remains on the vine, so neither can you unless you remain in Me. I am the vine, you are the branches. Whoever remains in Me and I in him will bear much fruit, because without Me you can do nothing."

QUESTIONS FOR REFLECTION OR DISCUSSION

1. What is your favorite quote from Jesus in Chapter Twenty-five? Why?

2. Which of Jesus' quotes in Chapter Twenty-five did you find most surprising? In what way did it surprise you?

3. Have you ever attempted to evangelize family members or friends? Were you successful? Why or why not?

4. Have you ever attempted to evangelize mere acquaintances, or strangers? Were you successful? Why or why not?

5. The Chapter mentions three methods of evangelization. With which method would you be most comfortable as an evangelizer? What about as an evangelizee?

Chapter Twenty-Six

WHAT ARE THE KEYS TO WISDOM AND UNDERSTANDING?

Martha Martha, you are anxious and worried about many things. There is need of only one thing. Mary has chosen the better part, and it will not be taken from her.

Do you ever get the impression that society is getting stupider? I don't mean *intellectually* stupider. I'm sure the amount of education the average person receives nowadays is as high as it has ever been. I mean stupider in terms of common sense, and just the things people do.

Take rage, for example. Road rage – going berserk because you don't like the way some other person is driving, and responding in such a way that it puts his life at risk, your life at risk, and possibly the lives of any other motorists who happen to be in the vicinity at risk. The purpose behind driving is to get from one place to another safely. Since when did disliking the way another person is driving become an excuse for trying to maim or kill?

Children's sports rage is another idiotic modern development – getting uncontrollably angry at a coach, an umpire or referee, another child's parent, etc. What happened to playing sports because they are fun?

Celebrity worship is another of society's pitfalls in stupidity. There is basically now an entire media industry around the culture of celebrity. While I understand the notion of appreciating somebody's talent and the ways they use that talent to create music, art, or entertainment, to act as though they are worthy of great adulation is just ridiculous. They are human beings just like us; to honor them as if they are gods and goddesses is quite absurd, and at the same time demeaning to ourselves by making us seem subservient.

How about acute intoxication to the point of death? Of course people have been getting drunk, high, and stoned for ages and ages. Those who have the misfortune of becoming addicted have always been at risk of dying from an overdose or from the ravages of long-term use. But I'm talking about a different phenomenon now, one that I think is a more modern development. Not people from broken families or abusive homes who seek solace in intoxicants and become hooked, but young people from "normal" backgrounds, college students, even high school students, who go on drinking binges that result in death by alcohol poisoning, or by accidental or intentional misadventure. What is the attraction in this type of self-abusive and self-destructive behavior? Perhaps a spiritual void inside.

I could fill an entire book with the foolishness we modern people carry on, but as Mussolini was quoted after Betty Hutton gave birth to sextuplets in Preston Sturges' comedy classic "The Miracle of Morgan's Creek", "Enough is sufficiency". Let us move on to Jesus' prescription for how society might get back on a wiser course.

One place we can start is with Jesus' rejoinder to Satan when that devil tried to tempt Him in the desert: "It is written, man does not live by bread alone, but by every word that comes forth from the mouth of God." I don't think nowadays people are steeped in the word of God. I realize I am generalizing there. Members of certain religious groups are fervent Bible readers, and in recent decades many Catholics have begun catching up. But I think in general, if you took into account the number of people who identify themselves as Christian, of one denomination or another, and then asked how many of them read the Bible on a regular basis, the number would be frighteningly low. I say frightening because our eyes and ears are being besieged daily by garbage spewing forth from the entertainment industry, and we need some moral guidance to balance it out. If people are not getting that guidance, is it any wonder that so many people behave in an unsavory manner?

As I've mentioned before, the Commandments that God gave us remain the basis of our moral law, and Christians are still today called to obey and follow them. That might be a problem for some people. For many today, the idea of freedom is being able to do whatever they want without anyone telling them otherwise. The distinction between freedom and license has become blurred into irrelevance. I sense that many people reject God for this simple reason: They don't want to be told how to behave. It's not convenient for them to be told what is right and what is wrong. But as Jesus says, "[W]hoever breaks one of the least of these commandments and teaches others to do so will be called least in the kingdom of heaven. But whoever obeys and teaches these commandments will be called greatest in the kingdom of heaven." If we refuse to listen to what God says to us, we help perpetuate immoral conditions on earth, and risk depriving ourselves of the immortal condition in heaven.

Indeed, true wisdom, the wisdom that endures, does not come from the world, but from the Word.   Jesus says, "Ask and it will be given to you; seek and you will find; knock and the door will be opened to you. For everyone who asks, receives; and the one who seeks, finds; and to the one who knocks, the door will be opened." But we must take the time and make the effort to seek God's wisdom, to understand, and to follow. Jesus exhorts us to do so out of our own best interests. He tells us:

> Everyone who listens to these words of Mine and acts on them will be like a wise man who built his house on rock. The rain fell, the floods came, and the winds blew and buffeted the house. But it did not collapse; it had been set solidly on rock. And everyone who listens to these words of Mine but does not act on them will be like a fool who built his house on sand. The rain fell, the floods came, and the winds blew and buffeted the house. And it collapsed and was completely ruined.

As is often the case, Jesus' focus is not on what happens here on earth, but what happens after our days here are finished. Hence, speaking of houses that stand and houses that collapse, He is speaking metaphorically about our immortal souls. Our eternal fate takes precedence over our earthly dwelling. Similarly, Jesus says, "Blessed are those who hear the word of God and observe it."

In urging us to keep the commandments, Jesus confirms the importance of living our lives on earth as a springboard to eternal life. Thus does He say, "I tell you, My friends, do not be afraid of those who kill the body but after that can do no more. I shall show you whom to fear. Be afraid of the one who after killing has the power to cast into Gehenna." In cautioning His contemporaries about the pitfalls that await those who do not heed the Word, Jesus said, "At the judgment the queen of the south will arise with this generation and condemn it, because she came from the ends of the earth to hear the wisdom of Solomon; and there is something greater than Solomon here."

Again let me emphasize that I am not trying to frighten anyone, but rather to lovingly encourage all to behave in a manner that will be acceptable to God so that we may all attain eternal life together. If we call ourselves Christians, we really ought to listen to Jesus and abide by what He tells us to do. Otherwise, I'm not sure how much good the name will do us. Jesus tells us, "You are My friends if you do what I command you."

Jesus is not looking for lip service from His followers, but rather for a commitment to live a righteous life. "You justify yourselves in the eyes of others," He says, "but God knows your hearts; for what is of human esteem is an abomination in the sight of God." Left to his own devices, man will too often bring forth things that defile. "From within people, from their hearts," says Jesus, "come evil thoughts, unchastity, theft, murder, adultery, greed, malice, deceit, licentiousness, envy, blasphemy, arrogance, folly. All these evils come from within, and they defile." Christians are by no means immune from committing these sins. We must listen to, and act on, Jesus' words to remain in God's good graces.

The wisdom and understanding that Jesus would impart on us is that the ways of this world and the things of this world do not bring lasting happiness and satisfaction. It is more important, He tells us, to work not for food that perishes, "but for the food that endures for eternal life, which the Son of Man will give you." In a similar vein, Jesus counsels us not to be caught up in the things of this world:

> If even the smallest things are beyond your control, why are you anxious about the rest? Notice how the flowers grow. They do not toil or spin, but I tell you, not even Solomon in all his splendor was dressed like one of them. If God so clothes the grass in the field that grows today and is thrown in the oven tomorrow, will He not much more provide for you, O you of little faith? As for you, do not seek what you are to eat and what you are to drink, and do not worry anymore. All the nations of the world seek for these things, and your Father knows that you need them. Instead, seek first His kingdom, and these other things will be given to you besides. Do not be afraid any longer, little flock, for your Father is pleased to give you the kingdom.

God wants us to have eternal life and lasting joy, and not to be caught up in the mundane. Remember that when Jesus was confronted by busy, anxious Martha about needing her sister Mary's help to serve their visitors, Jesus told her, "Martha Martha, you are anxious and worried about many things. There is need of only one thing. Mary has chosen the better part, and it will not be taken from her." What better part had Mary chosen? *She sat beside the Lord at His feet, listening to Him speak.* (Hence the title of this book, in case you didn't know it.)

So for Jesus, the key to wisdom and understanding is to be focused on the things of God, not the things of man. All our accomplishments, acquisitions, and conquests are transient, and therefore bring only transient joy to our lives. If you are happy about having a nice car, soon you will want to get a nicer, newer one. If you are interested in getting a nice house, soon you will want to get a nicer, bigger one. If you want to have a paramour, eventually you will want a younger, hotter one. Jesus would have us strive for something more meaningful. "If you remain in My word," He says, "you will truly be My disciples, and you will know the truth, and the truth will set you free."

QUESTIONS FOR REFLECTION OR DISCUSSION

1. What is your favorite quote from Jesus in Chapter Twenty-six? Why?

2. Which of Jesus' quotes in Chapter Twenty-six did you find most surprising? In what way did it surprise you?

3. Have you ever had the experience of seeking joy from some material possession or pursuit, only to find it did not bring you the joy you expected?

4. Have you ever, in times of trouble or turmoil, turn to the word of God for guidance? If so, what guidance did you receive?

5. Do you agree with the author that our society seems to be getting stupider? Are there any pet peeves you have about the direction in which society is heading? Do you think Jesus' words can help turn society around? Why or why not?

Chapter Twenty-Seven

DO YOU PLACE MUCH IMPORTANCE ON PRAYER?

In those days He departed to the mountain to pray,
and He spent the night in prayer to God.

I grew up in a praying family. I remember my father always kneeling at his bedside, praying before retiring for the night. I remember the night time mantra in my house as I was growing up: "Don't forget to say your prayers, don't forget to brush your teeth." My years with the Sisters of Christian Charity at St. Nick's grammar school reinforced in my mind the importance of prayer. In addition to the Our Father and the Hail Mary, I was happy to recite the prayer to my Guardian Angel: "Angel of God, my guardian dear, to whom God's love commits me here, ever this day be at my side to light and guard, to rule and guide. Amen." As I got a little older I developed a more conversational style of prayer, talking to God about things in addition to reciting the standard prayers. Even when, as a young adult, I stopped going to Mass on a regular basis, I continued to pray almost every night. In my thirties I became extremely fond of the Prayer of St. Francis and made it one of my staples. From time to time I let my prayer life slip, by giving it short shrift or ignoring it completely. When that happens, I find my life becomes a little uncentered. I also tend to feel guilty when I neglect to pray for the sick, and have been known, in my more insane moments, to blame myself when someone I had stopped praying for dies.

I suppose that now, as western society is becoming more secular, the number of people who pray on a regular basis is probably falling. This I think is an unfortunate development, both for people as individuals and for the world as a whole. Communing with God is important to our spiritual well-being. Even Jesus -- God incarnate -- found it necessary in His human life to pray. There are many instances in the Gospels of our Lord praying to the Father.

For example, in the Gospel of Matthew, we are told that after the feeding of the five thousand, Jesus "made the disciples get into the boat and precede Him to the other side, while He dismissed the crowds. After doing so, He went up on the mountain by Himself to pray." Similarly, when Jesus heard of the death of John the Baptist, He withdrew in a boat to a deserted place by himself.

In the Gospel of Mark, we are told, "Rising very early before dawn, He left and went off to a deserted place, where He prayed." And also, "In those days He departed to the mountain to pray, and He spent the night in prayer to God."

Of course we know that in the Garden of Gethsemane, before His arrest, Jesus prayed fervently: "My Father, if it is possible, let this cup pass from Me; yet, not as I will, but as you will. My Father, if it is not possible that this cup pass without My drinking it, Your will be done."

Jesus also prayed from the cross, saying, "Father, forgive them, they know not what they do."

So what is my point? Simply, if Jesus, Son of God, felt the need to pray when He was on the earth, think how much more we frail humans need to pray for help and guidance. But not only did Jesus show us by His example the importance of praying, He also provides some valuable lessons about *how* to pray.

As we have seen above, Jesus would frequently go off on His own to pray on a mountain or in a deserted place. Similarly, we read in Mark's Gospel that when the Apostles returned from their mission, they gathered together with

Jesus and reported all they had done and taught. Jesus said to them, "Come away by yourselves to a deserted place and rest a while." So we can glean from this that Jesus was a proponent of a meditative type of prayer, as well as prayerful retreats.

The Gospels also provide us approximately a dozen teachings from Jesus about the types of things we should pray for, or how we should pray. Here are two of them.

➢ When you pray, do not be like the hypocrites, who love to stand and pray in the synagogues and on street corners so that others may see them. Amen, I say to you, they have received their reward. But when you pray, go to your inner room, close the door, and pray to your Father in secret. And your Father who sees in secret will repay you.

➢ In praying, do not babble like the pagans, who think that they will be heard because of their many words. Do not be like them. Your Father knows what you need before you ask Him. This is how you are to pray: Our Father in heaven, hallowed be Your name, Your kingdom come, Your will be done, on earth as in heaven. Give us today our daily bread; and forgive us our debts as we forgive our debtors; and do not subject us to the final test, but deliver us from the evil one."

This of course is the passage from Matthew's Gospel relating Jesus giving us the Lord's Prayer, also known as the Our Father.

Another description of Jesus' instructions concerning prayer is found in the Gospel of Matthew and goes as follows: "Ask and it will be given to you; seek and you will find; knock and the door will be opened to you. For everyone who asks, receives; and the one who seeks, finds; and to the one who knocks, the door will be opened. Which one of you would hand his son a stone when he asks for a loaf of bread, or a snake when he asks for a fish? If you, then, who are wicked, know how to give good gifts to your children, how much more will your heavenly Father give good things to those who ask Him."

There is a variation on these instructions in Luke's Gospel, in which the ending of this prayer goes, "If you then, who are wicked, know how to give good gifts to your children, how much more will the Father in heaven give **the Holy Spirit** to those who ask Him?" Luke's ending, in my judgment, makes the prayer more sensible. It would seem likely, based on all His other teachings, that Jesus was speaking to His disciples about asking God for spiritual guidance and wisdom, not material goods and earthly success. Indeed, if we were to interpret the prayer to mean God will give us whatever we ask for in a worldly sense, then Christianity would have disappeared almost as soon as it began, as Jesus would have been immediately exposed as a fraud. Why? Because we don't get everything we pray for.

Along those same lines, I note that some of our atheist brethren are wont to use the Matthew version of this scene as proof there is no God, since we often ask the heavenly Father for good things that we don't get. The argument goes something like this: "Jesus said unambiguously that if you ask for something it will be given to you. But I asked for something and it wasn't given to me. That proves there is no God." But as I said, I believe what Jesus wants us to ask, seek, and knock for is spiritual guidance and wisdom.

What other advice does Jesus give us about praying? He tells us, "When you stand to pray, forgive anyone against whom you have a grievance, so that your heavenly Father may in turn forgive you your transgressions." He tells us, "Pray for those who mistreat you." He tells us, "The harvest is abundant but the laborers are few; so ask the Master of the harvest to send out laborers for His harvest." He tells us, "The hour is coming, and is now here, when true worshipers will worship the Father in spirit and truth; and indeed the Father seeks such people to worship Him. God is Spirit, and those who worship Him must worship in Spirit and truth."

Jesus also tells us we should be persistent in our prayers. He relates this story:

> Suppose one of you has a friend to whom he goes at midnight and says, "Friend, lend me three loaves of bread, for a friend of mine has arrived at my house from a journey and I have nothing to offer him," and he says in reply from within, "Do not bother me. The door is locked and my children and I are in bed. I cannot get up to give you anything." I tell you, if he does not get up to give him the loaves because of their friendship, he will get up to give him whatever he needs because of his persistence.

Despite Jesus' advice that we be persistent in our petitions to God, however, it is important that we also remember that Jesus recommends we be humble in our prayers. Consider what Jesus tells us about the Pharisee and the tax collector. "The Pharisee prayed, 'O God, I thank you that I am not like the rest of humanity ...' But the tax collector stood at a distance and would not even raise his eyes to heaven, but beat his breast and prayed, 'O God, be merciful to me, a sinner.' The latter went home justified, not the former; for everyone who exalts himself will be humbled, and everyone who humbles himself will be exalted."

Let me also mention Jesus' prayer on the night of the Last Supper, which encompasses all of Chapter 17 of John's Gospel. Here Jesus gives us a great example of the conversational style of prayer, in which He thanks the Father for His ministry and for His disciples, and prays for the salvation of the world. I have used parts of this prayer throughout the book, but it is worth reading in its entirety as a model for your own praying. Not that we would expect to match the Lord in the quality of our prayers, but, as they say, there's no harm in trying!

Most religious traditions suggest that we pray upon waking in the morning and when retiring at night time. Praying by making an examination of conscience during the course of the day is also a favored practice. We also pray when we gather as an assembly in Church on Sundays and other days.

At what other times should we pray? It is an old Hollywood cliché that one should say his prayers when he is about to be killed. Indeed, Elmer Fudd advised Bugs Bunny as much on many occasions: "Say your pwayers, wabbit!"

Jesus seems to agree that prayer at the hour of our death is a prudent thing. His exchange with the "good thief" [14] crucified to His right indicates as much. 'Jesus," said the thief, "remember me when You come into Your kingdom." "Amen, I say to you," Jesus replied, "today you will be with Me in paradise." Of course this is a heartening story of mercy and redemption, but let it also teach us that no one can console us like Jesus when it is our time to leave this earth. My wife, who is a doctor, has been with many patients while they were in the hospital suffering their final illness. Her experience has been that the spiritual and prayerful patient is far more likely to be at peace, and this peace also extends to the family of the dying.

Thus there are many lessons we can learn about prayer from Jesus. We can and should pray in private, but it is also

---

[14] I suppose it is debatable whether this thief was really good, but there are two things we know he was: repentant and believing, and for this he was rewarded.

good to pray as an assembly. We may pray through silent meditation or with words. When we pray in words, we should use meaningful words. Our prayers should be for spiritual rather than material blessings. We should not come to God in prayer when we are harboring resentments against other people. We should pray in a humble way, not in an arrogant or demanding way. We should pray when we are troubled, and we should pray for other people who are troubled. We should pray for our enemies, for a change in their lives for the better. We should pray often, and we should not give up if our prayers are not immediately answered.

Lastly but by no means leastly, we should pray for God's will to be done on earth. The Lord's Prayer doesn't say "thy kingdom come, *my* will be done", does it? In today's world there has never before been so *little* emphasis on prayer, yet there has never before been so *much* emphasis on getting what we want. The mind boggles that we want to cut God out of our lives and out of our society, yet we are baffled by the heartaches we suffer and the proliferation of evil in the world. DUH! Pray more and pray fervently. We are told that in the various Marian apparitions, the Blessed Mother advises us to pray for peace. Perhaps if more of us took that advice to heart, instead of cynically scoffing at it, peace would in fact have a chance.

QUESTIONS FOR REFLECTION OR DISCUSSION

1. What is your favorite quote from Jesus in Chapter Twenty-seven? Why?

2. Which of Jesus' quotes in Chapter Twenty-seven did you find most surprising? In what way did it surprise you?

3. Do you pray regularly? What do you find to be the most effective method of prayer for you?

4. Do you find that there are certain types of your prayers that are answered, and certain types that are not answered? Which of your prayers tend to be "successful"?

Chapter Twenty-Eight

WE ALL HAVE OUR LIVES TO LIVE; DO YOU REALLY EXPECT US TO WORRY ABOUT DOING GOD'S WILL?

Not everyone who says, 'Lord, Lord' will enter the kingdom of heaven, but only the one who does the will of My Father in heaven.

Do you ever feel overwhelmed by life? You probably do. I know I do. You have to earn a living and pay your bills. You have to take care of your children, if you have any – take them to school, pick them up from school, take them to practices and games, make sure their homework gets done, make sure they eat. You have to keep your spouse/significant other happy, if you have one. Maybe you have aging parents to worry about as well. And at some point you have to take care of yourself, too. So yeah, it can be overwhelming at times. Can we really be expected to make the time to seek and do God's will? With so much else on our plates, you must be kidding, right?

I think the question of seeking and doing God's will brings us face to face with the basic existential question: why are we here? What is the meaning of life? It is a question that can shake us to our very foundation if we choose to think about it. I don't think too many people want to think about it, because it can lead to an existential crisis. If you believe in God, then the most basic response to why we are here can be found in the old Baltimore Catechism: <u>to know, love, and serve God in this world so that we can be happy with Him in the next</u>. If you don't believe in God, then I'm not sure what the answer is. I suppose it would depend on your philosophy.

If you were a social humanist, you would probably say the answer is to do the most good for the most people, leave the world a better place, things like that. But why? If there is no God, then what difference would it make? To make you feel better about yourself? So that people will say you were a capital fellow?

If you were a hedonist, you would probably say the answer is to have as much fun and get as much pleasure out of life as you can. But that seems pretty shallow and selfish. Yet at the same time, if there is no God, what difference does it make? You might as well make yourself happy, right?

Some non-believers may use this line of reasoning to argue that they are better than I am. They do things for their fellow man or for the environment because they are enlightened individuals; I only do good things because I think some spirit in the sky wants me to. But in my view it's really the same thing. We are both enlightened by the revealed word of God; they simply don't acknowledge that God is the author of this philosophy. Perhaps they are unwilling or unable to subscribe to a worldview in which there is something bigger than man.

But for the theists out there, let's circle back to knowing, loving, and serving God in this world so that we can be happy with Him in the next. If we believe that there is a God in the Christian sense, a God who desires a personal relationship with His people, then the Catechism answer is probably a pretty accurate statement as to why we are here. And if that is the case, then seeking and doing God's will would have to be pretty high up on our "Things to Do" list. Because God won't really be impressed by the cost of your house, or the size of your portfolio, or the fanciness of your car, or whether your kids are star athletes or get into the best schools. He certainly won't be impressed by how many people you have slept with. (He might however be disgusted.) Because in God's eyes this is all vanity. This is why I say if we really ask ourselves what is the meaning of life, it can shake us to our very foundation. Would we come to realize, as Mr. Cosmo Castorini did in the movie "Moonstruck", that our lives are pretty meaningless?

You may recall that Mr. Castorini was a successful plumber in Brooklyn, and he had a lot of money (even if he didn't like to spend it). But Mr. Castorini, when revealed to be a philandering husband, offered up this reason for his sinful ways: "A man understands one day that his life is built on nothing." Luckily for Mr. Castorini he had a God-fearing wife who loved him.

We don't want our lives to be built on nothing. So what about doing God's will? If God has created this world and given us life, it stands to reason that seeking and doing His will should be the guiding principle of said life. Then we will know our lives have meaning and are not built on nothing. Listen to what Jesus says, and then ask yourself if you should find time in your busy life to do God's will.

We can start with the underlying premise of this book, which is that I would like everyone to get to heaven. Jesus tells us, "Not everyone who says, 'Lord, Lord' will enter the kingdom of heaven, but only the one who does the will of My Father in heaven." That is a fairly direct and unambiguous invitation to do God's will. Unless of course you don't want to go to heaven.

Jesus Himself came to earth on a mission to do God's will, as He said on numerous occasions. Jesus said, "My food is to do the will of the one who sent Me and to finish His work," and also, "I came down from heaven not to do My own will but to do the will of the One who sent Me." Jesus went so far as to be nailed to a cross as a sacrifice for our sins in carrying out God's will. Jesus prayed in the Garden of Gethsemane, on the night we now know as Holy Thursday, "My Father, if it is possible, let this cup pass from Me; yet, not as I will, but as You will. My father, if it is not possible that this cup pass without My drinking it, Your will be done."

Okay, let me assume for the moment that we want to do God's will and book our passage to heaven. This gives rise to a question: How do we discern God's will? The answer is, we discern God's will from the scriptures and from the counsel Jesus gives us. As you read what Jesus says, I hope you will discover that what God asks of us is not really all that difficult, provided we approach it with this thought in mind: it's not all about us.

If we wish to discern God's will, we can start with those things called the Commandments. Remember, Jesus says, "[W]hoever obeys and teaches these commandments will be called greatest in the kingdom of heaven." Obey and teach the commandments. Check. What else do we know of God's will? Jesus tells us, "[T]his is the will of My Father, that everyone who sees the Son and believes in Him may have eternal life, and I shall raise him on the last day." So it is God's will that we all get to heaven. Indeed, Jesus reiterates this in the parable of the lost sheep:

> If a man has a hundred sheep and one of them goes astray, will he not leave the 99 in the hills and go in search of the stray? And if he finds it, amen I say to you, he rejoices more over it than over the 99 who did not stray. In just the same way, it is not the will of your heavenly Father that one of these little ones be lost.

Thus we can say it is God's will that we all obey and teach the commandments, and it is God's will that we all join Him in heaven, which is like saying the same thing twice, since obeying and teaching the commandments will get us to heaven. What else can we learn from Jesus regarding God's will? We can learn how He would have us live in relation to one another, which has two components.

The first component is how we treat our fellow man. For example, as Jesus tells us, "[L]ove your enemies, do good to those who hate you, bless those who curse you, pray for those who mistreat you. To the person who strikes you on one cheek, offer the other as well. From the person who takes your cloak, do not withhold even your tunic. Give to everyone who asks of you, and from the one who takes what is yours do not demand it back. Do unto others as you would have them do to you." How many of us can honestly say we abide by that teaching? Jesus wants us to suppress the desire to fight back or get revenge against people who have hurt us. It requires that we humble ourselves and swallow our pride. It requires that we make loving others more than just a nice notion to be applied among friends. Jesus also gives us specific directions as to people who are less fortunate than we are: Give food to the hungry, give drink to the thirsty, welcome the stranger, clothe the naked, care for the sick, and visit the imprisoned.

But Jesus also lets us know that we should have our hearts in the right place when we are showing our love for our fellow man. "Take care not to perform righteous deeds in order that people may see them," Jesus says, "otherwise, you will have no recompense from your heavenly Father. ... when you give alms, do not let your left hand know what your right is doing, so that your almsgiving may be secret. And your Father who sees in secret will repay you." Here again Jesus urges that we be humble, not boastful, and that our concern for others be genuine, rather than a means to bring the attention back upon ourselves. In true Christianity this is nothing less than our job. In one of my personal favorite Gospel verses, Jesus says, "When you have done all that you have been commanded, say, 'We are unprofitable servants; we have done what we were obliged to do.' " We don't pat ourselves on the back, we don't take any bows. We serve others and move along.

The other component of God's will for our lives in relation to others is sharing our faith in order to (oh no, not again) bring our brothers and sisters to heaven. This is a true test of love – do we want our brethren (and sistren?) to join us in paradise? I realize talking about our faith and trying to spread our faith is an unpopular pastime. Let's talk about our friend Tim Tebow again. Some people maintain that Tim was hated by the media and blacklisted from the NFL because he is a Christian. This, however, is not the case, as

NFL rosters are loaded with Christians. The problem people had with Tim was not that he is a Christian, but that (a) being Christian is the main thing in his life, (b) he wants to talk about being Christian, and (c) he is sincere about it.

In other words, society is willing to tolerate Christianity, as long as it stays in Church, where it belongs. Except that's not the only place it belongs, because Jesus wants us to save (or try to save) everybody, including the "haters" who don't want to hear it. So we must strive to be, as Jesus tells us, "the light of the world, a city set on a mountain [that] cannot be hidden." This is why our behavior as Christians is so important. If we respond to hate with hate, our faith is not alive, it is just words. In all things we must act as Jesus would have us act. "Your light must shine before others," says Jesus, "that they may see your good deeds and glorify your heavenly Father." It is by rising above the fray and holding to our convictions in the face of challenges and persecutions that we can change the world. "Peace be with you," says Jesus. " As the father has sent me, so I send you."

Here are some other pointers Jesus would have us keep in mind in our quest to seek and do God's will. Apologies if you've heard some of them before:

- ➤ "No one can serve two masters. He will either hate one and love the other, or be devoted to one and despise the other. You cannot serve God and mammon."

- ➤ "Whoever loves father or mother more than Me is not worthy of Me, and whoever loves son or daughter more than Me is not worthy of Me."
- ➤ "Whoever wishes to come after Me must deny himself, take up his cross, and follow Me. For whoever wishes to save his life will lose it, but whoever loses his life for My sake will find it."

These are difficult teachings, especially for those who are involved in raising a family. You gotta love your kids, you gotta put food on the table. Of course Jesus realizes this, but the lesson is that our worldly attachments must not stand in the way of our obligation to God. Remember how I mentioned about the existential crisis shaking us to our foundation? If God created the world, and if God gave us life, then whatever we have we owe to Him. Consequently, we should use what we have in His service, rather than letting it be a barrier that comes *between* us and Him. This means placing spiritual things above worldly things, and sacrificing what we want for ourselves in favor of what God wants from us.

Remember the parable of the Good Samaritan. The person who went out of his way, inconvenienced himself, and sacrificed his time, energy, and money for the stranger in need was the "hero" of the story. I think we all recognize Good Sam as a hero, I think we all see him as someone to emulate. But I don't think we would all make that same heroic sacrifice if it was placed before us. It's a lot of trouble, man; I got things to do.

We should also learn from this lesson that Jesus gave his Apostles at the Last Supper. Jesus took a towel and tied it around his waist. Then He poured water into a basin and began to wash the disciples' feet and dry them with the towel around His waist. Afterward He said to them, "If I therefore, the master and teacher, have washed your feet, you ought to wash one another's feet. I have given you a model to follow, so that as I have done for you, you should also do." In other words, it is God's will that we serve others.

With a nod to the secular humanists who will say "see, we told you so", there are certain rewards that come with finding and doing God's will. Listen again to what Jesus says: "Everyone who listens to these words of Mine and acts on them will be like a wise man who built his house on rock. The rain fell, the floods came, and the winds blew and buffeted the house. But it did not collapse; it had been set solidly on rock." Jesus also tells us, "Whoever does the will of My heavenly Father is My brother, and sister, and mother," and also, "You are My friends if you do what I command you." Presumably, we are all longing to be Jesus' friends, to be considered part of His family, and to share His eternal joy.

The day that Mr. Castorini understood that his life was built on nothing was "a bad, crazy day." Let's try to avoid having our judgment day be a bad, crazy day. We don't want to hear these words: "Mr. Jones, I would like to bring you into My kingdom to share eternity with Me. However, in reviewing your history, it appears that your life was built on nothing. I'm not sure I can justify bringing you in with all these good people, who built their lives on doing My will."

So keep in mind that despite our busy lives, we are still called to prioritize doing God's will. We can sum up our Christian mandate to our fellow man with this quote from our Teacher: "This is how all will know you are My disciples, if you have love for one another."

QUESTIONS FOR REFLECTION OR DISCUSSION

1. What is your favorite quote from Jesus in Chapter Twenty-eight? Why?

2. Which of Jesus' quotes in Chapter Twenty-eight did you find most surprising? In what way did it surprise you?

3. Have you ever spent time quietly contemplating God's will for your life? If so, can you describe the experience?

4. What do you think is God' will for your life? How did you come to that conclusion?

5. Has your concept of God's will changed over the course of your life? How so?

6. How many people whom you know personally would you say make a sincere effort to prioritize doing God's will? Are there any other traits you would say these people share with each other?

Chapter Twenty-Nine

WHAT WOULD YOU SAY IS THE BIGGEST MISTAKE PEOPLE MAKE AS THEY GO ABOUT LIVING THEIR LIVES?

"Get behind me, Satan. You are an obstacle to Me.
You are thinking not as God does, but as men do."

One of the basic tenets of Christian living is that Christians are to be *in* the world, but not *of* the world. Essentially this is an acknowledgment that our spiritual life is more important than our material life, and that our primary allegiance should be to the things of God rather than the things of man.

The earth has been the scene of a struggle between good and evil since we were first expelled from the Garden of Eden. The seeds of corruption have been sown by Satan, and, sadly, man, given his human frailty, has often been prone to falling into evil. We look around us and see the disastrous effects of our sinfulness – anger, violence, greed, covetousness, pride, self-absorption, lust, promiscuity. Warfare, terrorism, man's inhumanity to man, murder, theft, pornography, adultery, abortion, broken families, lost souls. Ultimately it all comes back to our inability, or unwillingness, either as individuals or as a group, to avoid the trap of sin. Why do we sin? Because we want something – money, power, possessions, people, control, sex, freedom without responsibility – that we do not have, and to which we are not entitled.

Christians are as prone to sin as anyone else, because they are human. Being human, they are susceptible to falling under the spell of worldliness. The new car, the bigger house, the younger lover, the fatter wallet, the footloose and fancy-free lifestyle, all the trappings/traps that a true Christian shouldn't be concerned about. We shouldn't be concerned about them, but we become concerned about them because we are human. When we start coveting the things of this world, we lose our way; we forget the true Way.

Jesus tells us, "Do not store up for yourselves treasures on earth, where moth and decay destroy, and thieves break in and steal. But store up treasures in heaven, where neither moth nor decay destroy, nor thieves break in and steal. For where your treasure is, there also will your heart be." Jesus knows what he is talking about. When we start focusing on and caring about material things, we find ourselves being led into sin.

There are so many things that Jesus says to us that we fail to understand, or choose not to understand, as they relate to our daily lives. Jesus tells us that we cannot serve God and mammon, and that we should not worry about our material needs. We should instead "seek first the kingdom of God and His righteousness, and all these things will be given to you besides." Yet we continue to chase wealth and possessions because that is the way of the world, as if any of that can bring us happiness or peace.

God does not want us to be consumed with riches, luxuries, and a life of ease. Rather, he desires that we serve Him by serving others. This can be challenging and difficult at times, but Jesus tells us, "[W]hoever does not take up his cross and follow after Me is not worthy of Me. Whoever finds his life will lose it, and whoever loses his life for My sake will find it." The true Christian life is not about us, and it is not about our things. Consider again the parable of the sower, and the seed that fell among the thorns and was choked. Jesus explains that the seed sown among the thorns represents "the one who hears the word, but then worldly anxiety and the lure of riches choke the word and it bears no fruit." Is this the 21st century American Christian? Will we fall victim to the rampant consumerism that afflicts our society, and measures us by how well we keep up with the Joneses?

Speaking of the Joneses, remember poor departed Mr. Jones from the last chapter – will our lives be built on nothing?

You may have noticed that I have a bad habit of droning on about the trappings of the accumulation of wealth. This is probably because my family had little, and also because I noticed, as I got older, that there are many wealthy people who are miserable and miserly. Let me clarify, however, that wealth in and of itself is not the problem, as I have stated before. Rather, the problem arises when there is a disproportionate desire to acquire wealth and make it the end-all and be-all of life, and a failure to use wealth charitably. There are very many people who use their wealth in altruistic, God-centered ways. **Those of us with limited resources owe a tremendous debt of gratitude to the well-to-do who**

generously share their wealth with the world, in service to the less fortunate. That point cannot be overstated.

If we as Christians want to leave a mark on society, we must keep in mind our priorities. Jesus says, "You shall love the Lord, your God, with all your heart, and with all your being, with all your strength, and with all your mind, and your neighbor as yourself. Do this and you will live." This is our mandate.

The problem, then, is not material things per se, but rather a worldly way of looking at life. Peter the Apostle, the rock upon whom Jesus chose to build His Church, learned this lesson in a rather mortifying way. We read in the Gospel of Matthew that when Jesus began to inform His disciples that He had go to Jerusalem, where He would suffer greatly and be killed, Peter took Him aside and began to rebuke Him. I always get a little jolt when I read that passage. Peter rebuking Jesus? Some Galilean chutzpah. "God forbid, Lord," says the Rock of the Church. "No such thing shall ever happen to You." But there is an old saying, He who rebukes last rebukes best. Jesus turned and said to Peter, "Get behind me, Satan.

You are an obstacle to Me. You are thinking not as God does, but as men do." Ouch!

For my money, that re-rebuke by Jesus is one of the most important and most overlooked lessons in the Gospels, nay, in the history of religion. <u>If only we could learn and remember to think as God thinks</u>, how much better our world would be. We could free ourselves of all the mundane nonsense that clutters our minds and disturbs our peace. We would realize living our lives for God is the way to lasting peace and happiness. So why is this lesson, so important according to me, so overlooked? Because it's also darned inconvenient. I don't want to think as God does, I have to get my nails done. Or, as George Bailey says to Mary Hatch in one of the more painful scenes from "It's a Wonderful Life", "I wanna do what *I* wanna do!" But if George *had* done what **he** wanted to do, they wouldn't have made a movie about him!

Those of you who are old enough to remember the legendary Chicago Bears halfback Gale Sayers may recall the quote that was the underpinning of his autobiography: "The Lord is first, my friends are second, and I am third." [15] I can't help feeling that for too many people in the world today the mantra is "I am first and the hell with the rest of you." But Mr. Sayers' quote accurately reflects our Christian heritage, that God is supposed to come first, and concomitant therewith service of our neighbors. Thus Jesus says, "Many who are first will be last, and the last will be first." If we put ourselves first, we curry no favor with the Lord.

We owe our religion in large part to early Christian martyrs, who gave their lives under Roman persecution rather than disavow all knowledge of the Lord. We don't like to notice or admit it in modern America, but devout Christians continue to be martyred this very day for proclaiming, or refusing to renounce, their faith. It goes without saying that martyrs put God ahead of themselves. Would we? Hell, we'd renounce our faith to keep our big-screen TVs, let alone our lives!

---

[15] Old fogeys like me will recall bawling our eyes out watching the ABC TV-movie "Brian's Song," starring James Caan as Brian Piccolo and Billy Dee Williams as Sayers. Both great college backs, they wound up together on the Bears' roster, where Sayers became the superstar and Piccolo the afterthought. But they became roommates, and despite being of different races they developed a remarkable friendship, still a fairly unusual thing in 1965. Their friendship endured and grew through Sayers' career-threatening knee injury and Piccolo's battle with, and death from, cancer.

Where else will God-like thinking help us in our daily struggles? One area is being on the go 24 hours a day, seven days a week. As we all know by now, the technology that was supposed to make our lives easier has instead enslaved us. Thanks to our computers, smartphones, and Internet connections, we no longer have to be at our places of work to do work. So our bosses (or ourselves if we are our own bosses) generously let us work from home as well. Every day. At all hours. This is sick. Even God rested on the seventh day. Bringing me to another humdinger from Jesus: "The Sabbath was made for man, not man for the Sabbath." We tend to see Sunday as just another obligation. "Oh, it's Sunday. We have to go to Church. But I have so much else to do! I'll have to skip Church." Hah! God's idea is more like this: "It's Sunday. Please come to Church to say hello to Me and My other friends. Then go home and take the rest of the day off." In essence, our Sabbath should be a respite from working, doing chores, going shopping, attending our children's sporting events, and the various other things that exhaust us. We need that respite. But instead of tipping our hats and saying, "Thank you, Lord," we go about doing all the same "stuff" we do the other six days. We make ourselves worn down and bitchy.

I'm also going to take this opportunity to acknowledge once again my dear friend Mary. You remember Mary, right? She's the one who sat beside the Lord at His feet, listening to Him speak. Mary had a sister named Martha, who wanted Jesus to tell Mary to help Martha do the serving. And Jesus said, "By golly, you're right, Martha. Who does that lazy ne'er-do-well sister of yours think she is, listening to what **GOD** has to say about stuff, instead of setting the table for YOU." No, actually, that's not what Jesus said. What Jesus really said was, "Martha Martha, you are anxious and worried about many things. There is need of only one thing. Mary has chosen the better part, and it will not be taken from her." That's what Jesus said (or the Aramaic equivalent thereof). Listening yet, people?

Here are some of Jesus' statements as recorded in John's Gospel, to shed a bit more light on the "God's thinking versus Peter's thinking" quandary:

> "The one who is of the earth is earthly and speaks of earthly things. But the one who comes from heaven is above all. He testifies to what He has seen and heard

… the One whom God sent speaks the words of God."

"Do not work for food that perishes but for the food that endures for eternal life, which the Son of Man will give you."

"It is the Spirit that gives life, while the flesh is of no avail. The words I have spoken to you are Spirit and life."

"Whoever loves his life loses it, and whoever hates his life in this world will preserve it for eternal life."

"In the world you will have trouble, but take courage, I have conquered the world."

Thinking as God does versus thinking as man does. It is a question of focus. Is our focus *here*, on our earthly dwelling, or on heaven, our (hopefully) forever home? Jesus wants us to know that we are here on earth temporarily, usually for somewhere between 0 and 110 years. Where we will be for eternity should be somewhat more important than what happens to us for the relatively insignificant span of time we are here. I realize it is hard to look at it that way while we are "down here", but from a strictly mathematical perspective, infinity trumps 100 +/- years, for sure.

Here is an interesting and I would say somewhat esoteric passage from Luke's Gospel that I will discuss further in the next chapter, but that puts an interesting spin on the "here versus there" view of life.

> At that time some people who were present there told Him about Galileans whose blood Pilate had mingled with the blood of their sacrifices. He said to them in reply, "Do you think that because these Galileans suffered in this way that they were greater sinners than all other Galileans? By no means! But I tell you, if you do not repent you will all perish as they did! Or the eighteen people who were killed when the tower at Siloam fell on them – do you think they were more guilty than everyone else who lived in Jerusalem? By no means! But I tell you, if you do not repent, you will all perish as they did!"

What is fascinating to me about this passage is that Jesus poses the question in terms of why did these things happen to these people, but rather than answering the question he posed, he turns the question on its head. He basically tells us it doesn't make any difference why these things happened – why Pilates' soldiers killed these particular Galileans, or why a building fell on these particular people. Instead, what matters is that we repent so that when we *do* die, as we all will, we will not perish. Because at the end of the day, the cause of our death here on earth is much less important than how we lived our lives while we were here.

So in short, the biggest mistake we make in our lives, in Jesus' view, is that we place our focus on the world. We think about worldly things, we pursue worldly treasure, we crave worldly goods, we seek worldly esteem. We should turn our focus to God, and think instead about what *He* wants from us, and for us. Pursue *spiritual* treasure, and seek *God's* esteem. As Jesus laments, "You justify yourselves in the eyes of others, but God knows your hearts; for what is of human esteem is an abomination in the sight of God." We must repent, then, and redirect our focus.

QUESTIONS FOR REFLECTION OR DISCUSSION

1. What is your favorite quote from Jesus in Chapter Twenty-nine? Why?

2. Which of Jesus' quotes in Chapter Twenty-nine did you find most surprising? In what way did it surprise you?

3. When you confront situations in your life, do you ever try to think about them as God would? Do you think it would be helpful to do so?

4. What did Gale Sayers mean when he said that he was third? On the Sayers' scale, where would you say you are? And where is God?

5. What would you consider the biggest obstacles to you keeping God number one?

Chapter Thirty

SO, WHAT ABOUT THOSE BAD THINGS THAT HAPPEN TO GOOD PEOPLE?

"Your heavenly Father ... makes His sun rise on the bad and the good, and causes rain to fall on the just and the unjust."

Bad things happen to good people. They do. There is no denying it. I suspect that this simple, unavoidable fact of life is responsible for a great number of people falling away from the Church and questioning their belief in God. For the Church teaches that God is all-knowing, all-seeing, all-powerful, and all-loving. If that is so, why should anything bad ever happen to people who are good? I suppose we could take the question a step further, and ask: if God is *really* all-loving, why should bad things happen **at all**, even to *bad* people? After all, God does love bad people too. Hates the sin, loves the sinner.

The conundrum of bad things happening to good people is the subject of an excellent book by Rabbi Harold Kushner entitled, appropriately enough, "When Bad Things Happen to Good People". I suggest you read it, if you haven't already.

Nevertheless, because of the strong influence this topic can have on apostasy, I do want to cover it here and see if Jesus can shed some further light on it for us. It is a daunting and exhilarating task to take on such a troubling issue. Because, in the final analysis, we are not only examining why good people suffer, but also whether the fact that good people suffer somehow proves that there is no God.

If you, like me, spend any time reading through the comments at online news sites, you will understand why this is an issue. For invariably, when some tragedy occurs, a commenter will post a statement to the effect of "prayers go out to the victims and their families." Then, a responding commenter, most likely a "troll" on the lookout for just such comments, will post something to the effect of "where was your God when this happened?" Because in some people's minds, God is the intergalactic policeman, fireman, security guard, crossing guard, traffic cop, and emergency medical tech. Or, to say that more accurately, in some people's minds, God **should be** the intergalactic policeman, fireman, security guard, crossing guard, traffic cop, and emergency medical tech. The fact that God is not these things proves to them that God does not exist. Stated conversely, some people feel that if there were a God, nothing bad would ever happen.

It is interesting that such a theory can gain any traction in the minds of thinking individuals, for it is a truly bizarre theory. Nevertheless, bizarre though it may be, it is a theory that holds sway with many non-believers. A corollary theory to which many seem to subscribe is that if human beings do anything evil, this also proves God doesn't exist. I have a friend from my high school days who professes to be an atheist. He was raised Catholic, but became an agnostic while in college (at a Catholic institution, naturally). He claims to have made the "conversion" from agnostic to full-fledged atheist after 9-11; that is, September 11, 2001, when the terrorist attacks by al Qaeda took down the Twin Towers and killed nearly 3,000 people.

I don't mean to be dense, but I do not understand how an event like 9-11 can make someone an atheist.   I am starting from a position with which, I think, everybody would agree, which is that there is evil in the world. I also assume virtually everybody, no matter how nostalgic, would agree that evil in the world is nothing new. If you have no more than a rudimentary knowledge of the Old Testament, you know that Adam and Eve were tempted to sin and, as a result of their disobedience to God, were expelled from the Garden of Eden. You may choose to accept the story of Adam and Eve as fact or as merely a mythological story of man's fall, but either way the result is the same. Man disobeyed God and brought evil and death into the world. There has been a battle between good and evil ever since. Evil has often prevailed, to the detriment of the good and innocent.

Consider some other Biblical stories as they relate to good and evil. Cain killed his brother Abel, who was favored by God. God sent a flood to destroy almost all of creation because men preferred evil to good. God destroyed the cities of Sodom and Gomorrah for their evil doings. God's own chosen king, David, sent a loyal soldier to certain death because David had decided to take the soldier's wife to be his own. An unquestionably evil act. The New Testament tells of John the Baptist, imprisoned and beheaded by King Herod. John's crime? Speaking the truth.

Then there is Jesus Himself, arrested, tried, condemned, and crucified for trying to spread the Word of God, and for doing loving acts of healing and forgiveness. The Son of

God, the Son of Man, the Word made flesh, the second person of the Holy Trinity, however you choose to refer to Him, **allowed Himself** to be put to death by evil men.

If at some point you believed in God, you believed in Him despite knowledge of all the evil things that had happened throughout history, including evil things that happened to very holy people. Is it at all reasonable or logical, therefore, to be persuaded that God does not exist because of a murderous plan carried out by evil men? I say, you can only come to this conclusion if this is the conclusion to which you *want* to come.

Indeed, we only have to go back 70 years in world history to consider other, greater deeds of evil carried out by men. The killing of 6,000,000 Jews and other "undesirables" under Hitler's Third Reich in Germany, the killing of a similar number under Stalin's regime in Russia, and various instances of genocide or "ethnic cleansing" in more recent times. If one could believe in God despite all this evil and atrocity, how then do the events of 9-11 push one over the edge to atheism? Is it because 9-11 happened to Americans? In New York City? That's just East Coast arrogance. Or is it because the evil individuals who perpetrated the acts did so in the name of God?

I'm sorry, but the fact that evil individuals use a perversion of God's message as a justification to kill does not prove God does not exist. God tells us how to live. Some people don't follow what He tells us. That doesn't mean God doesn't exist. It's like saying if I teach my son the rules of safe driving, but he doesn't obey the rules of safe driving and someone gets killed, that proves I don't exist. It's nonsense. The fact that my son contends he was driving the way I wanted him to drive doesn't change the outcome. I still exist; he is either a liar or delusional. Similarly, 9-11 does not prove God doesn't exist, it only proves that the perpetrators either lied about their motivation or had been deluded as to what God wanted of them. Many in our world are deluded in this regard, and at the heart of the delusion is hatred, not the non-existence of God.

Throughout history, many evils have been carried on by men in God's name. This, however, is because there are evil men, not because God does not exist.

But I have not addressed the underlying problem of bad things happening to good people. Why do bad things happen to good people? I discussed this issue with a good friend of mine, Eileen Barroso, our local youth group leader, and she gave me a simple yet profound response: bad things happen to good people because bad things happen.

What exactly does that mean? First off, we are mortal human beings, that is our lot in life. We will all die. Therefore, if you consider dying a bad thing, then I'm afraid it is existentially unavoidable that bad things happen to good people. You may or may not choose to believe we became mortal because of the sin of Adam and Eve, but, either way, the reality is that human beings are not indestructible and immortal.

The second thing is, we humans are given free will, along with the ability to understand that our choices have consequences. Even though I am a good person, if I put a loaded gun to my head and pull the trigger I am probably going to die. Maybe the gun will misfire and I will be spared, but is it reasonable for me to expect God to come down from heaven and block the bullet from penetrating my head? No, it isn't. Does that mean God doesn't exist? No, it doesn't. I like lemon meringue pie. I especially like lemon meringue pie from Greek diners, where the meringue is extra-sugary and impossibly high. If I go to a diner once in a while for a slice of lemon meringue pie, it is a fairly innocuous treat. Like many things we enjoy, when done in moderation it is not harmful. But if I have two slices of lemon meringue pie every day at lunch and two more slices every day at dinner, pretty soon I am going to pack on a bunch of pounds, raise my cholesterol to an unhealthy level, develop diabetes, and become a medical timebomb. Is it reasonable for me to expect God to say, "John is a good guy, so he can eat all the lemon meringue pie he wants and never gain weight and never have any health consequences"? No, it isn't. Does that mean God doesn't exist? No, it doesn't. I choose to exercise my free will. I am not immune from the consequences of my choices.

Bad things happen to good people for the simple reason that God does not suspend the laws of nature for good people. I suppose one could argue that maybe He should, since that would inspire more people to be good. But then we would again come up against the issue of free will. If God were to bribe us to be good, could we honestly take credit for being good? And if we chose to do good in order to get an *earthly* reward, would our goodness still merit an eternal reward too? Hmm. It's complicated, isn't it? I think the system works better if we do good because God asks us to, not because He bribes us to. I think the Old Testament Book of Job, one of the earliest treatments of bad things happening to good people, shows that God agrees. [16]

I admit that life would be a lot easier for me if *I* were permitted to have free will, but everyone else had to do what they were told. Unfortunately, that's not life. God gave *all of us* free will. This means we not only have to deal with the consequences of our own bad decisions, we also have to deal with the consequences of other people's decisions; including, unfortunately, irresponsible people, stupid people, and evil people. If a person gets behind the wheel of a car while drunk; or if a sober person behind the wheel of a car decides to send text messages, or tweet, or post something to Facebook while driving; and if said irresponsible driver crosses the double yellow lines and is going to crash head-on into a car being driven by a good person, is it reasonable to expect God to come down and push the good person's car out of the way? No, it isn't. Does that mean God doesn't exist? No, it doesn't.

---

[16] If you have not read the Book of Job, do so some time.

Some people will use the fact that there are starving children in the world to argue that God doesn't exist. "Why would your God create a world where children are starving?" Since they don't believe in God, they cannot get angry at Him for this, so instead they get angry at people who believe in God. As if it's our fault for believing in a God who would let people starve. Either way, however, the anger is misplaced. God did not create a world with starving children in it; rather, starving children in the world are a by-product of man's selfishness and distorted priorities. Starving children do not prove there is no God. Our world produces more than enough food to feed everybody in it. Sadly, the more accurate question is not, why does *God* let children starve, but rather, why do *people* let children starve. People and nations possess the resources to get food to all the starving children. They choose not to. This does not mean there is no God. It means people fail the test.

We have no choice but to accept the fact that we live in an imperfect world because we are imperfect beings. Sometimes bad things happen to us and others because of our imperfections. Life is **not** just a bowl of cherries. Which leads me to a story.

Some people say we can learn a lot from our mistakes. Well, I have heard innumerable homilies in my life, innumerable really good homilies, too. But most of them, even the really good ones, are long forgotten. Nevertheless, I can tell you about a homily I heard some 44 years ago, and the reason I can remember it is because it relates to a mistake I made.

I was at Sunday Mass with my brother Chris at St. Nicholas Church in Jersey City. I was about 11 years old. The Mass was being said by a young priest named Father Nicholas DiMarzio, who later went on to become Bishop of the Diocese of Brooklyn. (That's in New York, son.) Anyway, Fr. DiMarzio began his homily by saying something like, "There's a song that's been playing a lot on the radio lately …." And I was so smart and clever, in a nano-second I just *knew* Father was going to use his homily to go off on the song "Jesus Christ, Superstar", from the rock musical of the same name, which was big at the time. But I was WRONG!! Father DiMarzio spoke to us about Lynn Anderson's hit song "Rose Garden" (which was written by Joe South). Father mentioned the lyrics "I never promised you a rose garden; along with the sunshine, there's gotta be a little rain sometime."

Forty-four years later, that homily still resonates with me. Because it's true. God never *did* promise us a rose garden. Quite the contrary; Jesus tells us, "Blessed are the poor in spirit, for theirs is the kingdom of heaven. ...Blessed are they who mourn, for they shall be comforted...Blessed are they who are persecuted for the sake of righteousness, for theirs is the kingdom of heaven. Blessed are you when they insult you and persecute you and utter every kind of evil against you because of me. Rejoice and be glad, for great will be your reward in heaven. Thus they persecuted the prophets who were before you."

Did I mention that St. John the Baptist was beheaded by King Herod? Jesus told the people that among those born of women, none was greater than John. So, did God come down to stop the blade from killing John? No. And when Jesus heard of John's execution, did He call down armies of angels to crush Herod's kingdom? No, He withdrew in a boat to a deserted place by Himself. I think I might have mentioned that Jesus was also executed, crucified by the Romans at the behest of the Jewish leaders. And most of those who were closest to Jesus, and many others who were His disciples in the early years of Christianity, also suffered persecution and martyrdom. So where do we get off thinking nothing bad should ever happen to people just because they are good? And if something bad *does* happen, to us or to a loved one, or to the world at large, then that proves there is no God? I think perhaps this is Me-generation madness.

What, then, would life have to be like in order to prove God's existence to these doubters? Everyone would have to be happy all the time? Everyone would have to get exactly what they want? In Frank Capra's 1937 movie "Lost Horizon", based on the novel of the same name by James Hilton, Ronald Colman's character learns that in Shangri-La, he can have Jane Wyatt just because he is attracted to her. She becomes his, just like that! And if she is presently with another man, that man simply has to relinquish her. That's utopia for ya.

Well, it may work like that in the movies and in Shangri-La, but I'm not so sure it would work so well in real life. You're telling me if someone wants my wife he is permitted to have her, and I'm supposed to be o.k. with that? (It's probably an ideal situation if you're Henny Youngman.) And does my wife have any say in this? Suppose she doesn't want either one of us? But let me get back on track.

So we were saying if God existed, nobody would ever get injured or sick. Planes would never crash, nobody would ever get murdered, there would be no wars, no terrorism, no hunger. Everyone would die peacefully in their sleep, but not until all their family members and friends wee perfectly ready to accept their passing. Is this the safe, harmonious world that would prove God's existence? Presumably we would still have our free will – we don't want a society of automatons, right? -- but everything would turn out perfect no matter how irresponsibly or stupidly we behaved. Sounds great. Not feasible, but great nonetheless.

I want to talk about an episode of the classic 1960s television show "The Twilight Zone" entitled "A Nice Place to Visit." In that episode, Larry Blyden played a small-time criminal who seemed to have ended up on the wrong side of a shootout with the police, but then awoke in a glitzy hotel. The plot of the story was reprised by a superb songwriter, Elliott Murphy, in his song "Sacrifice", so I will let Elliott tell you the rest:

On TV was a petty thief shot by the police,
He came to in Las Vegas in a penthouse suite.
He had a magic butler, gave him all that he desired,
A feast of wine and women 'til his passions were expired.
He couldn't understand how a crook like him
Had died and gone to heaven when his life was full of sin,
And when he shot pool and every ball quickly fell
He saw his butler was the devil
And the penthouse was in hell.[17]

The point of the Twilight Zone episode is, when you get everything you want without working for it, without any challenge, without any struggle, it can feel more like hell than like heaven. The point of Elliott's song is that life is full of ups and downs, and that in order to enjoy the ups we have to make, and endure, some sacrifices. Otherwise it's all rather POINTLESS. And my point, echoing Father DiMarzio's, is that God never promised us a rose garden, and if we think everything has to be perfect in order to accept that God exists, we are truly delusional (not to mention oblivious to the lessons of the Gospels).

I suppose one could put forth this counter-argument: everything doesn't have to be perfect to convince me there is a God; as long as bad things only happened to bad people, I

---

[17] © Elliott Murphy 1990. Used by kind permission of the artist.

would believe in God. But this adds a whole new dimension of controversy to our conundrum, which is, who is good and who is bad? Or, equally importantly, **who decides** who is good and who is bad? I think you would find it difficult to build a consensus. Do we leave it to God to decide? Well, if God loves all His children, the bad as well as the good, maybe He does not want to make that decision either. And there is also a logical problem here, which is this: if bad things can only happen to bad people, is anybody bad anymore? Presumably, the key criterion that helps define for us who is a bad person is that he (or she) does bad things that hurt good people. But we no longer allow bad things to happen to good people, only to bad people. So now how do we define a bad person? Is a bad person someone who does bad things that hurt bad people? But what if those bad victims *deserve* to have bad things done to them? Does that make the person who does the bad things to them a good person? Or maybe a mediocre person? The situation quickly becomes untenable.

The unfortunate reality is that it is neither metaphysically realistic nor desirable for God to stop every bad thing from happening before it happens.

Human decisions and human actions have consequences. Unless we want to become a society of unthinking, unfeeling robots, we are stuck living with the bad consequences as well as the good, because people have free will.

However, we also have to address the reality that bad things can also happen to good people without being the result of the exercise of free will by anybody. Mainly I am talking now about freak accidents, natural disasters, and illnesses. Suppose a six-year-old child loses his mother to one of these, or suppose a mother loses her six-year old child to one of these. We can assume losing a child or a parent is a bad thing, and let's assume for the sake of argument that the six-year-old child and the mother are both good people. Why does God let this happen? Or, can there be a God if this happens? In times of tragedy we have all heard, and perhaps spoken, platitudes meant to bring some consolation to grieving family members. "It was God's will." "We don't know why this happened, but God must have a reason. Some day we will understand." "God must have needed an angel in heaven." These and similar platitudes would offer little consolation to the six-year-old, or to his mother. If anything, I would think they would more likely make them hate or reject God. "Why is it Your will that my mommy should die?" "How can You need my mommy in heaven more than I need her on earth?" "Why is it Your will that my little boy should die? He never did anything bad to anyone."

Pretty tough questions, and in this regard I have to agree with Rabbi Kushner's assessment that oftentimes things happen on earth that are NOT in keeping with God's will. God does not have control over everything that happens on earth. I feel this way because I think the earth is in large part the devil's domain, not God's. If you look around at the state of affairs in our world, I don't think my theory is particularly far-fetched. Let me take one brief detour outside the realm of the Gospels to the first letter of John, chapter 5, verse 19, where it is written, "We know that we belong to God, **and the whole world is under the power of the evil one**." (Emphasis mine.)

Now let's go back to the Gospels, specifically to the scene in which Jesus gives us the prayer that has come to be known as the Our Father. I just want to focus on one phrase: "Thy will be done, on earth as it is in heaven." Even if you don't have a law degree, I think you can see the implication that the Father's will is done in heaven, but not necessarily on earth. That, I assume, is why Jesus tells us to pray that God's will be done on earth. If everything that happens on earth *is* God's will, then we wouldn't need to ask God for His will to be done on earth.

Nor do you need a degree in rocket science to see that God's will is **not** being done on earth, even if many well-meaning people suggest otherwise. For if God's will were being done, there would be no hatred, no violence, no wars, no genocide, no starvation, no abortion on demand, no Internet pornography, etc., etc. Please don't tell me it's all part of God's plan.

So how do we rectify this situation? Sadly, we can't. I don't mean we can't in a theoretical sense, but in a realistic sense. Theoretically we could all (I mean ALL) pray the Our Father three times a day, and we could ALL use our intellect and wisdom to discern God's will and then, having discerned it, we could ALL set out to do God's will. We could ALL, in the exercise of our free will, choose to do good instead of evil every time we face that choice. But unfortunately that is not realistic, because many times God's will is at odds with our own will. And when God's will is at odds with our own will, whose will will usually win out? You know the answer to that one.

Let's imagine that one day God decided to address the world. The Big Broadcast of 2016. God comes over the PA and says, "If everyone in the world will stop sinning, there will be no more disease, accidents, and death. There will no longer be any suffering of any kind. All evil will be eradicated from the earth." How long would it be before the first person sinned? I'm pretty sure the over/under would be like 1 second. In the final analysis, we humans see the doing of God's will on earth as a very overrated thing, notwithstanding that we pray for it every day. God's will is that a married man should not have sex with his single, attractive co-worker. The married man's will is that he *should* have sex with her, if she is willing, or maybe even if she isn't. It is not God's fault that the sinful man decides to do evil, nor are any of the consequences of his decision God's fault, they are man's fault.

We can look to Jesus' words for confirmation of all these things. Is there evil in the world? Jesus says, "Do not worry about tomorrow; tomorrow will take care of itself. Sufficient for a day is its own evil." Jesus also says, "The world hates Me because I testify to it that its works are evil."

All right, so there is evil in the world; but aren't people inclined to shun evil and do good? Jesus says, "And this is the verdict, that the Light came into the world, but people preferred darkness to light, because their works were evil." Does this mean the devil holds sway in the world, as John's epistle suggests? Jesus says, "You belong to your father the devil, and you willingly carry out your father's desires. He was a murderer from the beginning and does not stand in truth, because there is no truth in him. ..[H]e is a liar and the father of lies. ... whoever belongs to God hears the words of God, for this reason you do not listen, because you do not belong to God." Jesus seems to tell us that there is an ongoing struggle between the people who are (or try to be) of God and the people who are agents of darkness.

Can our allegiance to Jesus protect us from the devil? The Gospel does tell us that Jesus prays for the protection of His disciples: "I gave them Your word, and the world hated them, because they do not belong to the world any more than I belong to the world. I do not ask that You take them out of the world, but that You keep them from the evil one." But does Jesus' prayer for the protection of His disciples guarantee they will face no *earthly* harm? NO!

What was Jesus' own destiny? "From that time on, Jesus began to show His disciples that He must go to Jerusalem and suffer greatly from the elders, the chief priests, and the scribes, and be killed and on the third day be raised." And what fate might be expected to befall Jesus' followers?

Listen:

"Whoever finds his life will lose it, and *whoever loses his life for My sake will find it.*"

"*Whoever wishes to come after Me must deny himself, take up his cross,* and follow Me."

"Whoever does not carry his own cross and come after Me cannot be My disciple."

"Brother will hand over brother to death, and the father his child; children will rise up against parents and have them put to death. *You will be hated by all because of my name.*"

So, at least as I read it, following Jesus, and, by implication, being one who does God's will, may not lead to a good outcome – a good *earthly* outcome, I should say. Denying yourself, carrying your cross, being hated by all, losing your life. Doesn't have a real Rose Garden-y feel to it. We are fortunate – those of us in the West at least – that we no longer live in a time when following Jesus means risking your life, though it does risk ridicule and hatred. Of course there is no guarantee we will not one day again face death for our convictions. Hopefully this esoteric statement by Jesus does not become prophetic in our time: "In fact, the hour will come when everyone who kills you will think he is offering worship to God." Given what goes on in the Middle East, it is not so far-fetched.

The point is, it is apparent from Jesus' own words that good people, even the very best, are not immune from bad happenings. Did not Jesus say to the audience at the Sermon on the Mount, "[Y]our heavenly Father ... makes his sun rise on the bad and the good, and causes rain to fall on the just and the unjust"? If we are all subject to the same misfortune, whether we are good or bad, what then is the reward for our righteousness? It's like I've been telling you, eternal life.

Remember the story from Luke that I mentioned in the last chapter, about the Galileans killed by Pilate and the Jerusalemites who had a tower fall on them? Why did these bad things happen to these (presumably) good people? Jesus didn't even go there. He said:

> Do you think that because these Galileans suffered in this way that they were greater sinners than all other Galileans? By no means! But I tell you, if you do not repent you will all perish as they did! Or the eighteen people who were killed when the tower at Siloam fell on them – do you think they were more guilty than everyone else who lived in Jerusalem? By no means! But I tell you, if you do not repent, you will all perish as they did!

In other words, Jesus' perspective is that when, how, or why we die is hardly relevant, not particularly meaningful. Bad things happen. God is not in control of everything. Ultimately, we all die. But the important thing is for us to be in a right place with God, so that when we *do* die, regardless of the circumstances, we will merit eternal salvation. As Rose Castorini says to her husband Cosmo ("Moonstruck" again), "Cosmo, I just want you to know, no matter what you do, you're gonna die, just like everybody else." But while our deaths are inevitable, our souls need not perish.

Jesus made this priority clear to His disciples when He said, "I tell you, My friends, do not be afraid of those who kill the body but after that can do no more. I shall show you whom to fear. Be afraid of the one who after killing has the power to cast into Gehenna." We might also note that when, at the pool called Bethesda, Jesus healed a man who had been ill for 38 years, Jesus said to him, "Look, you are well; do not sin anymore, so that nothing worse may happen to you." Did Jesus mean the man had been ill for 38 years because of his sins? I think not; I think Jesus is saying there are worse things than being ill, such as eternal damnation. So stop sinning.

We can learn the same lesson from the familiar story of the rich man and Lazarus. Lazarus was a poor beggar. He suffered greatly on earth. When he died, he was carried away by angels to the bosom of Abraham. The rich man knew little of earthly suffering, but he also died. However, he did not go to the bosom of Abraham, but to the netherworld, where he was in torment. The rich man raised his eyes and saw Abraham far off, and Lazarus at his side. The rich man asked Abraham to have pity on him and send Lazarus to dip the tip of his finger in water to cool the rich man's tongue, for he was suffering torment in the flames. Abraham replied, "My child, remember that you received what was good during your lifetime while Lazarus likewise received what was bad; but now he is comforted here, whereas you are tormented." You see, with God eternal life is far more important than what happens here. Since Lazarus went to heaven, we can probably assume he was a good person. On earth, however, despite his goodness, Lazarus received what was bad.

Are you familiar with the story of Saint Bernadette Soubirous? Saint Bernadette is the young French girl to whom the Blessed Mother appeared at Lourdes. As recounted in the book and movie "The Song of Bernadette", Our Lady said to young Bernadette, "I cannot guarantee you happiness in this life, only in the next." Who are we to expect better than Saint Bernadette? We certainly have no right to expect better, but we want better just the same.

Nevertheless, bad things do happen to good people; they always have. Illnesses, accidents, personal tragedies, premature death. This is a consequence of the evil in the world, and of humans being a fallen race. The relationship between evil and illness is exhibited in the Gospels, where, for example:

➤ Jesus was brought many people who were possessed by demons, and He drove out the spirits by a word and cured all the sick;

➤ Jesus drove out a demon from a mute person, and the mute person spoke;

➤ Jesus cured a lunatic boy who suffered seizures by driving out a demon;

➤ Jesus cured a woman who for eighteen years had been crippled by a spirit by driving out the spirit; and

➤ Jesus gave the Twelve authority over unclean spirits to drive them out and to cure every disease and illness.

In none of these cases is there any suggestion that the victims of the evil spirits or illnesses were not a good people. Indeed, with regard to a blind person whose sight Jesus restored, Jesus was specifically asked, "Rabbi, who sinned, this man or his parents, that he was born blind?" Jesus answered, "Neither he nor his parents sinned; it is so that the works of God might be made visible through him. …"

Jesus' mission, you must remember, is to bring us all to eternal life. He says, "Whoever hears My word and believes in the One who sent Me has eternal life and will not come to condemnation, but has passed from death to life." He also tells us, "I came into the world as light, so that everyone who believes in Me might not remain in darkness."

Unfortunately, as long as Satan holds power over people, life on earth will be a sacrifice, not a party. God does not promise us a rose garden. Along with the sunshine, there's gonna be a little rain sometime.

I know there is nothing I have said here that will console the six-year old who has lost his mother, or the mother who has lost her six-year old boy, because bad things do happen to good people, and oftentimes there is nothing we can do about it. Listen to the brilliant closing words from Thornton Wilder's novel The Bridge of San Luis Rey, which British Prime Minister Tony Blair used to console the USA in the aftermath of 9-11: "There is a land of the living and a land of the dead and the bridge is love, the only survival, the only meaning."

No matter how much God loves us, and no matter how much we may love one another, every one of us will die in the bodily sense. This unavoidable fact of life brings great sadness and emotional pain, even for those of us whose religion teaches that those who have died have gone to a better place. But we have a promise of better things to come, because Jesus tells us, "In the world you will have trouble, but take courage, I have conquered the world."

QUESTIONS FOR REFLECTION OR DISCUSSION

1. What is your favorite quote from Jesus in Chapter Thirty? Why?

2. Which of Jesus' quotes in Chapter Thirty did you find most surprising? In what way did it surprise you?

3. Why do you think bad things happen to good people? Has your faith in God ever been shaken by something bad that happened to a good person?

4. Do you think the world would be a better place if humans did not have free will? Would you prefer to live in a world in which you had no control over your life, with the trade-off that nothing negative would ever happen?

5. Why do you think some Christians think bad things should never happen to them, even know they are aware that Jesus and many of His early followers were martyred?

6. Do you believe that everything that happens in the world is a manifestation of God's will? Do you think there is a hidden reason for evil things that happen? Why or why not?

7. Did this chapter change your thinking in any way about why things happen?

Chapter Thirty-One

DO YOU HAVE ANY WORDS OF COMFORT FOR THOSE WHO ARE SORROWING AND GRIEVING?

"But I will see you again, and your hearts will rejoice, and no one will take your joy away from you."

It is 1862 and we are in Southern Indiana. The Confederate troops are heading our way, and the local Quaker congregation is in a quandary. Will they fight alongside their neighbors, to defend their land and the Union? Or will they adhere to their strict pacifist beliefs? Everyone is quiet; the tension in the meeting house is so thick you can cut it with a knife. Suddenly a young boy jumps up and breaks the silence, saying "God is love!" If, like me, you had no social life, you might recognize this as a scene from the 1956 motion picture "Friendly Persuasion", from the book by Jessamyn West.

God is love, and it is through God that we come to love one another. We are God's children, and though we are sinners God loves us unconditionally, despite our faults and moral failings. We live in an imperfect world, where we are made to suffer physically, emotionally, and psychologically because of our fallen condition. God sees our suffering, and because He loves us He is grieved by it. Although He is often unable to prevent our suffering, He offers us consolation and hope for the future.

God sent His son Jesus to earth as a sacrifice for the expiation of our sins, and to open the gates of heaven to those who believe in Him and do His will. Because He came to earth in the form of man, Jesus, like us, knew what it was to suffer and sorrow. When John the Baptist was executed by Herod, Jesus went off to a deserted place by Himself to mourn. When His friend Lazarus died, Jesus was greatly perturbed and wept at his tomb. On the night before He was to be crucified, Jesus struggled mightily with his fate in the Garden of Gethsemane, enduring His personal "dark night of the soul". Kneeling before God, racked with doubt, He prayed, "Father, if you are willing, take this cup away from me." Then He added, "Still, not my will but yours be done." Then God sent Him an angel from heaven to strengthen Him. How often does God also send angels our way to help us when we are suffering?

It is when we are grieving that we most need to feel God's love and the consolation of angels, whether they be heavenly angels or the earthbound variety.

Nobody knows us better than God, and nobody understands us better than God. When we are grieving, nobody consoles us better than God. What does Jesus say to us when we need consolation? "Blessed are the poor in spirit, for theirs is the kingdom of heaven. Blessed are they who mourn, for they shall be comforted. Blessed are the meek, for they shall inherit the earth. Blessed are they who hunger and thirst for righteousness, for they will be satisfied." Jesus understands us when we are down, when we are grieved, when we are weak, when we feel defeated. "Come to Me, all you who labor and are burdened," Jesus says, "and I will give you rest. Take My yoke upon you and learn from Me," He continues, "for I am meek and humble of heart; and you will find rest for yourselves. For My yoke is easy, and My burden light." What wonderful words these are to hear from our God when we are suffering, when we are in doubt, when we are not up to the task, on those days when you just can't manage to do much of anything except cry.

When we have lost all hope, as Jairus did when he thought his daughter had died, Jesus says to us, "Do not be afraid; just have faith." When we feel we have no place to go and we are at the end of our rope, we can turn to God, and He will rejoice, as the father of the prodigal son rejoiced. When we are the flesh failures, the ones who couldn't cut it, the hopeless beggars, Jesus will have us carried away by angels to the bosom of Abraham. For God loves us amid all our imperfections, all our screw-ups, and all our tragedies.

In an earlier chapter we spoke about praying. We can and should pray when we are sorrowing and grieving, for strength, for courage, and for consolation. Jesus tells us we shall be comforted when we mourn. There is a wonderful song called "Thankful for the Roses", by Anthony Liguori, Jr., and Joseph Durante, which includes this line: "tears are a way God gives us to pray for things that words just can't say." There is healing power in our grief, and God helps carry us through the most difficult and sad situations we face. He also offers the consoling promise of eternity.

Remember that by God's reckoning, thinking as God thinks rather than as man thinks, eternity is more important than our temporal existence on earth. Even as we mourn the death of a loved one, we ought to keep our eyes focused on our everlasting residence, where by the grace of God we will be with our loved ones once again. "Do not let your hearts be troubled," Jesus exhorts us. "You have faith in God; have faith also in Me. In My father's house there are many dwelling places," He continues. "If there were not, would I have told you that I am going to prepare a place for you?"

When Jesus was preparing His Apostles for his imminent trial and execution, and His return to the Father, He said to them, "In a little while the world will no longer see Me, but you will see Me, because I live and you will live.

"On that day," He went on, "you will realize that I am in My Father and you are in Me and I in you." Then He also said, "If you loved Me you would rejoice that I am going to the Father; for the Father is greater than I."

This last statement is very reminiscent of what we hear many people say to us when a loved one has died. "He is in a better place." And while the Gospels may not support the platitude that someone's suffering and death was God's will, they do support this more important platitude. When someone we love dies, it is natural for us to grieve, for we are sad that he is going away and we will not see him again. But in reality, if he has lived a righteous life, he **is** going to a better place, where his earthbound limitations and suffering are no more.[18] Jesus makes this analogy:

> When a woman is in labor she is in anguish because her hour has arrived; but when she has given birth to a child she no longer remembers the pain because of her joy that a child has been born into the world. So you also are now in anguish. But I will see you again, and your hearts will rejoice, and no one will take your joy away from you. On that day you will not question Me about anything.

What a wonderful consolation that is. *"No one will take your joy away from you."* And did you notice the last line in the passage? "You will not question Me about anything! " We will be so overjoyed in heaven that everything else, all our questions and concerns, will just slip away.

"I am the resurrection and the life," Jesus tells us. "Whoever believes in Me, even if he dies, will live, and everyone who lives and believes in Me will never die." This is why it is so crucial that you, me, all of us, get right with God. The love and the joy in His everlasting presence will wipe away any sorrow and grief we experience in our earthly lives. What could be better than to be reunited with

---

[18] To reiterate the words of Ronald Colman qua Sidney Carton in "A Tale of Two Cities": "It is a far far better rest I go to than I have ever known."

the ones we love and rejoice in God's divine light? If we believe God's word, then even in the midst of our mourning there is the joyful hope of a heavenly reunion with those we love. This is the promise God gives us.

God is love. His love consoles us.

QUESTIONS FOR REFLECTION OR DISCUSSION

1. What is your favorite quote from Jesus in Chapter Thirty-one? Why?

2. Which of Jesus' quotes in Chapter Thirty-one did you find most surprising? In what way did it surprise you?

3. Was there a time when you were grieving, and you felt peace and consolation from God? Talk about it.

4. Have you ever had the sense, when you were at the end of your rope, that God was carrying you? If so, what were the circumstances?

5. Do you feel God has ever sent you an angel of the spiritual kind to help you when in need? How about an angel of the human kind? Discuss these experiences, and what made you think they were from God.

Chapter Thirty-Two

HOW ABOUT PEOPLE WHO HAVE SPENT THEIR LIVES TRAVELING DOWN THE WRONG PATH; IS THERE ANY ENCOURAGEMENT OR CONSOLATION FOR THEM?

"There will be more joy in heaven over one sinner who repents than over ninety-nine righteous people who have no need of repentance."

God loves us, and like anyone who truly loves, God forgives us when we go to Him for forgiveness. If you read the Gospels, you will find that mercy and forgiveness are recurring themes throughout. God is merciful and forgiving, and He expects the same from us. Jesus tells us, "If you forgive others their transgressions, your heavenly Father will forgive you. But if you do not forgive others, neither will your Father forgive your transgressions."

When we dealt earlier with the requirements of a worthy prayer life, we mentioned Jesus' admonition, "When you stand to pray, forgive anyone against whom you have a grievance, so that your heavenly Father may in turn forgive you your transgressions." We are asked to emulate God in this sense: "Forgive and you will be forgiven."

Just how merciful is God? "God so loved the world that He gave His only Son, so that everyone who believes in Him might not perish but might have eternal life. For God did not send His Son into the world to condemn the world, but that the world might be saved through Him." The Son came down from heaven not to do His own will, but to do the will of the One who sent Him. What then is the will of the Father? "That everyone who sees the Son and believes in Him may have eternal life, and I shall raise him on the last day." How was it that Jesus saved us? By being a good shepherd. "A good shepherd lays down his life for the sheep. … This is why the Father loves Me, because I lay down My life in order to take it up again." Jesus went all the way to Calvary, to die on the cross as a sacrifice for our sins. As Jesus Himself says, "The Son of Man did not come to be served, but to serve and to give His life as a ransom for many."

Great is the depth of God's mercy. By now you are familiar with the story of the prodigal son, who returned home after squandering his share of his father's estate by extravagant and wanton living. When he returned to his father, tail between his legs, his father greeted him jubilantly. But the older son, the good son, was miffed by the attention his younger brother received. His father tried to assuage number one son's hostility. "My son, you are here with me always," said the father. "Everything I have is yours. But now we must celebrate and rejoice, because your brother was dead, and has come to life again; he was lost, and has been found."

I suppose most of us who are parents would be equally joyful at the return of the wandering squanderer, or squandering wanderer. But at the same time, perhaps we can relate to the older brother's feelings as well. I know this parable rubs some of the unprodigal sons the wrong way, those who have always been faithful and done the right thing. Why should this disrespectful sinner get special treatment? Why not just turn him away at the gate? Having grown up as a goody-two-shoes, I am sympathetic to the complaints of the non-prodigals: I'm a better person, a better son, a better Christian than he is, I should get the special treatment, not he!

At the same time, I have over the years developed a peculiar knack for falling in love with movie actresses who brought about their own demise through excessive alcohol or drug intake. I wonder, if I get to heaven, whether I'll find out why that is. But in any case, I always pray for God's mercy and forgiveness for these fallen stars. I can tell you that if you love troubled people, you can't help but hope for their redemption and salvation. And at the same time, you hope that God, in His mercy, has a soft spot for these unfortunates as well. Therefore, that part of me, the part that loves and prays for the lost souls, rejoices in the story of the prodigal son.

As Jesus made clear, it was for these troubled souls that He most especially came to be a Light. "Those who are well do not need a physician," says Jesus, "but the sick do." As Jesus told the Jewish leaders who resented His association with "undesirables", "Go and learn the meaning of the words, 'I desire mercy, not sacrifice.' I did not come to call the righteous but sinners."

As the parable of the prodigal demonstrates, our God is a God of second chances. To reaffirm the theme of extreme forgiveness, recall the parable of the lost sheep. "If a man has a hundred sheep and one of them goes astray," Jesus queries, "will he not leave the ninety-nine in the hills and go in search of the stray? And if he finds it, amen I say to you, he rejoices more over it than over the ninety-nine who did not stray. In just the same way, it is not the will of your heavenly Father that one of these little ones be lost." Again, if we are one of the ninety-nine who did not stray, we might not like this fervent pursuit of the one who did stray. But if we are sincere in our love for our fellow man, we will acknowledge that God's mercy is an awesome thing. For Jesus reiterates, "There will be more joy in heaven over one sinner who repents than over ninety-nine righteous people who have no need of repentance. ...I tell you, there will be rejoicing among the angels of God over one sinner who repents...."

As we see in Jesus' encounter with Zacchaeus, the crooked tax collector, the Son of Man came to seek and to save what was lost. That little guy, universally despised because of his chicanery, climbed a sycamore tree so that he could catch a glimpse of Jesus. In return, Jesus turned Zacchaeus' life around. All our Savior asks is sincere remorse and a humble commitment to change. We discussed some chapters ago the tax collector in the temple who stood at a distance and would not even raise his eyes to heaven, but beat his breast and prayed, "O God, be merciful to me, a sinner." Because of his humble contrition, he went away justified.

You have also heard the Gospel story of the woman caught in the act of adultery, who was going to be stoned by the Jews in accordance with their law. There is no question that she was a sinner, but Jesus had mercy on her and did not condemn her. He did, however, add a condition on His offer of forgiveness: "Go, and from now on do not sin any more." Sometimes I think that contingency gets overlooked in our zeal to acknowledge Jesus' mercy and kindness. But reminiscent of the Act of Contrition that Catholics are directed to say when seeking the Sacrament of Reconciliation, Jesus does require that we make an effort to avoid sinning, and to avoid the near occasions of sin as well.

I guess the one exception to that requirement is when we seek God's mercy in the face of death, when we run out of chances to sin again. Even at the hour of our death, regardless of the life we have led, God stands ready to forgive if we are truly contrite and remorseful. Notice the simple beauty of the exchange between Jesus and the "good thief" on the cross: "Jesus, remember me when You come into Your kingdom," asks the thief. "Amen, I say to you," Jesus replies, "today you will be with Me in paradise." These are undoubtedly some of the most comforting words found in the Gospels. A life of sin wiped away by the words of a merciful Savior.

There may be many of you reading this book who are in a similar situation to the good thief. Perhaps you have been on the outs with God for a long time, living a sinful life. Maybe you think it is too late to change your ways, that God will not take you back. But God loves you, and he wants you to come back. He is just waiting for you to ask his forgiveness and to accept His word into your life. Consider the parable of the vineyard workers. Those who went to work in the vineyard early in the morning received the same reward as those who went to work in the vineyard late in the afternoon. Those who worked a full day were not happy to learn of this arrangement. Like goody-two-shoes me, they figured they should get something extra for their long service. But Jesus tells them they have no cause to complain, for they have received the reward that was promised to them. If God chooses to be generous in His mercy towards those who reformed late in the game, that is cause for rejoicing, not complaint. For, as I said, if we truly love, then we must want **all** to be saved. If we have a problem with that, we need to look in the mirror and ask ourselves, am I loving others as Jesus teaches me to love them?

Listen again to Jesus' words, and notice how they call to you to come home to the Lord:

"I am the bread of life; whoever comes to Me will never hunger and whoever believes in Me shall not thirst";

"If you remain in My word, you will truly be My disciples, and you will know the truth, and the truth will set you free";

"Amen amen I say to you, whoever keeps My word will never see death";

"I am the resurrection and the life; whoever believes in Me, even if he dies, will live, and everyone who lives and believes in Me will never die."

Our God is a God of infinite mercy, and His Son came to earth on a mission to save souls, to bring us back to God, to spend eternity with Him. So, as Jesus was preparing Himself for the sacrifice He was to undertake and become, He prayed:

"Father, the hour has come. Give glory to Your Son, so that Your Son may glorify You, just as You gave Him authority over all people, so that He may give eternal life to all You gave Him."

Suppose you were Jesus, the Son of God. Suppose You humbled Yourself to become man, just so that You could be condemned to death for the sake of sinners. Wouldn't You want as many people as possible to take advantage of Your sacrifice? Wouldn't that be the most gratifying thing?

Jesus says it is never too late. Turn to the Father, humble yourself before Him, ask His forgiveness, and say YES to eternal life.

QUESTIONS FOR REFLECTION OR DISCUSSION

1. What is your favorite quote from Jesus in Chapter Thirty-two? Why?

2. Which of Jesus' quotes in Chapter Thirty-two did you find most surprising? In what way did it surprise you?

3. Do you find it troubling that one of the thieves crucified alongside Jesus was able to get into heaven despite his criminal ways? Why do you feel that way?

4. Do you ever worry that your life has been so sinful that God could never forgive you? Do you think Jesus would agree with that assessment of yourself?

5. Have you had any friends or relatives who died as a consequence of living a troubled life, such as a struggle with drugs or alcohol? If so, do you think they received forgiveness from God? Explain why you feel that way.

Chapter Thirty-Three

PLEASE HELP US FIGURE OUT IF WE'RE LIKELY TO GO TO HEAVEN OR HELL WHEN THE FINAL JUDGMENT ROLLS AROUND.

"For the hour is coming in which all who are in the tombs will hear His voice and will come out, those who have done good deeds to the resurrection of life, but those who have done wicked deeds to the resurrection of condemnation."

So here we are at the grand finale, the last chapter. Heaven or hell? The purpose of this book was to encourage you to listen to the lessons the Lord teaches, to take His words to heart and obey His commands, so that we can all enjoy eternal life together with God. This final chapter will address Jesus' teachings about final judgment, eternal life, heaven, and hell. This will be a long chapter, but not by my doing. It just so happens that Jesus has a lot to say about these topics. I hope this is not a surprise to you. I think it has become apparent through the previous chapters that Jesus' focus is a heavenly focus rather than a worldly focus. After all, His purpose in coming to earth was to show us the way to heaven!

I am of course assuming that all of us want to go to heaven (even if, as the saying goes, none of us wants to die).

Maybe that is an erroneous assumption, though I would hope not. Maybe some of you think that heaven would be a boring scene. The refrain from the Talking Heads' song "Heaven" suggests that heaven is a place where nothing ever happens. Albeit the song does not cast heaven in a negative light; still, I'm not sure it's an accurate description (though I do hope to find out some day). But if nothing else, heaven is generally described as a place of great joy and serenity, so why would you not want to go there?

As I said, Jesus has quite a lot to say to us concerning eternal life, so in order to give some structure to this final lesson I will attempt to organize Jesus' teachings into these categories: (1) the final judgment; (2) who will get to heaven; (3) who will go to hell; (4) what is hell like; and (5) what is heaven like.

(1) The Final Judgment

The first thing Jesus wants us to know is that there will in fact be a judgment. Jesus tells us, "[O]n the day of judgment people will render an account for every careless word they speak. By your words you will be acquitted, and by your words you will be condemned." Jesus also says,

> At the judgment, the men of Nineveh will arise with this generation and condemn it, because they

411

repented at the teaching of Jonah; and there is something greater than Jonah here. At the judgment the queen of the south will arise with this generation and condemn it, because she came from the ends of the earth to hear the wisdom of Solomon; and there is something greater than Solomon here.

Jesus also told His disciples, "Whoever will not receive you or listen to your words - go outside that house or town and shake the dust from your feet. Amen I say to you, it will be more tolerable for the land of Sodom and Gomorrah on the day of judgment than for that town."

Further discussing the judgment to come, Jesus warns us, "What profit would there be for one to gain the whole world and forfeit his life, or what can one give in exchange for his life? For the Son of Man will come with His angels in His Father's glory, and then He will repay everyone according to his conduct." Moreover, Jesus exhorts us to be on our best behavior at all times, because we do not know when the judgment will come. "Be sure of this: if the master of the house had known the hour of night when the thief was coming, he would have stayed awake and not let his house be broken into," says Jesus. "So too, you also must be prepared, for at an hour you do not expect the son of man will come." Similarly, Jesus cautions thus: "If the wicked servant says to himself, 'my master is long delayed,' and begins to beat his fellow servants and eat and drink with drunkards, the servant's master will come on an unexpected day and at an unexpected hour and will punish him severely and assign him a place with the hypocrites, where there will be wailing and grinding of teeth."

(2) Who Will Get to Heaven?

At the time of the judgment, the determination will be made whether we shall be with God in heaven, or be remanded to the netherworld, with the wailing and grinding of teeth. There is ample material provided in the Gospels to give us a good idea of where we might expect to spend eternity. With respect to the judgment itself, Jesus offers this parable to give us an idea of how it will go down:

> The kingdom of heaven may be likened to a man who sowed good seed in his field. While everyone was asleep his enemy came and sowed weeds all through the wheat, and then went off. When the crop grew and bore fruit, the weeds appeared as well. The slaves of the household came to him and said, "Master, did you not sow good seed in your field? Where have the weeds come from?" He answered, "An enemy has done this." His slaves said to him, "Do you want us to

413

go and pull them up?" He replied, "Let them grow together until harvest; then at harvest time I will say to the harvesters, 'first collect the weeds and tie them in bundles for burning; but gather the wheat into my barn."

Jesus explains the symbolism in the parable for us. The one who sows good seed is Jesus, the field is the world, and the good seed represents the children of the kingdom. The weeds are the children of the evil one, and the enemy who sows them is the devil. The harvest is the end of the age, and the harvesters are angels. Just as weeds are collected and burned up with fire, so will it be at the end of the age. "The Son of Man will send His angels," says Jesus, "and they will collect out of His kingdom all who cause others to sin and all evildoers. They will throw them into the fiery furnace, where there will be wailing and grinding of teeth." Jesus continues, "Then the righteous will shine like the sun in the kingdom of their Father. Whoever has ears ought to hear."

Perhaps the following is the better known telling of the coming judgment, but the effect is similar to the foregoing parable.

When the Son of Man comes in His glory, and all the angels with Him, He will sit upon His glorious throne, and all the nations will be assembled before Him. And

He will separate them from one another, as a shepherd separates the sheep from the goats. He will place the sheep on His right and the goats on His left. Then the King will say to those on His right, "Come, you who are blessed by My Father. Inherit the Kingdom prepared for you from the foundation of the world. For I was hungry and you gave Me food, I was thirsty and you gave Me drink, a stranger and you welcomed Me, naked and you clothed Me, ill and you cared for Me, in prison and you visited Me." Then the righteous will answer Him and say, "Lord, when did we see You hungry and feed You, or thirsty and give You drink? When did we see You a stranger and welcome You, or naked and cloth You? When did we see You ill or in prison and visit You?" And the King will say to them in reply, "Amen, I say to you, whatever you did for one of these least brothers of Mine, you did for Me." Then He will say to those on His left, "Depart from me you accursed, into the eternal fire prepared for the devil and his angels. For I was hungry and you gave Me no food, I was thirsty and you gave Me no drink, a stranger and you gave Me no welcome, naked and you gave Me no clothing, ill and in prison, and you did not care for Me." Then they will answer and say, "Lord, when did we see You hungry or thirsty or a stranger or naked or ill or in prison, and not minister to Your needs?" He will answer them, "Amen, I say to you, what you did not do for one of these least ones, you did not do for Me." And these will go off to eternal punishment, but the righteous to eternal life.

So right there we get a pretty good idea of the kind of moral accounting that will determine our eternal fate. If you are righteous, if you are charitable to your fellow men, no matter their station in life, you are on the right road. If you do evil, if you cause others to sin, if you ignore your fellow men in need, you may be headed where you don't want to head.

What else does Jesus tell us about what we must do to spend eternity with Him in heaven? Many things. Here are the pointers to keep in mind. We have seen many of these before in other contexts, but they are worth reviewing here as we cram for our final exam for entry to Paradise:

"Blessed are the poor in spirit, for theirs is the kingdom of heaven."

"Blessed are the meek, for they shall inherit the land."

"Blessed are the pure of heart, for they will see God."

"Blessed are the peacemakers, for they will be called children of God."

"Blessed are they who are persecuted for the sake of righteousness, for theirs is the kingdom of heaven."

"Blessed are you when they insult you and persecute you and utter every kind of evil against you because of Me. Rejoice and be glad, for great will be your reward in heaven."

"[W]hoever obeys and teaches these commandments will be called greatest in the kingdom of heaven."

"Enter through the narrow gate; ... How narrow the gate and constricted the road that leads to life. And those who find it are few."

"Not everyone who says, 'Lord, Lord' will enter the kingdom of heaven, but only the one who does the will of My Father in heaven."

"What I say to you in the darkness speak in the light. What you hear whispered, proclaim on the housetops. Do not be afraid of those who kill the body but cannot kill the soul; rather, be afraid of the one who can destroy both soul and body in Gehenna."

"Everyone who acknowledges Me before others I will acknowledge before My heavenly Father."

"Whoever loses his life for My sake will find it."

"Whoever wishes to come after Me must deny himself, take up his cross, and follow Me. For whoever wishes to save his life will lose it, but whoever loses his life for My sake will find it."

"Whoever humbles himself like this child is the greatest in the kingdom of heaven."

"If your hand or foot causes you to sin, cut it off and throw it away. It is better for you to enter into life maimed or crippled than with two hands or two feet to be thrown into eternal fire."

"Let the children come to Me, and do not prevent them; for the kingdom of heaven belongs to such as these."

"If you wish to be perfect, go, sell what you have and give to the poor, and you will have treasure in heaven."

"Everyone who has given up houses or brothers or sisters or father or mother or children or lands for the sake of My name will receive a hundred times more, and will inherit eternal life."

"This is the time of fulfillment. The Kingdom of God is at hand. Repent, and believe in the Gospel."

"Go into the whole world and proclaim the Gospel to every creature. Whoever believes and is baptized will be saved."

"But to you who hear I say love your enemies, do good to those who hate you, bless those who curse you, pray for those who mistreat you. To the person who strikes you on one cheek, offer the other as well. From the person who takes your cloak, do not withhold even your tunic. Give to everyone who asks of you, and from the one who takes what is yours do not demand it back. Do unto others as you would have them do to you. Love your enemies and do good to them ... then your reward will be great and you will be children of the Most High, for He Himself is kind to the ungrateful and the wicked. Be merciful, as your Father is merciful."

"You shall love the Lord, your God, with all your heart, and with all your being, with all your strength, and with all your mind, and your neighbor as yourself. Do this and you will live."

"When you hold a banquet, invite the poor, the crippled, the lame, the blind; blessed indeed will you be because of their inability to repay you. For you will be repaid at the resurrection of the righteous."

"For God did not send His Son into the world to condemn the world, but that the world might be saved through Him. Whoever believes in Him will not be condemned..."

"Whoever believes in the Son has eternal life."

"Whoever hears My word and believes in the One who sent Me has eternal life and will not come to condemnation, but has passed from death to life."

I told you Jesus has a lot to say on this subject! As you can see, Jesus provides us with many tips concerning the ways we can merit eternal life. He recommends that we be pure, be humble, be obedient, proclaim God's word, sacrifice ourselves on God's behalf, avoid sin, be charitable, be merciful, love God, love our fellow man, be repentant when we sin, and believe in Jesus and God. (I got about 54%; how'd you do?)

(3) Who Will Go to Hell?

What then might lead to our exclusion from the kingdom of heaven? Jesus tells us, "[W]hoever breaks one of the least of these commandments and teaches others to do so will be called least in the kingdom of heaven." He also warned his contemporaries, "[U]nless your righteousness surpasses that of the scribes and Pharisees, you will not enter into the kingdom of heaven."

Listen to what else He says on the subject: "You have heard that it was said to your ancestors, 'You shall not kill; and whoever kills will be liable to judgment.' But I say to you, whoever is angry with his brother will be liable to judgment, and whoever says to his brother 'raqa' will be answerable to the Sanhedrin, and whoever says 'you fool' will be liable to fiery Gehenna." I must admit, these are pretty strict standards Jesus lays down for us. Breaking the least of the commandments, being angry, calling people names – these are things I do every day. Jesus also says, "If your right eye causes you to sin, tear it out and throw it away. It is better for you to lose one of your members tan to have your whole body thrown into Gehenna. And if your right hand causes you to sin, cut if off and throw it away. It is better for you to lose one of your members than to have your whole body go into Gehenna."

I suppose we could chalk up these statements as rhetorical hyperbole used by Jesus to stress a point. But even disregarding the self-maiming aspect, He is again setting the bar very high. Basically, if we sin we are in danger of losing heaven.

Jesus does warn us, "The gate is wide and the road broad that leads to destruction, and those who enter through it are many. How narrow the gate and constricted the road that leads to life. And those who find it are few." So I think we see the message here is that we really do need to be on our best behavior to avoid condemnation. Following the crowd and saying, "Hey, everybody else is doing it," is not the recipe for gaining eternal life. This is why moral relativism is so dangerous. In the whole scheme of eternity, each generation is like a blip of time on the screen. It would be nice if God were to say to us at judgment time, "Everybody's doing whatever the hell they want these days anyway, so come on in, you ain't so bad!" But I am not sure He will. It's sort of like being a slugger during major league baseball's steroid era. The fact that "everybody was doing it" doesn't give you a pass with the Hall of Fame voters. I'll grant you that God is *probably* more merciful than most sportswriters, but I wouldn't want to bet my eternity on it.

Listening to the moral relativists seems to me a bit like listening to the false prophets Jesus warns us about. "Beware of false prophets, who come to you in sheep's clothing, but underneath are ravenous wolves," says Jesus. "By their fruits you will know them. Do people pick grapes from thornbushes, or figs from thistles? Just so, every good tree bears good fruit, and a rotten tree bears bad fruit. A good tree cannot bear bad fruit, nor can a rotten tree bear good fruit." There is a lurking danger with false prophets and moral relativists: "Every tree that does not bear good fruit will be cut down and thrown into the fire. So by their fruits you will know them."

Here is some more advice from our Lord with respect to passing muster at the pearly gates. He tells us, "[W]hoever denies Me before others, I will deny before My heavenly Father." He also has this to say: "Whoever loves father or mother more than Me is not worthy of Me, and whoever loves son or daughter more than Me is not worthy of Me; and whoever does not take up his cross and follow after Me is not worthy of Me. Whoever finds his life will lose it…"

As I said earlier, Jesus sets a very high standard for us to gain eternal life. These most recent statements might again be hyperbolic, but perhaps not. It is consistent with Jesus' frequently stated priority with the spiritual over the material, the heavenly over the worldly. It is not so much that we shouldn't love our family – of course we should; Jesus wants us to love **everybody**, so to suggest He doesn't want us to love our own family is patently illogical (there I go being a lawyer again). The greater point, though, is that God gave us the world and gave us our lives, and our first obligation is to know, love, and serve Him. If any worldly attachments, including our own families, interfere with that obligation, then we have a problem. Most of us have probably, at some point in our lives, encountered a situation where a parent or a sibling or a child of ours could bring us down and cause us to sin in one way or another. Despite la familia, we have to remain above the fray. We are not to overthrow our duty to God; that should always be job 1. There is a correct way to behave and an incorrect way to behave. As Christians, we are obliged at all times to choose the former.

Jesus also says to us, "[U]nless you turn and become like children you will not enter the kingdom of heaven"; and similarly, "[W]hoever does not accept the Kingdom of God like a child will not enter it." We should be innocent, pure, and humble, not worldly, arrogant, and corrupt. We should be trusting in the word of God, not cynical or defiant. Thus Jesus also warns us, "Whoever is ashamed of Me and of My words in this faithless and sinful generation, the Son of Man will be ashamed of when He comes in His Father's glory with the holy angels." In the world, the cool thing to do, the "now" way to be, is to disregard God and all that religious stuff. But as I said earlier, don't follow the crowd, follow your conscience, and follow the Word. Cool or not, it is the right thing, and in your heart you know it.

Another thing Jesus tells us is, "[I]t will be hard for one who is rich to enter the kingdom of heaven." We discussed this a bit earlier, and it is not the fact of being rich in and of itself that is a bar to the kingdom. If it were, Jesus would have said, "No one who is rich will enter the kingdom of heaven." But that is not what He said. He said it will be hard. It will be hard because riches can become a god for us if we let them. If worldly treasure is the paramount thing in our lives, we may undertake unscrupulous (and thus sinful) means to attain it. Similarly, we may feel compelled to do whatever we have to do to hold onto it. This may mean using unethical or illegal tactics (again, sinful) to protect what is ours. It may also warp our thinking, such that we do not use our blessings to help those who are less fortunate, which is an absolute essential in God's eyes. So if you are rich, be grateful, be generous, but never let your wealth, or the perceived importance of holding on to your wealth, cause you to behave in an ungodly way.

I'm sure you remember the stories about Galileans whose blood Pilate had mingled with the blood of their sacrifices, and the eighteen people who were killed when the tower at Siloam fell on them. What was Jesus' reaction to both these tragedies? "If you do not repent, you will all perish as they did!" So another key element to entering into the kingdom of heaven is to be repentant and give up our sinful ways. We must embrace living righteously and in keeping with God's word. For Jesus tells us, "If anyone hears My words and does not observe them, I do not condemn him, ... the word that I spoke, it will condemn him on the last day, because I did not speak on My own, but the Father who sent Me commanded Me what to say and speak." Jesus further says, "[W]hoever disobeys the Son will not see life, but the wrath of God remains upon him."

We will all be subject to our day of judgment. "The hour is coming," Jesus tells us, "in which all who are in the tombs will hear His voice and will come out, those who have done good deeds to the resurrection of life, but those who have done wicked deeds to the resurrection of condemnation." It is the oft-stated goal of this book to exhort you to seek the resurrection of life. Can we glean anything from Jesus' words about the difference between these two fates?[19]

---

[19] I and many, if not most, Catholics also believe in a third possible fate, called Purgatory, which I guess you could say is for people who were pretty good or not too bad during their lives on earth, but are not sufficiently sanctified to enter heaven. So they go through a waiting time, a time of further sanctification, before they can enter the Kingdom. Can we find any support for the concept of Purgatory in Jesus' words? Maybe. The Gospel tells of Peter asking Jesus, "Lord, if my brother sins against me, how often must I forgive him? As many as seven times?" Jesus answered, "I say to you, not seven times, but seventy-seven times." Jesus then tells the parable of the unforgiving servant, after which He says, "Unless each of you forgives your brother from your heart, My heavenly Father will hand you over to the torturers until you have paid back your whole debt." The concept of being tortured "*until* you have paid back your whole debt" certainly sounds (to me at least) like a penalty time that is short of eternity. As I understand hell, it is forever, your debt is never paid. Therefore, by comparison, terminable torture is better. Also, Luke's Gospel records Jesus saying this: "That servant who knew his master's will but did not make preparations nor act in accord with his will shall be beaten severely; and the servant who was ignorant

(4) What Might Hell Be Like?

As far as hell is concerned, some people theorize that it is not an actual place. Some may believe that if you do not earn eternal life, then your soul, your consciousness, dies when your body dies. End of story. Others say hell is simply the absence of heaven, that the descriptions of hell are a metaphor for knowing you lost the opportunity to spend eternity with God. I would like to think that that is true, that there is not really a place of physical torment for all time. No matter how badly a person may have sinned, I would hate to think of someone suffering in that milieu.

Just the same, metaphorical or not, Jesus makes reference on more than one occasion to eternal damnation as a place of wailing and grinding of teeth. It sounds like a rather unpleasant place. Jesus also says, "Anyone who does not remain in Me will be thrown out like a branch and wither;

---

of his master's will but acted in a way deserving of a severe beating will be beaten only lightly. Much will be required of the person entrusted with much, and still more will be demanded of the person entrusted with more." Here again, Jesus introduces the concept of differing levels of punishment, which is inconsistent with a black and white/heaven or hell destiny. For the sake of people like me, who try to be good but know we are not so good, I hope Purgatory is an option! Not that I *want* to be beaten or tortured for **any** length of time, but at least in Purgatory there's a Light at the end.

people will gather them and throw them into a fire and they will be burned." Hell as a place of burning is a repeated motif that makes it sound like a pretty terrible place to be. In the parable of the wheat and the weeds, you may recall, Jesus talks of the sinners (the weeds) being thrown into the furnace.

We can get a glimpse of the difference between heaven and hell by re-visiting the story of Lazarus and the rich man. When Lazarus died, he was carried away by angels to the bosom of Abraham. When the rich man also died he went to the netherworld, where he was in torment. The torment seems to have been related to a fiery fate, for he asks Abraham, "Send Lazarus to dip the tip of his finger in water and cool my tongue, for I am suffering torment in these flames." Lazarus, by contrast, was comforted at Abraham's side. It seems to me that Lazarus got the better deal.

(5) What Might Heaven Be Like?

Billy Joel sang that he would rather laugh with sinners than cry with saints because sinners are much more fun. That may be the case in some respects on earth, but in the afterlife it's more likely the sinners who are crying. I would urge you to remember that eternity is a very very long time. In all respects, heaven sounds like the preferred destination. What does Jesus say about heaven? "Do not let your hearts be troubled. You have faith in God; have faith also in Me. In My Father's house there are many dwelling places." He also said to His Apostles, "If you loved me you would rejoice that I am going to the Father; for the Father is greater than I." And again He told them, "I will see you again, and your hearts will rejoice, and no one will take your joy away from you. On that day you will not question Me about anything."

Heaven, it would seem, is a place of peace, comfort, and great joy. Think of the times in your life when you have felt the most happiness and contentment, and that is what I imagine heaven is like. There is a feeling I occasionally get (I assume I am not the only one, but I couldn't swear to it), which I would describe as an ineffable sense of joy and contentment that rises from my solar plexus into my brain. It may come while listening to a nice piece of music, but it's just as likely to come while sitting in the living room with my family, watching TV, and nobody's fighting with each other. It's a sort of "God's in His heaven and all is right with the world" kind of feeling that I wish would come more often and stay longer. I assume heaven will be like that, only better. Because all is *never* right with the world, but in heaven we will be with God, where His will is always done.

I also like to think that in heaven we will share in God's eternal nature. So, contrary to the Talking Heads' notion of nothing ever happening in heaven, my vision is that we will be spirits, able to travel around freely, unconstrained by time or place. So it will not be a place where nothing ever happens, but rather a place where *everything* is *always* happening, if we want it to. Theoretically, in my concept of heaven, you could be anywhere you wanted to be, at any time you wanted to be there. No moment in history would be out of your reach. Imagine that. I would sit in on those early Rolling Stones recording sessions and find out once and for all which guitar parts Brian was playing and which parts Keith was playing.

Perhaps it would not be too far-fetched to also hope that, in some small measure, we would also be able to watch over and assist our loved ones on earth. But alas, this is only speculation.

One thing I do know, however, is that the people who claim to have visited heaven and returned to earth after a death or near-death experience describe heaven as a truly wonderful and joyful place. Indeed, many people who say they had a glimpse of heaven also say they were reluctant to return to life on earth. All I can say here is that if you are such a person, please share your story with the world, even if only in your own little corner of the world. You can provide people with such a profound sense of peace by allaying their fears about death and what comes next. But more than that, you can reinforce in them the need to conduct themselves on earth in such a way that they can merit eternal life. I cannot imagine being blessed by such an experience and then keeping it to myself. Getting the truth out – heaven is for real, do what you can to get there – is more important than anything.

The smart money says that heaven is a way better place than hell. In heaven the saints will be laughing, not crying. In hell the sinners will be crying, not laughing. My hope and my prayer is that you will listen to Jesus' words, take them to heart, and conform your lives to them. Equally important, share His words with anyone you know who also needs to hear them.

Remember, it is God's will that we will all share eternity with Him. He has given us the roadmap to get there, but He can't do the driving for us. It is up to us to follow the Way.

QUESTIONS FOR REFLECTION OR DISCUSSION

1. What is your favorite quote from Jesus in Chapter Thirty-three? Why?

2. Which of Jesus' quotes in Chapter Thirty-three did you find most surprising? In what way did it surprise you?

3. Do you think you will have eternal life? Is eternal life something you think about much? Does it affect the way you behave?

4. Do you believe there is a heaven? If so, what do you think it is like?

5. Do you believe there is a hell? If so, what do you think it is like? Do you ever worry about ending up there?

6. Does the possibility of hell affect the way you behave? If so, in what way?

ACKNOWLEDGMENTS

Did you read the whole book? Did you like it? You probably don't want to hear about Martha and Mary, Gehenna, the parable of the sower, and Jonah and the Ninevites ever again, right? But hey, if you thought the book was worthwhile, please tell your friends and family.

Many people contributed to the completion of this book over the years. The first acknowledgment must go to Jesus and then to His Apostles, disciples, and first century martyrs who helped spread the faith. Then to those who gave me my formation – my parents, Frank Rizzo from Hoboken, NJ, and Lilian "Betty" Rizzo from Chipping Norton and Oxford, England; the Sisters of Christian Charity at Saint Nicholas School; the Jesuits at Saint Peter's Prep and College; and all the priests whose homilies inspired me, at Saint Nick's Jersey City, Saint Francis de Sales Lodi, and Corpus Christi Hasbrouck Heights. Also, Bishop Roderick Caesar of Bethel Gospel Tabernacle in Jamaica Queens, to whose radio program I have frequently listened on WMCA 570, in awe of his spiritual acumen.

I would also like to acknowledge my wife, Maria Ramos, for her endless support and encouragement, and those who have offered their time, suggestions, and guidance in reading drafts of my manuscript: Patricia Lynn Baghdo, Joseph Blythe, Ken Bransfield, Roxanne Kowalski, Deacon Anthony and Jeannette Liguori, Robert Spearing, and the late Father Cassian Miles, OFM. Rest in Peace, Padre.

Made in the USA
Middletown, DE
28 September 2015